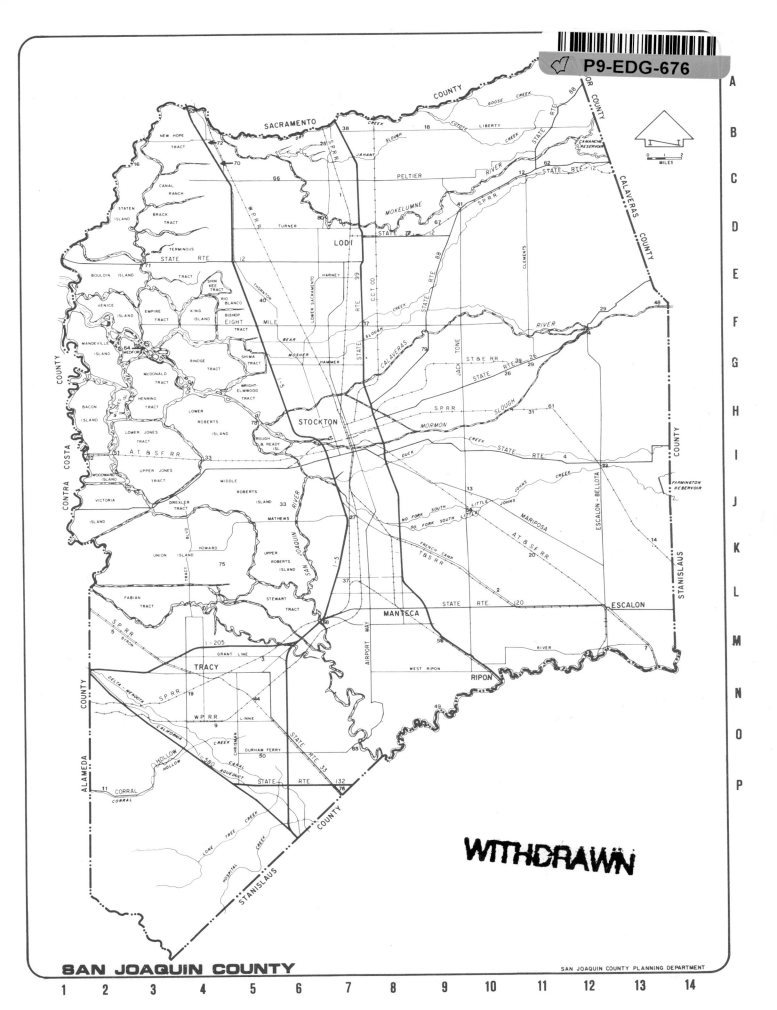

SAN JOAQUIN COUNTY

SAN JOAQUIN COUNTY PLANNING DEPARTMENT

P9-EDG-676

Cities & Towns of San Joaquin County

—⚬⚫ since 1847 ⚫⚬—

Raymond W. Hillman

Leonard A. Covello

Cities & Towns of San Joaquin County

⟶⋇ since 1847 ⋇⟵

**By Raymond W. Hillman
and Leonard A. Covello**

Published by Panorama West Books

2002 North Gateway, Suite 102

Fresno, California 93727

209/251-7801

Manufactured on acid-free paper in the United States of America

CONTENTS

STATUE OF SAINT JOACHIM IN THE CATHOLIC CEMETERY, HARDING WAY AND CEMETERY LANE
An object of rare beauty at the south entrance of the cemetery is this marble statue of Saint Joachim, whose name was spelled the Spanish way in the naming of the county. He was the husband of Saint Anne and the father of the Blessed Virgin Mary.

San Joaquin County was established as one of the twenty-seven original counties in California, February 18, 1850. *(Photograph by Raymond W. Hillman)*

FOREWORD

"When I want to understand what is happening today or try to decide what will happen tomorrow," wrote Oliver Wendell Holmes, "I look back."

As you read this fine history, you will find your perspective enlarged. You will see and understand how far San Joaquin County and its people have come and you will dare to imagine what can take place in its bright future.

A look at the map of the state of California shows that at the heart of this Golden State is San Joaquin County,

a county leading the state in asparagus and corn production;

a county blessed with some of the richest soil in the world, its leading produce being milk, grapes, tomatoes, eggs and almonds;

a county with one thousand miles of life-giving waterways not only irrigating farmland and bringing international shipping through the Delta, but also providing recreation to scores of people from across the country;

a county that is a transportation hub, served by a major metropolitan airport, three transcontinental railroads, an internationally significant inland deep-water seaport, over 160 trucking firms, and two major highways—State Highway 99, spanning California, and Interstate 5, linking the Canadian and Mexican borders;

a county encompassing 1,440 square miles and 921,000 acres within its boundaries;

a county with a cosmopolitan population of over 407,000, unique in its ethnic diversity;

a county that is fifteenth largest in a state of

THE SETTING OF SAN JOAQUIN COUNTY IN 1879

Like much of the San Joaquin Valley, the region surrounding Stockton was originally covered with broad, flat grasslands interspersed with park-like groves of valley oak trees. Only vestiges of these stands remain today and are preserved mainly in Oak Grove Regional Park on Eight Mile Road near Interstate 5, Caswell State Park on the Stanislaus River near Ripon, and Micke Grove Park near Armstrong Road and Highway 99. Tens of thousands of valley oaks were cut down to prepare the fertile valley plain of the county for grain farming.

The Livermore Range, south of Mount Diablo, is shown in the distance in this monochrome lithograph from Thompson and West's *Illustrated History of San Joaquin County*.

fifty-eight counties and which has the potential to be a leader among its peers;

a county rich in its own history and holding a significant place in the history of California and of the nation;

a county and a people with a great future.

Leonard Covello and Ray Hillman have prepared for us an extraordinary pictorial and narrative study of San Joaquin County, its communities and its people. Their efforts have produced a "county family album." This "family" is comprised of all the communities of San Joaquin County, past and present. The reader is given a comprehensive summary history of each community showing its evolution from the earliest days to the present. Emphasis has been placed upon human involvement in the social, political, cultural, commercial and architectural transitions that our county has made since the Yokuts Indians and the French Canadian trappers first made this area their home.

In birth, one does not have the opportunity to choose one's home, but I feel very fortunate to be a native of San Joaquin County and to have had the opportunity to grow up in such a wonderful and beautiful setting. I am proud of the fact that I am a fifth generation native, my wife Sandra is a third generation native, and our son, Matthew, is now the sixth generation of our family to grow up in this historically bountiful county.

Much has taken place in this county since the last book on the county's history was written in 1923, and Leonard Covello and Raymond Hillman have prepared a fresh view of San Joaquin County from its early beginnings to the exciting decade we are part of today. Their effort has provided all of us with a comprehensive resource from which we can learn and teach our children. Researched from obscure as well as more readily accessible published and unpublished materials as well as the recollections of long-time residents, this book is a real contribution to the literature of our region. All of us, native and non-native, can share a common bond and can truly and proudly identify ourselves as residents and citizens of San Joaquin County.

Douglass Woods Wilhoit, Jr.
Supervisor, San Joaquin County
Stockton, California
1985

RIBBON CUTTING FOR HIGHWAY I-5, OCTOBER 12, 1979

The long-awaited dedication ceremony honoring completion of the 1,380 mile route took place at the Mokelumne River Bridge northeast of Lodi within sight of the long abandoned gold rush river crossing of Benson's Ferry.

The new highway links three countries and representatives from each were present as follows: (left to right) Rafael Reyes Sindola, counsul general of Mexico at Sacramento; Andrianna Gianturco, director of transportation, State of California; H. J. Horne, consul general of Canada at San Francisco; R. G. Harvey, deputy minister of the British Columbia Department of Highways.

SAN JOAQUIN COUNTY MUSEUM, HELPING TO PRESERVE OUR HERITAGE

Micke Grove is a major facility supported by San Joaquin County, just west of Highway 99 off Armstrong Road. It was once known as Pixley's Grove and was deeded to the county in 1938 by Mr. and Mrs. William G. Micke, vineyardists.

One of the outstanding features in the park aside from a zoo, Japanese garden and other attractions, is the San Joaquin County Historical Museum, established in 1966 to obtain and interpret collections on the agricultural development of San Joaquin County.

The buildings (above) are situated on twelve acres within the park. The three matching structures house exhibits on agriculturally related subjects including a large Holt combined harvester built in Stockton during the mid 1920s. The Erickson Building in the background houses displays on county ethnic groups and settings of period furniture as well as the administrative offices. Additions to this building completed in 1985 with funds

from the Helen Weber Kennedy Estate house important collections of furniture and personal effects of Mr. and Mrs. Charles M. Weber. Weber was the founder of Stockton.

One exhibit, left, includes a rare twelve-foot diameter windmill made about a hundred years ago by the John S. Davis Company, a major Stockton firm and one of several manufacturing windmills widely used throughout the city and county. The "auto top" buggy was first prize in a raffle during the 1906 Lockeford Picnic.

Some of the principal exhibits are based on the Locher Tool Collection, the largest west of the Mississippi, the Clack Crawler Tractor Collection (featuring Caterpillar products) and the Tope-Gregory Ethnographic Collection. A special interest is California flora with the Walled Garden, a botanical garden, and the recently dedicated Sunshine Trail for the blind.

Museum exhibits are open from 1:00 p.m. to 5:00 p.m. Wednesday through Sunday. Visitors making prior arrangements are taken through by a trained volunteer tour guide.

THE HAGGIN MUSEUM PRESERVES THE HERITAGE OF SAN JOAQUIN COUNTY

One of California's art and history museums is located in Stockton's Victory Park on Pershing Avenue, just off Interstate 5. Named for Louis Terah Haggin, a prominent nineteenth and early twentieth century California attorney, it is operated as a private nonprofit institution by the San Joaquin Pioneer and Historical Society.

The museum opened in 1931 and has been vastly expanded over the years. It now has about 34,000 square feet of exhibit space. The major collections of nineteenth century American and French paintings and decorative arts include the work of Albert Bierstadt, E. L. Henry, Thomas Moran, Rosa Bonheur, Paul Gaugin, J. G. Vibert, and others. Extensive exhibits of California and local history also are on view.

The newest addition, Holt Memorial Hall, opened in 1976 and is dedicated to Stockton's contribution to the mechanization of American agriculture. One of the centerpieces of this exhibit is a Holt "75" track-type tractor built in Stockton about 1918. Thousands of these seventy-five horsepower units were manufactured for agricultural as well as military use. This is a particularly representative style of early Holt products.

Other exhibits relating to San Joaquin County in this hall and elsewhere in the museum are a 1904 Haines-Houser combined harvester, the second oldest on view in the United States; Benjamin Holt's experimental machine shop; and the four rooms of Victorian furniture from the Jennie Hunter ranch house near Linden. There is a particularly important collection of nineteenth century fire engines, including the second oldest steam pumper in the United States (1861). The American Indian Gallery, featuring California Indians, opened in 1981. It includes outstanding artifacts on the Yokuts, the original inhabitants of the San Joaquin Valley. Since 1948, the museum has operated the Petzinger Library, which has become a major repository of one-of-a-kind materials, including biographical data on pioneer residents of the county, industries of the nineteenth and twentieth centuries, the development of Stockton and surrounding communities, and more. The photograph, map and manuscript collections are extensive. This facility is available by appointment to advanced researchers.

With advance arrangements, groups may tour the exhibits with one of nearly fifty trained volunteer guides from the museum's Docent Council. The museum is open free from 1:30 p.m. to 5:00 p.m., Tuesday through Sunday. *(Courtesy the Haggin Museum, Stockton)*

GRANDSTAND AT THE COUNTY FAIRGROUNDS NEAR PRESENT CHARTER AND AIRPORT WAY, 1947
   Sulky racing was a featured event that started at the fairgrounds in the 1860s. In 1958, this c. 1920 wooden grandstand was replaced by the present facility for thoroughbred racing. Two extension ladders for installing aerial wires for a special event are leaning against the stand in this photo.

A PRIZE-WINNING EXHIBIT ON VERNALIS AND ITS AGRICULTURE FEATURED AN EARLY FALSE
FRONT GENERAL STORE/POST OFFICE THAT STILL STANDS IN THE TOWN
   While horse racing has been a tradition at the San Joaquin County District Fair, the annual event has also provided an important opportunity for local residents to learn of their surroundings. The exhibits of livestock, home arts and the booths organized to represent various communities have done much to disseminate information and instill local pride. In the early days, these exhibits were set up in Hunter Square and later in the Agricultural Pavilion opposite Saint Mary's Catholic Church.
   Today, the fairgrounds are not only busy during the traditional August fair time, but also for other events throughout the year. The annual Stockton Ag Expo, featuring the latest in farm machinery, drew 35,000 visitors in January 1985.

ACKNOWLEDGMENTS

Each of the following has kindly cooperated with review of parts of the manuscript or has given information or other encouragement during research of this book. The town in parentheses next to a name is the subject community for which that person provided data or other assistance.

Those who have provided photographs are given credit under the illustrations throughout the book. Pictures without credit lines are from the Covello Collection of historic photographs.

A. C. "Doc" Alders (Farmington)
George Barber (Thornton-Benson's Ferry)
Louise Jahant Bennett (Acampo)
Michael Bennett (San Joaquin County Historical Museum)
Angelo Brovelli (Forest Lake)
Bob Brunetti (Ripon)
Darrell Christy
Merral Clark (Escalon)
Christopher Colombo (Escalon)
Emery Conrad (Lodi-Clements)
Evelyn Costa (Tracy)
Guard C. Darrah (Woodbridge)
Olive Davis (Linden)
Jay Davison (Terminous)
Karen deJong (Clements)
Keith Dennison (Haggin Museum)
Mrs. George di Carlo (Linden)
Erva Dike (San Joaquin River Club)
Albert Henri "Frenchy" Disdier (Woodbridge)
Alma and Diane Freggiaro (Waterloo)
Charlie Eilers (Linden)
Leo Friedberger (Clements)
John Fujiki (French Camp)
Jabez Gibson (Clements)
Clarence E. Gordon (Clements)
Clyde C. Hall (Lathrop)
Del Haskell (Ellis)
Alan Hawkins (Tracy)
Anne Whittier Hayes, Hugh E. Hayes
Ted Heil (Victor)

Ruth Herbert (Farmington)
Frank Hillendahl (San Joaquin River Club)
Ray A. Hillman, Sr.
Ruth E. Hillman
Walter Hogan (Escalon)
Harry Holt (Holt)
Parker Holt (Holt)
Benton A. Hooper (Manteca)
Roy Hull (Vernalis and Banta)
Les Johnson (Escalon)
Ron Kaiser (Linden)
Delmar Knoll and Sons (Victor)
Gunter Konold (Stockton)
Clifford W. Koster (Tracy)
William Lange (Lodi)
Lodi Public Library, Reference Desk Staff
Aletha Mapes (Linden)
Milton McCann (Terminous)
John McCarthy
Mr. and Mrs. John Meek (Undine)
Edward Charles Merlo (Woodbridge)
Rich Mettler (Victor)
Father Jerome Meyer (Morada)
Ron Miller (Stockton)
Clem V. Mulholland (Ripon)
Ray Murphy (Vernalis)
Tom Nicolas (French Camp and Lathrop)
Christine Peterman (San Joaquin River Club)
The Petzinger Library (Haggin Museum)
Marion Ray Ray (Stockton)

Clarence Rennels (Manteca)
Robert Rinn (Lodi)
Rose Roskin (Terminous)
Setsuko Ryuto
Sacramento Public Library, Reference Desk Staff
William W. Salmon (Undine)
Apolinar Sangalang (Lathrop)
Al Schaeffer (Vernalis)
Hal Schell (Terminous)
John Schlotthauer (Victor)
George Schmeidt (Acampo)
Robert Shellenberger (remote areas)
John Philip Sousa (Forest Lake)
Steve Stocking (Acampo)
Stockton Public Library, Reference Desk Staff
Neva Summers (Ripon)
John and Helen Talbot (Lodi)
Dorothy Taylor (Lyoth)
Evelyn Thompson (Manteca)
Carl Trinkle (Vernalis)
Bill Wade (Lodi)
Ted Wallace (Stockton)
Ralph Wetmore (Lodi)
Earle E. Williams (Tracy and Carnegie)
Clifford Wisdom (Vernalis)
Richard Yoshikawa (French Camp)
Paul Zimmerman (Lodi)

PART I

TH

NCORPORATED
COMMUNITIES

STOCKTON
LODI
MANTECA
TRACY
RIPON
ESCALON

STAR AUTO STAGE DEPOT, WEST SIDE OF COURTHOUSE, c. 1918

Pacific Greyhound Lines, established in 1931, can trace its beginnings to this Stockton firm which was a consolidation of local jitney bus drivers just after World War I. Star Auto Stages took leadership in organizing inter-city service in California. In 1919 the line was purchased by the organizers of Yellow Cab Company of San Francisco and an associate. As a result, more lines were linked with Star Auto Stage routes including Los Angeles, Portland and Seattle. In 1927 the first transcontinental bus line to New York City was established.

A small portion of the Hotel Stockton arcade can be seen above the bus on the right, which, by the way, had headlights that burned carbide gas. Both "stages" shown are bound for Modesto. *(Collection of Doris Williams)*

STOCKTON
CALIFORNIA'S SUNRISE SEAPORT

The rush for gold coincided with the development of Stockton. Its far-sighted founder, German immigrant Charles M. Weber, commissioned a townsite encompassing an entire square mile in 1848-49 and established the present street pattern, parks and town lots before the great surge of growth began. This land was just a small portion of nearly 50,000 acres comprising Weber's "El Rancho del Campo de los Franceses." (French Camp Ranch). Second largest of all, this Mexican land grant encompassed the heart of San Joaquin County. At the time, the region was considered to be on the very edge of the frontier where few would venture.

The very early survey gave Stockton the distinction of being the first planned community in California. The name Stockton was bestowed at the time, to honor United States Navy Commodore Robert F. Stockton. He never visited this region and received the honor for helping to save Weber's life during the war with Mexican forces for California. Thus, the city of Stockton became the first in the state to receive a name that was not of Spanish or Indian origin.

Orderly growth was important when the community was rapidly expanding with its role as a major transportation and supply center for the Southern Mines of the famous Sierra Nevada gold belt. Such a role was assured, as Weber situated the town at the closest point to the Sierra Nevada foothills that river boats could reach. Stage coaches, pack mule trains and scores of freight wagons made connections at riverboat landings along what is now West Weber Avenue.

All provisions, miners' tools, building material, furniture and other freight bound for such mining camps as Jackson, Mokelumne Hill, San Andreas, Angels Camp, Columbia, Sonora and Mariposa first came to Stockton by river boat. By 1849, there was regular steamer service between Stockton and San Francisco. The first steam-powered riverboat tied up to an oak tree; its pilot is remembered only as Captain Warren, but it is also recorded that his river boat earned him $300,000 in just a few months.

GREAT SEAL OF THE CITY OF STOCKTON

In March 1851, the first mayor of Stockton, attorney Samuel Purdy, submitted the sketch for this seal and it was officially accepted by the board of aldermen, now known as the city council. Stockton is a public corporation and this is the corporate seal used on all official documents. Within just a few months Purdy was in Sacramento serving the first of two terms as lieutenant governor.

The design is very representative of our region and has never been officially changed, although it was redrawn by the mid 1920s and the Tule elk turned around. The Diablo Range forms the background, 3,849-foot Mount Diablo rising behind the horns of the elk.

Such elk, also known as dwarf elk, abounded in the valley, especially in the Delta region, with herds once numbering in the thousands. The numbers of elk and also pronghorn antelope dwindled quickly, as they were a ready source of meat for commercial hunters during the gold rush. The Tule elk almost became extinct in the late 1860s, but the Miller & Lux Cattle Company kept a pair; most of those surviving today at Tule Elk State Park near Tupman in Kern County and elsewhere are descendants of those two elk. There are no Tule elk surviving in San Joaquin County today. *(Courtesy Stockton City Council and the Office of the City Clerk)*

The original City of Stockton official press with a bond on which it was used circa 1890.

THE WEBER HOME

Ralph Yardley portrayed this accurate scene in his marvelous series of pen and ink sketches for the *Stockton Record*. The Weber home, constructed of adobe and redwood in about 1850, was the first residential showplace in Stockton and the first elaborate dwelling built on the San Joaquin Valley floor. It was located on Weber Point. The single story portion was the kitchen and dining room, preserved today at the San Joaquin County Museum. Charles M. Weber used the tower to observe the progress of riverboats coming to Stockton. In the distance is the bark *Otranto* which arrived laden with gold seekers in 1851. The pioneer residence fell into ruin after a new home was built in the early 1890s. The site of the original house is now the swimming pool of the Holiday Inn.

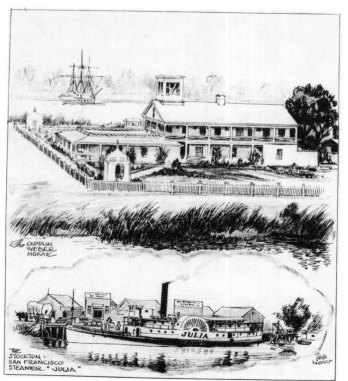

Weber was not a sea captain; his title was military. He served as a captain of Mexican auxiliary forces under General Jose Castro in the early 1840s, and, when there was an opportunity to win Caifornia for the United States, he served under army Captain John C. Fremont.

The side wheeler *Julia* was christened in honor of Charles and Helen Weber's only daughter in 1870 and was a familiar sight on the Stockton to San Francisco run for nearly twenty years. The couple had two sons, Charles and Thomas. Julia, a particularly important early Stockton woman, was very active and is remembered for her role in helping to establish Saint Joseph's Hospital, the Children's Home of Stockton and similar humanitarian projects. *(Collection of the Haggin Museum, Stockton)*

Adjacent to the river boat landings along the south bank of the Stockton Channel between present Madison and El Dorado streets was the principal business district. Major hotels such as the What Cheer House, the Corinthian, Saint Charles and other business establishments were located here upon the most valuable real estate in the city. By 1854, Stockton had a population of 7,000 and was the fourth largest city in California, next to San Francisco, Sacramento and Marysville, all principal gold rush supply and transportation centers.

Growth was to continue after the gold rush came to an end, about 1855. This was possible due to the city's strategic location at the head of year round navigation in the San Joaquin Valley and particularly because of the newly discovered resource of rich land for farming throughout much of the territory.

As a result of the overwhelming success of farming for the export trade, the city became a major commercial center; it was a focal point for grain warehousing, flour milling, grain and flour export and farm implement manufacturing. Sacramento and Marysville shared similar roles as trade centers for grain lands to the north.

When Stockton was included in the first transcontinental railroad system in 1869, its transportation facilities were further enhanced. Large manufacturing plants producing specialized machinery for the grain ranches were built along the railroad right of way.

Combined harvesters, remarkable horse-drawn machines that cut, threshed and sacked grain in one operation, were first mass-produced here in 1876 by Matteson & Williamson. One of these machines, built by Holt in Stockton during 1886, is now enshrined in the Hall of Agriculture at the Smithsonian Institution in Washington, D.C. Also very well-known was the Harris Manufacturing Company, the last to build combines locally; they built grain and bean harvesters to about 1950.

The Holt Manufacturing Company went on to greater feats of technology with the development of the first caterpillar track-type tractor, starting in the early twentieth century. Such units were mass produced here until a 1925 merger with Best Tractor Company to form Caterpillar of today. Holt had a large foundry, one of several that once operated locally. Beautiful iron castings on a cable car built by the Stockton Car, Machine and Agricul-

tural Works nearly a century ago can also be seen at the Smithsonian, a fine testimony of Stockton's role in American industrial productivity.

Several flour mills were built along Weber Avenue, the largest of which was Sperry's, producer of the famous "Drifted Snow Flour." They were among the major employers for decades until they closed in 1927.

Not all local industry served the farmers. El Dorado Brewing Company, opened in 1853 by Daniel Rothenbush, shipped Valley Brew beer to many parts of California and Nevada for 102 years.

In the late 1870s, a unique industry was founded by R. B. Lane. It was the California Paper Company, which was a pioneer recycling plant specializing in the manufacture of newsprint from rags, old paper and straw—a first for California.

There were several local wagon and carriage builders. The most famous was M. P. Henderson, who not only built stage coaches for use throughout the American West, but also constructed some of the famed Twenty Mule Team Borax wagons. By the late 1880s, Stockton was the second most industrialized city in California, after San Francisco.

Examples of twentieth century firms bringing fame to the city include R. G. LeTourneau, which was first organized about 1920 to develop landleveling equipment that has found usefulness in major projects all over the world. Tillie Lewis Foods, now an Ogden Food Products division, traces its beginnings to the late 1930s and has brought recognition to the community, not only because of its product line, including pioneering diet foods, but also because its president, Tillie Lewis, became one of the most prominent female industrialists in the United States.

Boat building is the oldest industry in Stockton and can be traced to 1850. Many of the paddlewheel steamers that plied the San Joaquin River, Sacramento River and the Delta between 1849 and 1938 were launched here. The best known are the river boats *Delta King* and *Delta Queen*, both of which exist today. Except for their steel hulls from Scotland and some machinery, they were built from raw materials in Stockton between 1923 and 1927. Several local shipyards were active filling government contracts during World War II. The largest, Pollock-Stockton, employed 5,000 persons, 18 percent of them women. Other important wartime developments along the channel were an army motor supply and repair depot, transferred

SOME OF THE PRINCIPAL BUILDINGS OF GOLD RUSH STOCKTON, 1854

These illustrations are from the border vignettes of a lithograph printed in San Francisco and published by local bookseller and stationer J. F. Rosenbaum. Rosenbaum's little shop is included.

All of these structures were located south of Weber Avenue, principally along El Dorado and Center streets. The only exception is the State Asylum, which was located at Grant and Flora streets. This huge building was unusually pretentious for the times and remained standing for over a century.

These brick buildings were constructed after the great fire of 1851, and the property owners, anxious to avert another disaster, rebuilt with fire proof material. To avoid as much fire damage as possible, the city government passed a zoning ordinance in 1855 forbidding the construction of wooden buildings in the

from Fort Ord to the Port of Stockton, and the mammoth Rough and Ready Island naval supply annex built in 1944. By 1943 fifty local firms were producing goods to supply the fighting forces.

Today, large custom yachts are built at the world famous Stephens Marine Inc. yard on the Stockton Channel. Stephens' neighbor, Colberg Inc., specializes in the construction and repair of commercial and government vessels.

Shipping activity can be seen almost daily at the Port of Stockton, opened in 1933 as the first inland seaport in California. It is still the largest such facility in the state and in recent years has become active and profitable once again, with twenty steamship companies serving it. A thousand people are employed, including the employees of the tenant firms at the port. Grain is the major cargo, followed by liquid (including aviation fuel), bulk (mainly fertilizer) and general cargo.

Although not permanently located here, the movie industry has been a regular visitor to Stockton and vicinity for more than sixty years. Scores of films have been made here, including the 1936 hit,

Steamboat 'Round the Bend starring Will Rogers. Productions of recent years include *Raid on Entebbe, Good Luck Miss Wykoff, Friendly Fire, Coast to Coast, Valley Girls, Dream Scape* and *Valentino Returns.*

Several state and local institutions have located here, the oldest being the State Hospital, the first publicly supported facility for the mentally afflicted in the West when it was opened in 1854. State Hospital Superintendent Dr. Margaret Smythe was just one of the famous people residing in Stockton; she served from 1929 to 1946.

Another, of more recent times, was the late Warren Atherton, attorney and influential Legionnaire. While national commander of the American Legion in 1944, he played a major role in the effort leading to the tremendously important GI Bill providing benefits to veterans.

One of the first woman attorneys, Laura De Force Gordon, practiced law and published a newspaper here in the 1870s. She later was the first woman to serve on the California Supreme Court.

Starting in 1868, Stockton became known for its

central business district. The first two-story brick building is shown, the pharmacy built by Erastus S. Holden at the northeast corner of El Dorado and Main streets. It remained standing, although considerably altered, until 1967. A notable wood frame building is the first mill of what became known as the Sperry Flour Company. In the early 1850s it was known as Sperry and Baldwin and operated at Commerce and Main streets.

good educational opportunities for Blacks, a reputation first developed by noted Black educator Jeremiah B. Sanderson. During 1985 a monument honoring Sanderson was unveiled near the school site at Washington and Monroe streets.

Another famous person was millionaire Japanese farmer George Shima, known as the "Potato King." In the early twentieth century, through his intensive and scientific methods of cultivation, he helped develop Stockton as the "Spud Capital of the World," a title long since lost to Oregon and Idaho.

The city has always had an unusually diverse ethnic population. By 1920 there were 840 Japanese, one of the largest Japanese populations in the United States. Their major commercial and social district was around Commerce and Market streets. During the 1930s, Stockton was nicknamed "Little Manila" because it had the largest population of Filipinos outside the Philippines. There are still many Filipino and Japanese families living here. The earliest ethnic groups were the Caifornia In-

dians, Mexican-Americans and the Chinese. The latter two have well-established roles in local business, farming interests, government and other areas.

Up to the late 1940s, there was considerable gambling in Stockton, conducted openly in several locations. Chinese lottery, card games and slot machines were common.

A host of cultural organizations have been established in Stockton to sponsor ballet, chamber music, drama, opera and other performing arts activities. One of the oldest is the Stockton Symphony Orchestra, which has been performing since 1927. Its first musical director, Manilo Silva, was responsible for guiding this group through its difficult formative years.

In 1930 the Fox-West Coast theater chain completed the 2,500 seat Fox on Main Street, an unusually elaborate facility intended to serve both as a movie palace and a vaudeville theater. The edifice is receiving continuing extensive renovation and is becoming part of local cultural life once again.

It is one of the last two remaining theaters of this type in the Central Valley.

A year after the theater opened, the Haggin Museum was dedicated and the first art and California history exhibits opened to visitors. The substantial brick building in Victory Park was erected as a result of combined efforts of the McKee family, San Joaquin Society of California Pioneers and many other donors. The Louis Terah Haggin collection of nineteenth century French and American art, a gift from Mr. and Mrs. Robert T. McKee, is one of the most outstanding in the United States. Over the years, major exhibits of Indian basketry, vehicles, store fixtures, industrial history, etc. relating to state and local history have been developed.

Another distinctive facility is Louis Park, the location of Pixie Woods, one of the finest children's parks in California. It has been steadily growing in size and in citizens' support since 1955.

During the past thirty years, numerous projects of the federal, state and local government have changed the face of Stockton. The West Lane post office, erected in 1969, is a regional processing center for the surrounding valley and foothills, including Stanislaus, Calaveras, Merced and Tuolumne counties. A $23 million facility will be completed in 1986 at Arch Road and Highway 99 on a 17 acre site, which will vastly extend the capabilities of this center. Not only will the role as a regional postal center continue but it will also become a vehicle maintenance garage for the post office fleet serving the surrounding area.

The State of California erected a major office building on Channel Street and also during the 1950s developed extensive new facilities at the Stockton State Hospital. The role of the hospital in training programs for 774 developmentally disabled as well as drug abuse patients has led to continuing activity and expanding facilities into the 1980s. Dameron Hospital, with 148 beds, has the most modern burn and eye clinics in a wide area. Saint Joseph's has 359 beds and facilities for open heart surgery and a twenty-four hour emergency room. In 1985 Kaiser Permanente Health Plan Inc. began construction of a hospital and medical center at West Lane at Hammer Lane.

A few of the major projects of San Joaquin County government within the city during the past twenty-five years have been the erection of a new Courthouse and administrative wing on the site of the domed 1890 Courthouse; the terminal

THE ORIGINAL TEMPLE ISRAEL, HUNTER STREET, ON PART OF THE PRESENT POST OFFICE FACILITY, c. 1880

Stockton has always had an important Jewish community and today retains the oldest Jewish synagogue building standing in the American West.

Shown here at its second location, this venerable structure originally occupied a lot near the intersection of Miner Avenue and El Dorado Street, where it was erected in 1855. After being moved to its second location, Hunter Street, it was again relocated to American Street opposite the Department of Motor Vehicles, where it became an apartment house, a purpose it serves to this day. It is the oldest non-residential building standing in Stockton today and is a registered Stockton Historical Landmark. (Collection of the Holt-Atherton Pacific Center for Western Studies, University of the Pacific)

EL DORADO STREET LOOKING NORTH FROM THE CROSSTOWN FREEWAY, 1983

Evidence of Captain Weber's excellent city planning, dating back to 1849, can be seen in this photograph. The street has been eighty-one feet wide ever since he founded the city. Even more impressive is the width of Weber and Miner avenues, each 115 feet wide. These east-west streets were major freighting routes between the river boat landings and the principal routes to the mines. Weber knew how beneficial it would be to have streets wide enough to turn around freight teams and wagons. Hazelton Avenue was 160 feet wide originally.

Shown at left is a portion of the Stockton Police Facility, which occupies an entire block. The former Lee Center, now the Franco Center, a residential and commercial facility, is at right. The tall building beyond it is the San Joaquin First Federal Tower, now Great American First Savings Bank, erected in 1975 as the most prominent of several banking institutions in the redevelopment district.

building and control tower at the Metropolitan Airport; and, most recently, the Michael N. Canlis Administration Building on Hunter Street. Runway expansion and construction of other facilities at the airport have been major projects of the board of supervisors since the 1960s.

The City of Stockton has undertaken numerous public works projects during this same period, resulting in four new libraries, including the Central Library, the Southeast, Margaret Troke and Fair Oaks branches; a new central fire station; a police facility; and several redevelopment projects, two of which are downtown west of El Dorado Street. The first downtown redevelopment covered a nine block area and was financed by two-thirds federal funding during the early 1960s. About ten years later, work began in a second area farther west.

Stockton's water supply underwent a major change at the close of the 1970s with completion of the Stockton-East Water District Treatment plant. this ended dependence upon ground water, which would be supplemented by a supply from New Hogan Dam in Calaveras County. The elaborate water treatment facility has received nationwide attention.

Stockton has been expanding its horizons since the early 1960s through its Sister City program. There are now three sister cities: Shimizu, a port city in Japan; Iliolo in the Philippines; and Empalme near Guaymas, Mexico.

Particularly dramatic since the late 1940s has been the growth of residential and commercial areas north of the Calaveras River. Starting with an 1,800 acre site, Sims and Grupe created the Lincoln Village subdivision. Growth continued with numerous other successful projects by this and other development firms, including Park Woods, Mayfair, Sherwood Manor and Lincoln Village West. With these came major commercial developments—Lincoln Shopping Center, Weberstown, Sherwood Mall and Village Square (now Marina Center), which would draw considerable retail business from old downtown. Construction commenced during the summer of 1985 on a project which will disburse the concentration of automobile dealerships downtown. Five will relocate to the innovative auto center at Highway 99 and Hammer Lane.

From the 1960s to the end of the 1970s, the population nearly quadrupled north of the Calaveras River so that the population here alone excelled that of Lodi, Manteca, Ripon and Tracy combined. While much of the growth has been in the north, some recent attention has been given to making the central district more of a population center through the constuction of new residential facilities. Particularly important toward this end has been the Filipino Center, Steamboat Landing and Delta Gateway apartments, which contain nearly 600 dwelling units altogether.

A considerable portion of Stockton's work force

PLATE XXXVI

A.W. SIMPSON.   "MANSION HOUSE" STOCKTON, SAN JOAQUIN Cº CAL.   GEORGE GRAY

THE MANSION HOUSE, NORTHEAST CORNER OF WEBER AVENUE AND HUNTER STREET, 1879

This is one of the many important monochrome lithographs prepared for the *Illustrated History of San Joaquin County* published by Thompson and West. The Mansion House was a major hotel when it was completed in 1873 as an investment of prominent lumber dealer George Gray. The Mansion House was stripped of its turret and ornamentation in the late 1940s but still stands today, just east of the old Hotel Stockton. The adjacent two-story building was a prominent grocery store and is no longer standing.

At the lower left a Stockton and Copperopolis Railroad locomotive puffs its way east on Weber Avenue for a thirty-eight mile run to Milton in Calaveras County. Steam locomotives were operated on Weber Avenue from 1870 into the early twentieth century by Southern Pacific, which soon acquired the Stockton and Copperopolis line.

This line was the first to serve the center of the city and the head of navigation, but it was not the first to reach Stockton. The first transcontinental railroad was built by Central Pacific through the eastern fringe of the community in 1869 on its way to Oakland via Altamont Pass. Two other transcontinental lines have been constructed through Stockton since this time, Santa Fe and Western Pacific. Today, all these lines are in operation with additional facilities provided by the Central California Traction Company, Stockton Terminal and Eastern and the Tidewater Southern. Western Pacific, part of the Union Pacific System since 1984, has particularly elaborate shops for the major overhaul of locomotives.

and buying power is concentrated in what is generally referred to as "South Stockton." While it was overlooked for decades, this area has gained increasing attention for its resources of open lands for residential development. Particularly extensive new construction was seen in the All Nations development on East Eighth Street near Airport Way, with 243 units covering thirty-two acres completed in 1982. In the same year Nabors Estates, twenty-one parcels between Commerce and Madison streets off Eighth, received considerable attention. Completion of softball diamonds at the San Joaquin County Regional Sports Complex in August 1985 was another important event for the southern section of the city. More softball and soccer fields will be added to the city-county-state financed Arch Road/Highway 99 facility.

In recent years, the Triangle, Air Metro, Grupe and other industrial parks have been developed on southern fringes of this area, where there is excellent highway and rail access.

Encouragement of infill residential construction has also had an effect in bringing new investment. The older residential areas, while still needing more understanding and improvements, have been receiving important assistance since the 1960s. Hundreds of properties in Knight's Addition, Sharpe's Lane, McKinley Park, Columbus Park and others have been improved. The "clean sweep" concept of redevelopment has been generally avoided and rehabilitation of existing homes has been widespread. Community Block grants, started in 1969, encouraged strong, active citizen participation.

Another program started at the same time that has made this portion of the city more attractive is the federally assisted Code Enforcement program (FACE), which has resulted in considerable upgrading of privately owned housing. All of these opportunities for neighborhood improvement have done much to encourage the organization of citizens' groups for better neighborhoods, and this spirit is continuing.

A steady industrial growth has accompanied residential developments. Within the city, various firms are engaged in manufacturing machinery, concrete pipe, wood and paper products, steel fabrication, ship building, food processing and bakery goods. There are many important firms: American Forest Products, Inc. produces lumber, furniture, pallets, shipping containers and mill work and has employed up to 450; Johns Manville

Products Corporation employs 350 in the manufacture of concrete pipe. There are three major canneries employing thousands seasonally. These include Del Monte, H. J. Heinz and Ogden Food Products (Tillie Lewis Food Division). One-half of the United States walnut crop is processed on Charter Way near Highway 99 by Sun-Diamond Growers of California, Inc., which operates the Diamond Walnut plant that has thirteen acres under one roof. Five of California's major grower and producer associations are in Stockton: California Beet Growers (sugar beet growers), Valley Honey, California Tomato Growers, California Asparagus and San Joaquin Cherry Growers.

New arrivals in the community have been Sumiden Wire, Ltd., employing 200, and Corn Products Corporation International. In the spring of 1981 this firm, one of the world's leading food processors, completed a facility to produce syrup and other products from local corn as well as huge train loads of corn from the Midwest. It is an ultimate in automation for the industry. Its corn products are extensively used as a substitute for beet sugar by the canning, commercial baking and soft drink industries.

Stockton gained more noteriety nationwide through California Cooler, a pioneer in the wine cooler market. In 1985, just four years after its founding, the company was sold to a major marketer of wine and whiskey, Brown-Ferman Corporation, for $55 million. Local financiers started California Cooler with $160,000.

Seven hundred to a thousand men have been employed by Sohio in the construction of modular steel buildings that started during 1982 on the north bank of the Stockton Channel near Louis Park. The site was part of the Pollock-Stockton shipyard. Thirty-eight of these buildings and the oil recovery equipment within them were used in Prudhoe Bay, Alaska. Reaching as high as eight stories, they were constructed by Bechtel Petroleum, Inc. for Sohio. They were taken north by barge to Alaska. The work for Sohio reached completion in mid 1985. Similar work at the same facility will continue for Chevron USA, which will have Wistmer-Becker fabricate structures for its Southern California offshore fields.

Another project of Chevron USA, the Standard Oil of California subsidiary, brought a rapid change to Stockton's skyline in the spring of 1983. It began drilling for natural gas with a 180 foot high rig at Aurora and Oak streets, near the center

GRAIN WAREHOUSING AND MILLING CENTER, SOUTH BANK OF THE STOCKTON CHANNEL, c. 1885
The photographer used the roof of the Capitol Flour Mill for his vantage point. The tallest building is the Crown Flour Mill built in the early 1880s and soon acquired by Sperry. The Eureka warehouses were operated by the Grangers Cooperative Union as a service to their grain farming members who wished to avoid high warehousing fees. This effort by the organization was particularly significant statewide.

THE WAREHOUSE, 1983
Below, this scene was photographed from about the same location. The oldest brick building on the channel (early 1870s) was expanded three times and by 1897 took its present proportions. This former Grangers warehouse was purchased by Sperry and Company about 1890 to serve its huge Union Flour Mill. The mill site is the parking lot for this complex. Grain was stored on the ground floor prior to milling, and flour for shipment by river boat was kept on the second story. In more recent decades, it was the San Joaquin Wholesale Grocers warehouse. Today, the extensively renovated structure is a mini Ghirardelli Square and a show place for Stockton. It presently contains several shops plus five restaurants, Wednesdays at the Warehouse, Chez Zabeth, The Fish Market, Antonio's Mexican Cuisine and Peta's Continental Cuisine. The new headquarters for the Stockton Chamber of Commerce was established here in 1984.

YOUNG LADIES AND A HOLT COMBINED HARVESTER, 1895

Stockton might well be called the "home of the combined harvester," as it was here that the first of these machines were mass produced in 1876. The machine shown here could cut, thresh and sack twenty-seven acres of grain a day.

One of the largest builders of combines to operate in Stockton was the Holt Manufacturing Company, which shipped units all over California, the American West and, eventually, to foreign countries including Australia and Russia. Their advertising was extensive, and particularly creative was the distribution of the above photo. To emphasize the ease with which Holt's combines could be operated, a crew of young ladies operated the machinery for four hours. It was pulled by a team of twenty-six mules and horses. The event took place east of Bieber (Lassen County), October 10, 1895. The original caption read in part, "Thus . . . the field of the 'new woman' is extending."

Shown from left to right are: Orra Dowell, driver; Gertie Sawyer, header tender; Lillie Dowell, sack sewer; Nellie Packwood, separator tender. *(Collection of Hugh Hayes)*

Satin flour sack made in Stockton for the company exhibit at the 1915 Panama-Pacific Exposition in San Francisco.

TYPICAL STEAMER LANDING, STOCKTON CHANNEL SOUTH BANK NEAR COMMERCE STREET, c. 1900

The sternwheeler *J. D. Peters*, named for an Italian immigrant who became a prominent banker and grain broker, is representative of a nineteenth century Stockton river boat. It was built in 1889 and remained in service until about 1936. The freight shed was owned by a well-known river transportation firm, the California Navigation and Improvement Company. Mills operated by the Sperry Flour Company can be seen over the roof top. The only structure left standing today is the office building for the Sperry Mills, the hip-roofed, single story building at left which is now the offices of Zuckerman, Hartmann and Walden. An important building historically and architecturally, it has been designated a Stockton Historical Landmark and, in addition, is listed on the National Register.

14

CALIFORNIA AND CHANNEL STREETS DURING A FLOOD, c. 1890
This was just one of a series of floods to engulf the central business district. The old horse car was a welcome service and, at the time, was in its last years before replacement by electric trolleys. The wet dog seems to be caught up in the excitement captured in this unusually lively photograph for the times. Well-known master photographer J. Pitcher Spooner recorded this scene.

of Stockton. The drilling operation bored three eight and a half inch holes which meander from eight to over 11,000 feet under 516 acres in the center of Stockton. During August 1985, the facility went into production as California's northernmost gas well.

Drawing much attention at the same time was American Savings and Loan, the principal operating subsidiary of Financial Corporation of America, the largest American savings and loan in the United States, with $27 billion in assets. In 1984 it survived the biggest bank run in history, losing $6.8 billion in deposits. The main offices of American Savings are in Stockton and occupy 645,000 square feet of office space in thirty-five separate buildings. Nearly 1,800 people were employed in 1985, making it the largest non-governmental employer in the county.

The traditional local role as a transportation center continues to grow in importance. Both the Southern Pacific and Santa Fe railroads maintain major freight transfer points at Stockton. Also very important are the thirty-eight regularly scheduled truck lines operating from Stockton.

This city of 176,934, the eighty-ninth largest in the United States, has been distinguished by its diverse ethnic groups, varied industry, important specimens of early architecture, major institutions of higher learning and culture—and a unifying factor, its trees, which bring so much character and beauty to its residential and commercial districts, covering forty square miles. Stockton's trees have for two years in succession earned its designation as "Tree City, U.S.A." from the National Arbor Day Foundation. Altogether these factors give Stockton a character and significance far beyond that which many visitors and local residents realize.

STOCKTON'S FIRST SKYSCRAPER, SAN JOAQUIN AND MAIN STREETS

Completed in 1908 as the first building expressly constructed for the Stockton Savings and Loan Bank (now the Bank of Stockton), this structure still looks much the same today. It is still owned by the Bank of Stockton, which was founded in 1867 and today is the second oldest bank in California operating under its original charter. The brick and terra cotta used in this edifice was made at Carnegie in San Joaquin County. The top two floors have always been used by the Yosemite Club, the oldest chartered men's club in California, dating from 1888.

The bank lobby still retains much of its original appearance including office furniture and beautifully matched marble from the historic quarries near Columbia in Tuolumne County. Well recognized for its historical and architectural importance, the building is a Stockton Historical Landmark; in addition, it has won a listing on the National Register.

A TRUE LANDMARK OF THE CITY—
THE HOTEL STOCKTON, c. 1910

This distinctive building, one of California's prime examples of Mission Revival Style architecture, is shown shortly after completion in 1910. It had 252 rooms, over 200 with bath, and served the traveling public with the theme of "comfort rather than elegance." Ideally situated at the head of navigation, it could be reached by those traveling from San Francisco or way landings by walking across El Dorado Street.

"IXL," painted prominently on the awnings, was the name of a clothing store that was in operation for many decades. Its space eventually became Ward Tyler's Sport Shop.

Few residents remember that the annex to the hotel under the once stately roof garden was City Hall for about fifteen years before the present City Hall was completed in the Civic Center during 1926.

In 1960 the hostelry closed and became a temporary courthouse and county office building while new facilities were being constructed across the street. It has remained county property ever since, providing offices for the public assistance, registrar of voters and other departments.

The building is one of the first to be designated a Stockton Historical Landmark.

The lobby was decorated in a Spanish Mission theme and the Indian pottery and mortars around the fireplace were actual artifacts. The fireplace is still there, and the pottery, including some c. 1800 specimens from the Southwest, was given to the Haggin Museum.

CONTRASTS ON HUNTER SQUARE, c. 1917 and 1981

Above, major buildings clearly visible, from left to right, are the Lauxen and Catts Furniture Store at San Joaquin Street and Weber Avenue, built about 1905; the San Joaquin County Courthouse-Stockton City Hall, built in 1890, which towers 172 feet above the streets; past the palms to the right, the IOOF building, built in 1866 and destined to stand only about three more years after this photograph was taken. The belfry next to the IOOF Hall is atop the central fire station of the time; its bell and clock mechanism, originally installed in the first Courthouse, are now at the Haggin Museum. On the opposite corner at the far right is the Sterling, a popular ladies' and children's clothing store.

Below, the only building familiar to the above view is the Elk's Building down Weber Avenue past the old Lauxen and Catts building, the facade of which was screened when it was the Bravo and McKeegan clothing store. The screening was removed a year after this photograph was taken and the original facade restored for State Savings and Loan. The scene is dominated by the County Courthouse and administrative wing, dedicated in October 1964. In the center of the picture, behind it, is part of the California Building, erected in 1916. The Michael N. Canlis Administration Building, completed in 1980, occupies the site of the IOOF building. In the distance beyond is the landmark steeple of Saint Mary's Catholic Church, removed for repairs a year after this picture was taken and replaced in 1985 after tremendous citizen support financed restoration and replacement.

UNIVERSITY OF THE PACIFIC CAMPUS, c. 1930

The most prominent feature is the old Baxter Stadium, built in 1929 and named for Thomas Baxter, who succeeded Benjamin Holt as Holt Manufacturing Company president. This was the home turf of legendary coach Amos Alonzo Stagg for fourteen years. Aside from the playing field, it had a quarter mile track and a baseball diamond. The adjacent gymnasium was completed in 1925 during initial construction of the campus. This campus replaced facilities in San Jose, California.

Since its first years in Stockton, the university has steadily grown, with major new buildings erected every few years. The landmark Burns Tower, a unique combined water tower and administrative building, was completed in 1964.

Upper left, across the sluggish stream that usually flows in the Calaveras River bed, is former farmland that has been almost completely covered with campus extensions and residential and commercial developments, particularly during the 1960s.

The University of the Pacific has extensive historical significance. It is California's oldest chartered institution of higher learning and was founded at Santa Clara as the California Wesleyan College in 1851. The following year it was renamed University of the Pacific and remained so until 1911, when it became College of the Pacific. This name remained in use for about half a century, until it was renamed University of the Pacific once again. The university became coeducational in 1871, an unusually early date. It relocated from San Jose to Stockton in 1924. Some of the landscaping on the new campus was done by John McLaren of Golden Gate Park fame.

Fall 1985 enrollment will approach 4,000. There was an additional combined attendance of 2,000 at the UOP McGeorge School of Law in Sacramento and the school of dentistry in San Francisco. The university employes about 1,500 people. More than 7 percent of the students were foreign students; Malaysia, Venezuela, Saudi Arabia and Indonesia were particularly well represented. The university offers doctoral programs in music, chemistry and pharmacy.

TROLLEY CAR ON MAIN STREET APPROACHING CALIFORNIA STREET, c. 1935
Stockton had electric streetcar service from 1892 to 1940. The lines gradually expanded throughout the city, with service radiating from the central business district to Victory Park on the west, Oak Park on the north, McKinley Park on the south and well east on Main Street. The car barn where this car and others were kept was on California Street; the old structure still stands and is a Centro-Mart store today. It is a designated Stockton Historical Landmark.

Streetcars disappeared from this scene in 1940, but all of the buildings in the background are still standing; while some have been remodeled, the Ritz Theater looks very much the same today.

CHINESE HERB STORE EXHIBIT AT THE HAGGIN MUSEUM

This authentically detailed period setting is composed almost exclusively from contents of the second to the last herb store to operate in Stockton. It was located in the Bow On Association building on Hunter Street opposite old Washington Park, a site now covered by the Crosstown Freeway. Acquired before clearance of the site in 1971, this is the only sizable reminder of the old Chinese business district of Stockton, which centered on Washington Street west of Hunter.

The fixtures date from about the turn of the century and came with some of the original processing equipment and stock. Each of the drawers in the photograph contains two to four carefully labeled compartments. This herb store and others like it were forced to close when trade with Red China ceased in the 1950s and many herbs, which grow nowhere else in the world, were not available. *(Courtesy Haggin Museum, Stockton)*

THE PORT OF STOCKTON, c. 1960

California's first inland port opened in 1933 as a result of tremendous financial support from Stockton residents as well as from state and federal sources. The project involved dredging a 26-foot deep, 100-foot wide waterway through islands and existing channels in the Delta to Suisun Bay. All new port facilities were built at the confluence of the Stockton Channel with the San Joaquin River. One hundred sixty-six ocean going vessels arrived at the facility during the first year, and the operation was so successful that the channel was deepened to thirty-two feet. Facilities were expanded as well, including warehouses, two lumber terminals, a grain terminal, cotton compress and 1,800 feet of concrete wharves.

Expansion and modernization of facilities have been steady over the years. Ships up to 900 feet long use the port as a result of 1985 channel deepening. The Stockton Elevators, shown in the distance, were erected in 1955 and are presently operated by Continental Grain as tenants of the port. It is the largest West Coast grain storage facility outside of Portland, Oregon. A little known fact about the structure is that the head house is 240 feet high, making it the tallest structure in Stockton. *(Photograph by Fred Feary)*

To the right, a Russian ship being loaded with grain at the Stockton Elevators, 1980.

21

SHIPYARDS IN STOCKTON

In the top photo are products of the second oldest yard in the city, Stephens Marine, Inc.: the thirty-six-foot *Graceta*, built in 1925, and the seventy-four-foot *Iwone*, launched during the eightieth anniversary of the firm in 1981. The *Iwone* was sent to Hong Kong but the *Graceta*, owned by Bob Hamilton, remains in Stockton waters as the oldest Stephens cruiser afloat.

Many types of government vessels were built by the nine yards in Stockton during World War II. These included minesweepers, net tenders, personnel barges, tugs for the army, rescue and salvage craft for the army and air force and other vessels, including this refrigerated freighter (center photo), built for the army in 1943. The freighter was a product of Hickinbotham Brothers Construction Division, operated by Guntert and Zimmerman near the head of the Stockton Channel. This firm continued steel fabrication at the former shipyard until 1985. A tug built by this company during the war serves the port of Stockton.

A "Rosie the Riveter" with an army tanker under construction at Kyle and Company Construction Division, 1943. This firm occupied the old river steamer construction and repair yard on the north bank of the Stockton Channel at Harrison Street.

THE RODGERS HOUSE, ONCE THE HOME OF A NOTED BLACK FAMILY

Located on South San Joaquin Street, two blocks south of the Santa Fe Depot, this house was built for famous Black mining engineer Moses Rodgers, his wife, Sara, and their five daughters. The family moved to Stockton about 1890 from the mining country at Quartzburg near Hornitos, Mariposa County, where "Mose" was superintendent of the Mount Gaines Mine.

The move was made to take advantage of unusually good educational resources afforded Blacks in Stockton. His daughters availed themselves of the opportunity: Adele became a professional nurse in Stockton; Lulu was accomplished in needlework; Vivian graduated from the University of California and taught at Hilo, Hawaii; Elinor spent much of her life as a teacher in the State of Washington; and Nettie became a modiste, styling dresses for well-known Stockton families. Such was the legacy of Moses Rodgers, who was born a slave in Missouri and found a great opportunity with the California gold rush. From this experience, he became a self-taught mining engineer and was so expert his advice was sought by investors from many parts of the state.

This home is a Stockton Historical Landmark.

THE SIKH TEMPLE, 1930 SOUTH GRANT STREET

Sikhs came from northwestern India, the land of Punjab, to become a prominent labor force in the Delta farmlands. This temple is the center of their lives. There has been a Sikh temple in Stockton since 1913; a year later it was established at the present location. The first, a clapboard building, served until 1929, when it was torn down and replaced by the present substantial brick edifice. This sanctuary, with its crystal chandeliers, is the principal temple for 250,000 Sikhs in the United States.

GENERAL MONCADO BUILDING, 2049 SOUTH SAN JOAQUIN STREET, 1983

This apartment building and meeting hall is a source of great pride to the local members of the Filipino Federation of America. Dedicated in 1963, the building was entirely financed through pledges of fifty-seven members of the federation. Today there are sixty-two apartments, federation offices, the General Moncado Meeting Hall, which holds 250, the federaton social hall, and eight apartments, added in 1969. The life-size marble statue of Dr. Hilario Camino Moncado in the courtyard was imported from Italy and unveiled in November 1983, replacing a profile made of steel plate.

Attorney, writer, publisher, lecturer General Hilario Moncado (1898–1956) was also founder of the Filipino Federation of America, first established in Los Angeles in 1925. Two years later, a branch was founded in Stockton. He remains perpetual president of the fraternity, which established strict codes covering diet, matrimony, appearance, etc. He is legendary to the history of the Philippines. From 1942 to 1944, General Moncado commanded guerillas in the Philippines and was known as Commander "X" of the resistance forces during the Japanese occupation. He also served as a senior delegate to the Philippine Constitutional Convention, which framed the constitution of the Republic of the Philippines.

First coming to California in 1915, he graduated from Lowell High School in San Francisco and later studied law. As an international golfer with a 3 handicap, he came to Stockton to play in 1948, and since 1951, the annual General Moncado Golf Tournament has been held here. *(Photograph by Raymond W. Hillman)*

MEXICAN DANCE GROUP PERFORMING FOR THE SPRING FESTIVAL, 1983

Los Danzantes de la Luna (Moon Dancers) are: (front) Debbie Bernardino and Gail Mettler; (back) Albert Vargas, Frank Rivera, Anthony Garcia and Albert Cadena. This group and others in Stockton maintain and encourage cultural traditions for an important Mexican-American population. Cinco de Mayo is a major event observed with a variety of activities including a huge parade through downtown Stockton. *(Photograph by Calixtro Romias)*

RAINY WEATHER DURING A PROTEST MARCH, WEBER AVENUE, 1965

Stockton joined the nationwide protest over civil rights violations in Selma, Alabama. This photo was taken at the height of the demonstrations. The two closest banners read, "Justice for our Brothers" and "Let Freedom Ring in Selma."

The landmark Hotel Stockton building has seen many events come and go since it was completed in 1910. The hotel had closed four years before this photograph was taken to be converted for use as a county office building, a purpose it still serves.

THE FIRST VIET NAM MONUMENT
IN THE NATION, CIVIC CENTER

Unveiled by the Stockton Junior Women's Club in 1973, this granite tablet has given distinction to Stockton for its pioneering efforts in memorializing the Viet Nam War. Fifty-nine San Joaquin County residents were killed in the war, and the name of each one has been inscribed on the monument.

On Veterans Day 1982, the monument received a tribute from the Vietnamese residents of Stockton in the form of the banner shown above. The gesture was repeated in 1983 and will probably become traditional in the large Vietnamese community. In mid 1983 there were 15,200 Southeast Asians living in San Joaquin County. (Photograph by Rich Turner, Stockton Record)

SAN JOAQUIN DELTA COLLEGE, c. 1979
One of the most spectacular developments in North Stockton, this is the third campus this institution has occupied. It started as Stockton Junior College in 1935 in rented facilities at the University of the Pacific. Shortly after the Second World War, a new campus was built on Kensington Avenue, south of the university. Known as San Joaquin Delta College since 1963, when it ceased to be operated by the Stockton Unified School District, it became part of the 107-campus state college system and serves students from San Joaquin County and from portions of Sacramento, Calaveras, Alameda and Solano counties. The 165 acre campus serves one of the largest districts of all the state community colleges. In recent years, there have been 18,000 day and evening students in attendance; 560 full time staff members are employed.

Humphreys College, named for educator John R. Humphreys, is another important educational institution. It has been operated by the Humphreys family since 1896. This private college now concentrates on associate degrees, bachelors degrees and a law school. About 450 attend classes on the seven acre campus, which includes student housing facilities. *(Courtesy San Joaquin Delta College)*

STOCKTON GENERAL MAIL FACILITY,
ARCH ROAD AND HIGHWAY 99, 1985

When completed in 1986, this project will
replace outgrown facilities on West Lane.
The building shown here will have over
175,000 square feet for mail processing plus
an enclosed dock terminal for trucks. Customers in San Joaquin, Stanislaus, Merced,
Tuolumne and Mariposa counties numbering 897,800 will be benefitted. This is the
fourth building expressly constructed for a
main post office in Stockton. The first, built
in 1901 at Market and California streets, was
replaced in 1933 by the "old" main post office built as a WPA project at San Joaquin
and Fremont streets. This in turn was replaced by the West Lane facility during
1966.

AN ARM OF HUGE QUAIL LAKE, LOOKING EAST FROM QUAIL LAKES DRIVE, 1983

This is part of the second water oriented Grupe Development Company subdivision; Lincoln Village West
was the first. Composed of several arms, the fifty-eight acre lake has three and a half miles of shoreline and is
six feet deep. The man-made lake basin was filled during 1975, ushering in commercial and residential
construction that continued into the 1980s.

A neighbor to this development is the Schmitz Development Inc. Venetian Gardens, flanking Pershing
Avenue. Here, two-story apartment complexes have been constructed along canals, providing a transition
between a major commercial district around St. Mark's Plaza and the single family residential district of Quail
Lakes.

GRAND CANAL BOULEVARD EAST
OF THE STOCKTON HILTON, 1983

A showcase development in the important commercial district off March
Lane is to be found along this beautifully landscaped boulevard. The arc
shaped commercial building is one of
two on the boulevard which provide
residential facilities above the shops.
These buildings and others along
Grand Canal Boulevard are an important adjunct to the 200 room Stockton
Hilton, opened New Year's Eve 1981.

THE INTERSTATE 5 AND CROSSTOWN FREEWAY INTERCHANGE, 1979

One of the most spectacular scenes of modern day Stockton illustrates the convenient access brought by I-5 to Stockton, one of the few cities the highway passes through on its route from Mexico to Canada.

This is the latest improvement to the highway system of Stockton, which includes State Highway 99, upgraded significantly in 1950 when Wilson Way was bypassed with a freeway link from Mariposa Road to the Calaveras River.

A long-awaited improvement is the Crosstown Freeway (right-hand lanes in photo), started with the intention of linking I-5 with Highway 99; it lies unfinished two and two-tenths miles short of Highway 99 more than fifteen years after it was started.

With $22 million allocated by the California Transportation Commission, construction will begin again in the spring of 1986 which will bring the Crosstown to Wilson Way; Highway 99 will not be reached until the 1990s.

VILLAGE WEST MARINA, 1983
Now the largest and most modern marina in the Delta, this facility had its beginnings in 1970, when a drag line rig dug a section from the Fourteen Mile Slough levee and water flowed into a man-made basin. By 1979, there were 630 slips and the marina had become the largest complex of covered berths in the world. *(Photograph by Cartwright Aerial Surveys, courtesy The Grupe Company)*

WATERFRONT TOWERS, 1984

An important development on the Stockton Channel in the early 1980s was this pair of office buildings built by the Schmitz Development Company, the first of four. Major firms of attorneys and public accountants plus New York Life occupy these five-story buildings.

Another major development along the channel is Channelbank North, a massive two-story office building overlooking the turning basin at the foot of Pershing Avenue. It reached completion in 1985. A principal tenant is Frank B. Hall & Company. These offices are part of the operations of one of the largest insurance brokerage and service companies in the world. *(Photograph by Raymond W. Hillman)*

SCENES IN THE STOCKTON SUBURB
OF MORADA: STAGI ESTATE AND A STAINED
GLASS WINDOW AT SAINT MICHAEL'S CHURCH

Just a short drive northeast of Stockton is lovely Morada; its name means "residence" in Spanish. At the turn of the century, grain farms occupied the area, but there was an opportunity for further development when the Central California Traction Company built its line through Morada's eastern fringes and established a waiting station near the present intersection of Alhambra and Morada lanes.

In 1909, the Morada Realty Company of Stockton was very successful in its efforts to sell parcels to local investors. Sidewalks were installed and a few houses built in the vicinity of Oakwilde and Plum avenues. At this early date, the firm was headed by William H. Brown, who correctly predicted that Morada would assume a position in the civic life of Stockton. Initial growth was slow, but by the mid 1920s, Davis School had to be expanded from one and a half classrooms to four. This brick building was replaced by the present elementary school in 1951, and there is now a second school, Morada Middle.

Saint Michael's Church on North Ashley Lane has held an annual fair for over seventy years, the oldest church festival in San Joaquin County. It was started as an Italian festival on Waterloo Road where the first Saint Michael's Church was built in 1902. During 1965, the church relocated to a new building near the Calaveras River in Morada. The stained glass windows, above, depict all twenty-one of the California Missions. On East Foppiano Lane is a second church, built by the Free Methodists.

The district has a distinct country atmosphere, yet it is very close to the city. Until the early 1940s there were many Japanese farmers in this vicinity, tending vegetable crops. Growth has been particularly significant since the mid 1950s, with development of Stockton to the north and improvements to Highway 99 shortening distances.

Palatial homes on spacious grounds are characteristic among more modest parcels. Many residents have a few chickens, sheep, horses or cows. Twentieth century home builders were not the first to consider this area uniquely attractive for residences—numerous Yokuts Indians artifacts have been found during construction. *(Photograph by Raymond W. Hillman)*

LODI
THE TOKAY CAPITAL OF THE WORLD

The very beginnings of what is now Lodi can be traced to 1859, when local rural families organized to establish a school. Built on the east side of present Cherokee Lane south of Turner Road, the Salem School also served as a church and community center. Ten years later this locale rapidly gained importance because of its proximity to a railroad crossing of the Mokelumne River.

In 1869, the Central Pacific Railroad planned to bypass Woodbridge in favor of a river crossing three miles to the east, and property owners here approached the railroad company in hopes of establishing a town. Pioneer settler of 1857, Ezekiel Lawrence, accompanied by other pioneers, Reuben L. Wardrobe, A. C. Ayers and John Magley, offered a townsite of 160 acres if a station would be built. The Central Pacific expected gifts of land toward the creation of settlements along its lines, and an arrangement was made without difficulty. The company was to receive a "railroad reserve" of twelve acres in the center of town plus alternate blocks of land throughout the townsite. At this time, there was only one structure on the land, a rough cabin built in 1868 by John Magley at what is now Pine and Sacramento streets.

The surveyors went to work, and streets were laid out from Washington to Church Street and Locust to Walnut Street. Following the beginnings of development by Magley, I. N. Stretch built a house and store on the same intersection just after completion of the survey. Additional early growth was effected not only by new settlers but also by the attraction of residents from fledgling communities nearby such as Woodbridge, Liberty City and Galt. Among the founders of what is now Lodi were John M. Burt and Dan Crist, both of Woodbridge. Crist, formerly the Woodbridge postmaster, assumed the same position here.

Woodbridge development was severely affected through the wholesale moving of wooden buildings from this community to what is now Lodi. The town's first hotel, the Hooker House, was also moved to the community but not from Woodbridge. In fact, the building had served two other communities—the Calaveras County mining camps of Lancha Plana and Campo Seco—and was on its way to a new settlement called Dover when its owner, "Uncle Dan" Crist, changed his mind and brought it to Lodi, in 1869. It was placed at the corner of Lockeford and Sacramento streets and also became the first post office.

Completion of the railroad station in December 1869 established the need for an official name. The name selected for the station sign was "Mokelumne," inspired by the nearby major river. The names Mokelumne and Mokelumne Station were used alternately by local government officials and commercial enterprises. Mokelumne Station, for example, was used by Wells Fargo and Company in its business. The name was in regular use until 1873, when confusion with two other towns—Mokelumne Hill in the foothills of Calaveras County and Mokelumne City to the northwest in San Joaquin County prompted a name change. It was proposed to rename the community Lodi. A change was officially endorsed in Sacramento by an assembly bill.

There are several stories behind why the name Lodi was selected. One of the most colorful is that it was inspired by a locally stabled trotting horse that had set a four mile record. However, its fame was in 1869, and it is doubtful that the enthusiasm continued to as late as 1873. A more plausible story is that two of the earliest families locating here were from Lodi, Illinois. Also, Lodi is a place in Italy where Napoleon won his first military victory by defeating the Austrians.

The principal buildings in the community by 1869 were the station, hotel, store and the Peck & Company stage office, operating coaches to Mokelumne Hill. A year later, there were fifty-six homes. The first two-story brick building was erected on Sacramento Street during 1876 for the Lodi Hall Association. The ground floor was occupied by the store, and the upper story was rented to local fraternal societies.

The earliest industries were a lumber mill and flour mill. A site on the south bank of the Mokelumne River near the Salem School was selected for the saw mill in 1877. This enterprise of the Lodi Land and Lumber Company sawed logs brought down river from the mountains during the rainy season. Powered by a steam engine, it had a capacity of 40,000 board feet of lumber per day.

A flour mill placed in operation in 1876 hints that economic growth of the area was dependent upon the success of agriculture. Through soil and climate, the region has some unique qualities. The sandy loam south of the river was soon discovered to be well adapted for vineyards and orchards. Complementing the soil was the climate, which was affected by its position directly east of Suisun Pass, the point where the Sacramento and San Joaquin rivers flow into a major tributary to San Francisco Bay. The great expanse of waterways cools the air at night, which is beneficial to the vineyards. Their fame developed slowly and was to center largely upon the Flame Tokay, first introduced from Algeria in 1857.

Vines were superceded in importance during the nineteenth century by grain and watermelons.

SACRAMENTO STREET IN 1876
One of the oldest surviving views of Lodi shows Sacramento Street opposite the Southern Pacific station in 1876. At this time, C. O. Ivory's store was also the Wells Fargo & Company express office. Note the folksy construction technique in nailing one end of Ivory's sign to the porch of the store and the other to the flag pole.

The flag flying over the intersection was brought from Woodbridge, where it flew during the Civil War. It is still preserved today as part of the collections at the San Joaquin County Historical Museum. (Courtesy Holt-Atherton Center, University of the Pacific)

BOOMING CANNON CELEBRATED THE CONCLUSION OF A BATTLE IN THE COURTS, 1876

An 1846 Mexican land grant, known as Los Moquelemos Grant, had a cloudy title which affected development of 50,000 acres surrounding Lodi. The federal government granted rights to the Central Pacific Railroad to alternate sections of land twenty miles on each side of the right of way, provided there was no established legal title before construction. As there was controversy over the validity of Los Moquelemos, the railroad claimed it in spite of numerous settlers and tested its action in the courts, eventually appealing to the United States Supreme Court. The final decision was handed down in the spring of 1876 in favor of the settlers.

The announcement touched off plans for a grand celebration in Lodi. With about 1,500 participants from Stockton, it became the largest public gathering ever held in the county up to that time. The speeches and grand barbecue were punctuated by much flag waving, music from the San Joaquin Band and the booming cannon (above) brought by the Stockton Guard. The long standing threat of railroad seizure of settlers' homes and land was over. *(Lodi News-Sentinel Collection)*

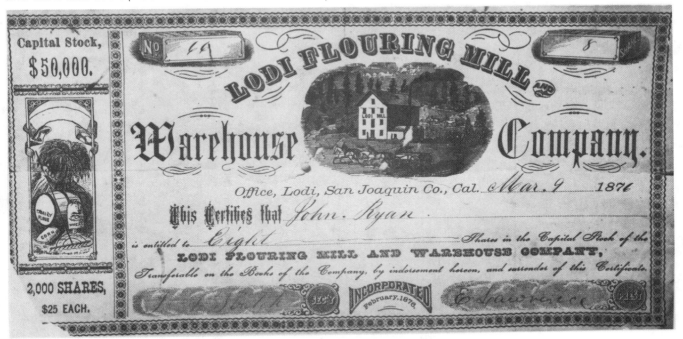

FLOUR MILLING—ONE OF THE FIRST INDUSTRIES

Considerable local production of wheat and the fact that the nearest mills were over fifteen miles away in Stockton inspired construction of a mill for Lodi as a stockholder's proposition. The building, which looked just like the illustration on the certificate except that a belfry was added, was constructed of brick at Lockeford Avenue and Sacramento Street. Inside were four sets of stones and a barley mill, all operated by steam. Two hundred barrels of flour were produced each day. Installation of roller mills to supplement the work of the stones and increase the efficiency of the operation took place in 1884. Operation continued until a fire destroyed the building in the early 1890s. Operators over the years were Ralph Ellis, George S. Locke, Corson, Lasell and Wright, Corson and Clark and C. H. Corson. *(Courtesy Lodi Public Library)*

"LODI'S SACRAMENTO STREET," c. 1879

Perhaps the most detailed early scene of the community still preserved is a twenty-four by thirty inch oil painting at the public library. Artist E. J. Munch captured the appearance of the town ten years after its growth was fostered by the coming of the railroad. The tiny passenger depot stands just behind the locomotive. Behind this building and across Sacramento Street is the Lodi Hotel. At the opposite end of the street is the large railroad freight shed. Towering in the distance up Main Street to the right is the Lodi Flouring Mill.

Although painted in a primitive style, the work is accurate and one of the most important early oil paintings of San Joaquin County. *(Courtesy Lodi Public Library)*

CHARLES AND REBECCA IVORY HOME, ELM AND SCHOOL STREETS

Probably the first elaborate home in the new community was built in 1871 for newlyweds Charles and Rebecca Ivory. Charles was a partner in Ivory and Greene, general merchandise. Surrounded with particularly attractive gardens, it was a showplace for many years. *(Reproduced from* An Illustrated History of San Joaquin County, *Thompson & West, 1879)*

Watermelons became symbolic of local produce during the 1880s, as they grew very well without irrigation, and such crops prepared the fields for plantings of wheat. These melons were quite unlike those of today, as they had a thin rind and a different texture, making them particularly desirable in distant markets. Watermelons labeled "from Lodi" brought a premium price. Other melon growing areas, remote from the town, discovered this and also labeled their product "from Lodi." This unfair practice cut the price, took the edge off the reputation and encouraged more extensive plantings of Tokay vines.

Fire brought disaster in 1887. Started in a planing mill, it spread through the center of town and burned all but three buildings in an area surrounded by Sacramento, Pine, School and Elm streets, the heart of the business district. There was no fire department, just a bucket brigade. All of the pioneer business buildings plus a newly constructed Odd Fellows Hall and many residences were lost. Reconstruction was soon underway, mainly in brick, particularly along Sacramento Street. Several of these buildings still stand today. Not all of the businesses on Sacramento Street depended upon the railroad, vineyards and the grain trade. There was also considerable cattle raising in the reclaimed lands of the Delta, and a large number of cowboys came to Lodi to patronize fourteen saloons operated there in the closing years of the nineteenth century.

Incorporation of Lodi was encouraged in 1906 by the need for a sewer system and public ownership of the utility company. Incorporation passed 2 to 1 by voters in November 1906, overturning strenuous opposition from the saloon keepers, who feared higher license fees, taxes and regulation. In celebration of the victory, church bells rang out; the *Stockton Record* reported: "When the church bells of the town are rung in honor of the result of an election, it serves to presume that it was no ordinary political contest."

At this time, the volunteer fire department could muster little more than a bucket brigade, and equipment was so sparse initially that their call to duty was the firing of a pistol until a bell could be obtained. The city fire department was established in 1911 as a volunteer service and equipped with two horse drawn combined chemical and hose wagons operated by eight men. By 1920, volunteers were serving with the Wide Awake Hose Company, the Alert Hose Company, the hook and ladder or the chemical engine company. It was in this year that the first motor driven equipment, a Seagrave pumper, was put into service. The volunteers were summoned by a special code of whistle blasts. The first paid employees were drivers; there were six by 1942. While most employees are paid nowadays, there are still eight volunteers.

Natural gas and water were first supplied to the town in 1891 by the Bay City Gas and Water Works. Electricity was added to the service ten years later with installation of a light plant capable of illuminating 500 globes. Only one of these was a street light, and it was installed in front of the Lodi Hotel. The "works" was purchased by the city in 1919. Considerable improvements were undertaken, and the utility was soon run at a profit, helping to defray the expenses of civic government. Water and power service is still under city jurisdiction. A great credit to Lodi is the fact that nearly half of the forty miles of streets were paved by 1923.

Other evidence of a progressive approach to projects for the public benefit was the completion in 1905 of the Lodi Opera House, which still stands as M. Newfield & Sons furniture store. During 1909, construction of a permanent library was underway through the Carnegie Foundation. This served until its replacement by a huge new building in 1981. In the same year, the first hospital was established by Dr. R. A. Buchanan in what had been two homes; it eventually became a thirty-five bed facility. Particularly well-known was the Mason Hospital, named for Dr. Wilton Mason, which opened in 1915 and closed in 1966. Lodi Memorial Hospital, named in honor of the forty-four Lodians who lost their lives during World War II, was established in 1952 with fifty-five beds. Lodi Community Hospital followed fourteen years later, with a capacity of fifty-six. Both have nearly doubled in size since opening.

A great variety of industry has contributed to the economic base of the community. One of the first during the twentieth century to establish national distribution and recognition was Supermold. Starting in 1927, this company began building the "super treader," a full circle retread mold for tires. This piece of equipment created the retreading industry and established the Super Mold Corporation, soon to become the world's largest manufacturer of such equipment. Its founders were H. J. Woock, E. A. Glynn and G. O. Beckman.

The Pinkerton Foundry, a general iron casting

operation established by James W. Pinkerton in 1934, is still operated today by his son, Jim Pinkerton. It produces hydrants, manhole covers, structural members and also ornate castings on a custom basis. Another local foundry is the Lodi Iron Works, with Vicki Van Steenberge as current president and owner.

Among other important industries are Pacific Coast Producers, canners and can manufacturers with 1,700 employees at peak; Holz Rubber Company, with 220 employees making industrial rubber products; Valley Industries, employing 250 in the manufacture of trailer hitches; and Goehring Meat Company, producers of Victor brand products. This firm also operates plants in Modesto and Hawaii.

Much has been done to preserve the vitality of the attractive, traditional business district. A fine improvement to this section was the extensive expansion and renovation of the post office, adding 17,000 square feet to the stylish 1930s structure. The $1.3 million project reached completion in August 1984.

SALEM SCHOOL AND BELL

The most prominent nineteenth century school building was the Salem School, erected in 1883 at Stockton and Walnut streets to supplement structures of 1859 and 1872. Five teachers were employed here. A three year high school, established in 1896, was held in the upper rooms of this building. These classes were the result of banding together school districts in northern San Joaquin County to establish a high school district. A permanent high school facility was developed on what was then the western limits of Lodi on twelve acres obtained from Thomas Hutchins.

The old Salem School was demolished in 1938 and its bronze bell, cast at Baltimore, Maryland, in 1883, was given a place at Lodi Municipal Lake. The clock was purely for effect; there were no works behind the faces! In later years, the ornate belfry was removed and replaced by a much plainer one.

This illustration is from the border vignettes of a print published by Beardsley, McMaster Company, Real Estate, 1880s. (Reproduced from a glass plate in the Covello Collection)

SALEM SCHOOL. LODI. CALIFORNIA.

36

A Greenbelt Initiative enated in 1981 to restrict encroachment upon prime agricultural land has restricted growth and caused a legal controversy that is still ongoing. There has been just a 2 percent growth here, one of the slowest in San Joaquin County—a boon or a bane, depending upon how one has been affected. Nevertheless, Lodi has come a very long way since the arrival of the first transcontinental railroad, construction of the steam powered flour mill and the opening of the saw mill that depended upon logs floated down the Mokelumne River.

WOMEN'S ACTIVITIES IN LODI

Women's activities were important to Lodi. Above, left, is newspaper founder and attorney Laura De Force Gordon (1838–1907). The Women's Club of Lodi is headquartered in the building pictured above, which was constructed especially for the organization in 1923. This Colonial Revival style building, located at the corner of Pleasant and Pine streets, has an auditorium seating 600.

A good measure of Lodi's twentieth century progress can be credited to the Lodi Women's Improvement Club, known since 1913 as the Women's Club of Lodi. It was organized in 1906 and in the first two years developed considerable energy and influence. The members not only attained their literary goals but also those of such civic improvements as street signs, the planting of trees in parks and along streets and cleanup campaigns. By 1923, there were 500 members. Their efforts were financed through concerts, vaudeville programs, social events, etc.

Lodi offered many opportunities to women in the nineteenth century. While the Lodi News Sentinel, published since 1935, can trace its roots back more than 100 years, it was not the first newspaper in Lodi. The first was founded by a woman. Mrs. Gertie De Force Cluff established the Valley Review as Lodi's pioneer newspaper and operated it for six years as a weekly. It was praised in the 1878 county directory: "It evinces good literary taste and spritely journalistic talent." The Cluff family was also associated with another newspaper in the 1880s with an eye-catching name, the Lodi Cyclone.

During 1878, Mrs. Cluff's sister, Laura De Force Gordon, started publishing the Daily Review. She was also active in publishing the Stockton Daily Leader, which, at the time, was the only daily newspaper in the world edited and published by a woman. Newspaper woman Gordon's significance went even further: she was one of the first two women admitted to the bar in California (1884) and the second ever to be admitted to the bar of the United States Supreme Court (1885). Susan B. Anthony was the first.

Other challenging work was undertaken by women in this community. Miss Daisy Pleas is believed to be the first woman watchmaker in California. She worked at George Hill's jewelry store on Sacramento Street from 1890 to 1950. Another triumph was the election of Mrs. Mabel Richey to the office of mayor in 1953. She was a former president of the Lodi Women's Club. Thirty years later, the second woman mayor of Lodi, Evelyn Olson, was elected to office by vote of the city council.

LOOKING NORTHWEST ACROSS TOWN, FALL 1907

Orientation to the railroad is well portrayed here; the principal business blocks along Sacramento Street can be seen facing the tracks at right. The photograph is easily dated, as Emerson Elementary School is under construction (left) in the then open country at Hutchins and Elm streets. This building served until replaced by Washington School. Emerson was dismantled in 1955; its site is now Emerson Park.

LOOKING NORTH ON SACRAMENTO STREET FROM PINE, c. 1900

A parade is in progress, and the participants are turning east onto Pine Street. Note the bearded man on stilts; one of the boys in the foreground has found the photographer more interesting. This view of the street shows some of the mudholes that were commonplace even on main thoroughfares in the days before the main streets were paved.

The Bank of Lodi can be seen on the corner. Across from it is the Hotel Lodi, built in 1871 and managed for decades by George W. LeMoin. During 1912 the hostelry was demolished so a new Bank of Lodi could be erected. Construction of a new Hotel Lodi, which LeMoin was also to operate, was unexpectedly delayed, leaving the community without first class accommodations for two years. *(Lodi News-Sentinel Collection)*

THE SAME LOCATION, 1982

While there have been many changes all of the buildings with the elaborate parapets are still standing next to the corner building, which replaced the old bank. *(Photograph by Raymond W. Hillman)*

39

GRAHAM'S DRUG STORE, c. 1895

Graham's, at the northwest corner of Sacramento and Elm street, was more than a drug store; there was a marble topped soda fountain (right) as well as the post office, Postal Telegraph and telephone switchboard. Shortly after the turn of the century, additional prominence was gained when the store became a stop on the electric traction line. All of these activities were supervised by the owner, Robert L. Graham. With the advent of electricity, the pharmacy gained significance by displaying the first electric sign in town. It was a trade sign in the shape of a druggist's mortar and pestle. *(Courtesy LeRelda Patton, Gladys and Janice Wood)*

THE "OLD TIMER" OF SACRAMENTO STREET, 1982

Known variously as the Granger's Building, the Lodi Hall Association Building and the Friedberger and Kaiser Store since its construction in 1876, this structure is often overlooked for its historical significance.

The most dramatic aspect of its history came during the great fire of 1887. It was one of three buildings left standing above the ashes of numerous businesses lost in the blaze that destroyed much of the main business district.

If it had not been for a quick thinking citizen, the fire would have spread farther to the north, beyond Elm Street, but it was checked at this building, which at the time was occupied by the Friedberger General Store. The plan was to cover the windows in the south wall so the fire would not invade the building. Among the stock were horse blankets which were taken outside and drenched in a watering trough and hung over the windows. They were kept wet by water thrown upon them from the inside. The building, with thick, brick walls, has stood many tests through the years and still stands at the corner of Sacramento and Elm streets. Note the long since bricked over window openings and the fading Bull Durham smoking tobacco advertisement painted on the brick wall. *(Photograph by Raymond W. Hillman)*

ON THE WAY TO VALLEY SPRINGS FROM LODI, 1902

The second railroad to reach Lodi was the narrow gauge San Joaquin and Sierra Nevada, which started service in 1882. The western terminus of this Southern Pacific controlled company was Brack's Landing west of Lodi. Three years later and forty miles away, it reached its eastern terminus, Valley Springs. It was extended about twelve miles to serve the Calaveras Cement Company in 1929 and still remains today as a little used standard gauge line. The 0-6-2 locomotive shown here was photographed on Lockeford Street at Sacramento Street. Southern Pacific acquired controlling interest in the line in the mid 1880s. *(Collection of Dr. Howard Letcher)*

TOKAY CARNIVAL, 1907

In the photo at the top of the page, a large crowd has gathered for the Tokay Carnival held in Lodi in 1907, the first of many special events held to call attention to the unique and outstanding product of local vineyards and wineries. The grand three-day event was largely the effort of a local businessman, Charles Ray, and was attended by James Gillette, governor of California. Many neighboring towns, including some from Calaveras County, participated with booths. Tons of grapes and green vines decorated not only the carnival grounds but homes and other buildings in town.

To commemorate the event, a temporary wooden arch, the Tokay Arch, was built across Pine Street at Sacramento Street, adjacent to the fairgrounds. It was soon replaced by a permanent mission style "welcome" arch, which has long been a distinctive and most attractive feature of the downtown business district and was listed on the National Register in 1981. The arch was featured on an artistic composition for a post card, c. 1915, shown above, right.

"Queen Zinfandel" for the 1907 carnival was Bertha de Almeda, shown here in her glorious purple robe. "King Tokay" was George Hogan, a prominent agriculturalist for decades.

(Top: From a glass plate in the Covello Collection. Above left: Collection of San Joaquin County Historical Museum, Micke Grove. Above right: Collection of the Haggin Museum, Stockton)

42

BLESSING THE GRAPES, c. 1937
Father Charles P. Hardeman of Saint Anne's Church officiates while Jackie Ritchie and Laura Ortez look on. By 1899 there were nearly 2,350,000 Tokay vines such as are shown here. The height of planting was in 1913. While there was a preference to the Tokay, there were extensive plantings of fifty other varieties of table and wine grapes. Presently 97 percent of the world's production of Tokay grapes grow within a ten mile radius of Lodi. *(Courtesy Lodi Grape Festival and National Wine Show)*

LODI GRAPE FESTIVAL AND NATIONAL WINE SHOW
A highlight of the annual three-day festival is the display of unusual grape murals. Composed of individual grapes arranged like tiles in mosaic, these works are up to eight by twelve feet in size. The event, which centers attention on the local wineries and vineyards, has been scheduled every September since the repeal of Prohibition in 1933. In 1935 the event moved to its own permanent grounds, which encompass twenty acres including the 14,000 seat Grape Bowl constructed as a WPA project.

More than 80,000 people are usually attracted to the nation's largest display of fresh grapes; more than 100 varieties may be seen. There is also a wine and brandy display, a prestigious and selective art show, and a spectacular exhibit of dahlias and other flowers. The State of California officially recognizes the festival as the San Joaquin County Fair; the extensive August event in Stockton is an agricultural district fair. *(Courtesy Paul Zimmerman, Lodi News-Sentinel)*

DR. MASON BROUGHT THE FIRST AUTOMOBILE TO LODI, c. 1900

Dr. Wilton Mason was one of the very first to drive an automobile in San Joaquin County. The three and a half horsepower Locomobile burned white gas and assisted the doctor greatly in attending to house calls. It arrived dismantled and in a crate. Dr. Mason and his two brothers had to reassemble it. Never having seen an automobile like this before, they accomplished the task only after considerable "animated discussion."

Dr. Mason is shown at the controls, beside his home at 209 North School Street; seated next to him is his sister, Bertha. Posing with more tried and true bicycles are, from left to right, his other sisters, Myrtle Anderson and Nellie Eaton, and brother, Lewis.

The arrival of this Locomobile caused great excitement, and onlookers flocked into town to see the phenomenon of the twentieth century. By about 1910, there were about three "horseless carriages" in town. *(Collection of the Mason family)*

OFF TO LODI FROM WEBER AVENUE IN STOCKTON, 1907

Starting in 1907 there was hourly service between Stockton, Lodi, Sacramento and way stations via electric railway. Passenger service on the Central California Traction line continued until about 1937. The company still exists today, as does most of the right of way, which is used exclusively for freight. The only surviving rolling stock from the days of passenger service is a combination baggage and passenger car preserved at the Western Railway Museum at Rio Vista Junction.

Other transportation links to Lodi were the Southern Pacific Valley Route and branch lines, as well as Western Pacific Railroad connections a short distance to the west. The Lincoln Highway, the first transcontinental auto route, connected Lodi with the rest of Central California. Those without motor vehicles of their own could travel the highway via Greyhound and Gibson River Lines during the 1930s. *(Courtesy Holt-Atherton Center, University of the Pacific, Stockton)*

**A HORSE DRAWN POPCORN AND
ICE CREAM WAGON
ON SACRAMENTO STREET
NEAR PINE, c. 1925**

Starting about 1911, P. S. Pierce operated this locally built wagon on the streets of town for many years. Although the vehicle is long gone, the tiny steam engine that operated its popcorn machine and peanut roaster still survives. It became part of the collection of the late Frank J. Troke, Stockton fire chief. Found incomplete and neglected, it was restored to operational condition by Troke and his friend, Glen Weagant. While the engine was important to operating equipment on the wagon, steam from the small boiler was also used to blow a whistle mounted on the roof, which was as important as the signs on the wagon in attracting customers, especially youngsters. *(Above, Lodi News-Sentinel Collection. Photograph to the right by Raymond W. Hillman)*

LOADING A REFRIGERATOR CAR WITH TOKAY GRAPES, c. 1905

Refrigerator cars were vital to the eastern market for table grapes grown in this region. This group is shown at work with boxes of grapes from the Frank H. Buck packing shed. Shown in the center is W. H. Thompson of the Frank H. Buck Company, fruit growers and shippers, established in 1888 and incorporated in 1902 with a capital stock of $100,000. This scene was recorded near Main and Locust streets.

MASON FRUIT PACKERS AND SHIPPERS, 216 NORTH SACRAMENTO STREET, c. 1915

Dr. Wilton Mason and his brothers, Herschel and Lewis, founded this firm, which forwarded fruit in refrigerator cars filled with ice manufactured in their own plant. The railroad cars were packed with grapes and other fresh fruit. Mason's also had an ice cream parlor in the building and offered home delivery of ice and coal. Their fleet of delivery trucks is shown above. Notice the blocks of ice suspended from tongs attached to scales on the back of the trucks. A Chinese laundry is located next door. (Collection of Mason family)

47

T & D THEATRE, c. 1921; LODI THEATRE, 1941

Until 1962, when finally closed by extensive fire damage, this building was a major entertainment center for the populace. This School Street landmark (shown above) was originally built in 1917 as the Lodi Theatre and shortly thereafter became the T & D, making it part of a chain that eventually totaled sixty theaters. The structure underwent many modifications over the years, especially when talking pictures were introduced in 1927 and again after the 1941 fire (shown below).

The Hotel Lodi, closed but still standing today, may be seen in the background. Of Colonial style architecture, it was constructed for the Lodi Investment in Company in 1914–1915. The architect, E. B. Brown, drew the plans for the Hotel Stockton a few years earlier. Officials of the investment company were W. H. Thompson, president; H. E. Welch, vice president; W. H. Lorenz, secretary; and George W. LeMoin, treasurer. Another of their projects was the Lodi Theatre. Interestingly enough, the old hotel itself has become a theater. In 1983, its ornate lobby and formal dining room were adapted for use by the Tokay Players, who relocated from the Pine Alley Theater, where plays were staged for seventeen years. *(Above, Lodi News-Sentinel Collection)*

BOTTLING, LABELING AND PACKING, ALL BY HAND, AT SHEWAN-JONES INCORPORATED DISTILLERY, STOCKTON STREET AND TURNER ROAD, c. 1940

This firm was established by an eastern investor and Lee Jones, a nationally-known Lodi area winery leader and wine and brandy industry pioneer. In 1939, with Jones remaining president, the firm became a wholly owned subsidiary of the National Distillery Products Corporation. Brandy, vermouth and other distilled products were distributed with the Lejon label, a contraction of Jones' name.

By the time he retired in 1949, the firm had received more medals for its products since the repeal of Prohibition than any other firm exhibiting at the California State Fair or the Los Angeles County Fair.

The fountain on the west side of the Lodi City Hall was erected through a bequest from Jones' widow, Georgina.

Today the old plant serves various industrial uses including Lustre-Cal (name plate manufacturers), warehousing for the Lodi Unified School District and Stokely-Van Camp. Tokay Foundry now leases the former distillery building. Lejon is now one of the labels of Allied Grape Growers of Fresno, one of California's largest producers. *(Courtesy Holt-Atherton Center, University of the Pacific, Stockton)*

"SCRAP GOING TO WAR," FEBRUARY 1941

Even before the United States was involved in World War II, there were organized activities for supplying manufacturers of war materials. Newspapers and cardboard were collected from diverse sources and baled at the local scavenger company headquarters, which was also the official tin can salvage depot. Tin cans were increasingly desirable throughout the war; tin and lead, both in short supply, could be reclaimed from them for reuse. Funds raised from the salvage of paper, metal, rubber and kitchen fat helped many organizations

and individuals raise funds during the war. Flattened tin cans were usually given away for processing. *(Courtesy Lodi Public Library, Celia M. Thompson Collection)*

LODI MUNICIPAL LAKE, c. 1970
Known for years as Smith Lake (Charles E. Smith, owner), this property became the site of a semi-permanent lake in 1901 when the Stockton and Mokelumne Canal Company completed a timber dam for irrigation purposes. This was replaced about ten years later by a concrete dam built by the Woodbridge Irrigation District. During 1934, the City of Lodi started acquiring the lake shore and completed the project in about ten years. Today, this is not only the finest park in the city but one of the most attractive in the entire county.

LODI'S NUMBER ONE INDUSTRY, GENERAL MILLS, 1984
It was a great moment in 1947 when General Mills started construction of a cereal plant on Turner Road in Lodi. The original twenty-acre site has since been expanded to eighty. The plant is one of six General Mills package food operations across the nation. Its role is to produce oat based cereals such as Cheerios and Trix, and flake cereals such as Wheaties and Total. Other foods made and packaged here are "helper" products, casseroles and side dishes, Bisquick, cake mixes, box frostings, ready to spread frostings, and specialty foods such as fruit bars and fruit rollups. The Lodi plant also has an extensive food service operation. Since 1967, it has been the West Coast distribution center for all General Mills products throughout the eleven western states. With 890 employees, it is Lodi's number one industry. *(Photograph courtesy General Mills, Lodi)*

A QUEEN ANNE VICTORIAN HOME BECOMES A BANK, 1150 WEST KETTLEMAN LANE, 1981

One of the finest turn of the century homes in Lodi stands near the intersection of Kettleman and Ham Lane. Built by local businessman and vineyardist Theodore Beckman, it once stood in the center of a 200 acre vineyard. Until 1978, the home remained in the Beckman family, who settled in the area a decade before the town was founded.

The landmark was then acquired by the Stockton Savings and Loan Association and converted to banking purposes during a lengthy reconstruction of the interior and careful rehabilitation of the facade. $10,000 alone was invested in a traditional staircase to offices in previously unused attic space.

Among the numerous challenges for adaptive reuse of the structure was the installation of a vault in the base of the tank house which towers above the rear of the home. A windmill was once perched upon one side of this structure to pump water into the tank for domestic use. Former Beckman land adjacent to the bank is now the Vineyard Shopping Center.

BOTTLING CHAMPAGNE AT GUILD'S CENTRAL CELLARS, 1980s

Guild Wineries and Distillers brought a new dimension to local wine production when they entered into large scale production and bottling of champagne in 1964. Guild is the largest winery operation in the Lodi district, employing 165 in the production of wines and brandy as well as champagne at three winery locations near Lodi. Guild is also the largest winery co-op in the world.

Guild, while the largest, is by no means the oldest. The first winery, the Urgon, was on Woodbridge Road on a site now occupied by the Lodi Winery. By 1919, there were many wineries around the community.

Prohibition was to bring about a suspension of winery operations. Even though there was considerable threat to all local businesses if the production of wines and brandy was prohibited, there was still amazing support for the program. Local vote tallied 559 votes for Prohibition and 337 against. The vote was testimony to strong feelings generated in local churches. Vintners' products were to be restricted to table grapes, wine grape sales for home use and vinegar and non-alcoholic grape products. After repeal in 1933, the industry was soon back on its feet, and in 1936, there were 900 growers serving fourteen wineries. By the late 1930s, Lodi was shipping more fresh grapes than any other part of the United States and possibly the world.

There are now nineteen wineries in the local wine district, which has been known as "America's Sherry Land" for the distinctive flavor of the local product. In addition, gold medals have been received for the brandy.

A UNIQUE MASCOT AT LODI HIGH SCHOOL, 1982

Lodi High's football team is known as the "Flames," honoring local importance of the Flame Tokay grapes. Team mascot and mascot of the entire school is "Ruby," the fire engine shown here. The 1949 American LaFrance pumper with a 750 gallons per minute capacity was retired in 1980, and through the generosity of Dr. and Mrs. R. E. Morton, who won it in a raffle raising funds for converting the old Lodi High campus into a community center, the apparatus found its way to Lodi High in December 1981. Principal Floyd Williams enjoys driving her. The pumper is being used in fund raising campaigns and similar events. (Photograph by Rich Turner)

MANTECA
CITY ON THE SAND PLAINS

Church meetings, elementary school classes, melons and rail shipment of fresh cream all had a part in the beginnings of Manteca. Its site originally gained a bit of distinction when a school house was built on the northeast corner of Louise Avenue and Union Road in 1857. The school also served as a church, but because of disruption of classes for funerals, a small wooden church was constructed on the southeast corner of the intersection in 1892.

By this time, the sandy soil had been discovered for its potential in raising melons, and through the effort of the "Father of Manteca," Joshua Cowell, dairying was introduced, resulting in the need for a facility to process and ship dairy products. In 1896, a wheelless, old box car became the skimming station at a stop known as Cowell Station since 1870, when Central Pacific Railroad was built through this region. Joshua Cowell first arrived on the sand plains in 1862, when they were sparsely settled. Other pioneers were Peter and Noah Clapp and David, Edward and Eldridge Reynolds. Cowell farmed the land for decades before a substantial portion of it was set aside for a townsite.

Joshua Cowell, known as "Uncle Josh" to the original residents, had an indelible part in the development of the town. The first building was a house at what is now the intersection of Yosemite Avenue and Manteca Road. He also constructed many of the earliest buildings.

By October 1897, Cowell Station had to be renamed due to confusion with a nearby stop on the same railroad line which was named for Joshua Cowell's brother Henry. The often told story about how the community received its present name through the misprinting of railroad tickets is probably not true. The tickets, according to local legend, arrived with the spelling "Manteca" instead of "Monteca," which was supposedly preferred by the residents as it was thought to be the Spanish word for butter. Manteca means lard, however, and as the story is told, despite the protest, Southern Pacific never changed the spelling. This entire story should bear little importance, as "monteca" cannot be found in any Spanish dictionaries. As the railroad was accustomed to using Spanish place names, it is likely a representative word believed to be Spanish was applied here through company initiative. Azorian Portuguese were California's dairymen and their word for butter, *manteiga*, could easily have been taken as Spanish and corrupted to the present spelling. Local input in the name selection can be discounted, as there were no Spanish or Portuguese dairymen in Manteca at the time.

Significant retail development was going to establish the town as a supply center for this section of the county, eclipsing Lathrop in a role that it had enjoyed since about 1870.

The first organized government was a board of trade, which was a cross between a city council and a chamber of commerce. Under its auspices, a volunteer fire department was organized in 1912. Along the line of boosterism, the same board appropriated $400 so that the town could have a

OFFICIAL SEAL OF THE CITY OF MANTECA
The seal, above, was adopted in the 1960s. It is based on designs submitted by local students. (*Courtesy City of Manteca*)

INDUSTRY TO SERVE THE FARMS

Bacilieri's Winery, above, built shortly after the turn of the century, was the first of these firms to serve the Manteca area. In 1914, the building was converted to become part of the Manteca Canning Company, below. Serving both fruit and vegetable farmers, this cannery was located at the corner of Oak and Vine streets. The tank tower at left was part of the community water system and served not only homes and fire plugs but the cannery as well.

Backing this major industrial enterprise were Achille Bacilieri, T. A. Nelson, F. M. Cowell and Louis Vestica. Activity centered upon canning local fruit and vegetables, including "Manteca Lady" tomatoes. Some of the products were shipped to the French front in World War I as well as to the Gold Coast of South Africa. In 1918 alone, 200,000 cans were filled at the plant, and further expansion was undertaken. Unable to cope with competition from larger firms and rising costs of operation, the plant closed on its golden anniversary in 1964. Two hundred lost their jobs by the decision. All of the buildings except one were demolished in the summer of 1967. The original winery was spared. Today it is the oldest building in Manteca and houses the seed coating operations of Cel Pril Industries.

BUSINESS DISTRICT OF MANTECA, c. 1905–6

Most likely this is the oldest available photo of Manteca. Just four or five years earlier, the settlement consisted of two houses and J. J. Overshiner's store, which was occupied by a general store and barber shop.

This was soon joined by a collectively owned Rochdale Store, consisting of a butcher shop and a general store. Ownership in the business was divided into 100 equal shares. Although the general store failed, the meat market was successful and eventually became privately owned. The first large building was the Palmer House, built in 1908 for a hotel which also offered space for the post office. With these beginnings, other businesses followed suit, some erecting two-story brick buildings, most of which still stand today along Yosemite Avenue.

One of these businesses was Thomas G. Lauritson's General Merchandise, which opened in 1916 and offered a variety of merchandise including gasoline and ice. It was much like a one stop market of modern times. In 1939, George Lauritson, son of the founder, established the Manteca Variety Store there, which continued in operation, in the same location, until 1976. In that year, Manteca's oldest retail business was closed, after being operated eight years by George's widow, Kathryn.

float for display during the 1915 Panama-Pacific International Exposition in San Francisco. This project no doubt was encouraged by the first prize won by an entry at the state fair. The Board of Trade might very well have continued as the local authority for a longer period of time before incorporation, but there was an emergency in 1918. This was a quarantine from the State Department of Health due to the failure of the local septic tank system. The cause was a rise in the water table due to irrigation of extensive lands nearby. It was imperative that a sewer system be installed, and the town would have to incorporate in order to fund the bond issue.

At this time, the local jail was an unused ice house in the 200 block of East Yosemite Avenue which had been donated about 1917. A new jail was among the projects approved by the new city council, along with curbs for Yosemite Avenue between Main Street (old Hogan Road) and the Southern Pacific track. There were also street signs, the paving of both Yosemite Avenue and Main Street and, in recognition of the automobile

age, all the hitching posts were removed.

A firebell was also purchased and installed at Joshua Cowell's home. At this time, the equipment was composed of two fire hydrants and two hose carts for the 400 feet of hose. Starting about 1918, an annual ball was held for the volunteer fire department. This was their only source of funds, but it was so successful that a combination pump and chemical apparatus on a Ford chassis could be financed in 1920.

Residents have always been admirably well served by utilities. Private enterprise by Achille Bacilieri established a water works just after the turn of the century. The utility was finally sold to the city in 1928. Electricity came in 1911 with the Sierra and San Francisco Electric Company producing power with generators operated by water wheels on the Middle Fork of the Stanislaus River. The utility was purchased by the Pacific Gas and Electric Company in 1920.

The first hospital opened at Yosemite Avenue and Veach Street in 1919 with eighteen rooms. No further expansion took place until 1962, when

GOODWIN DAM AND OLD MELONES DAM ON THE STANISLAUS RIVER, c. 1950

Irrigation water for agricultural lands surrounding Manteca is impounded behind these dams. Note the turkey buzzard soaring above the table mountain at left.

These dams are an integral part of a joint development of the South San Joaquin and Oakdale irrigation districts. They were established at about the same time, creating a fortunate circumstance, as their major facilities could be jointly developed. Goodwin Dam, appearing near the center foreground, was completed in 1913 for the massive project. Note the canals on each side of the river. The one at left brings water to the South San Joaquin Irrigation District while its counterpart on the right serves the Oakdale area. In the distance is old Melones Dam, completed in 1926.

The initial facility consisted of Goodwin Dam, a short distance up the Stanislaus from Knights Ferry in Stanislaus County. Completion of this structure was heralded by the governor of California, Hiram Johnson, who participated in a dedication ceremony before 4,000 spectators. With this completed, 300 miles of ditches, tunnels and flumes, including a sixty-eight foot high section, were needed for distribution. The system was operational by 1913 and provided thirty-five minutes of irrigation every thirty days throughout the 71,000-acre South San Joaquin Irrigation District.

Over the years, considerable improvements were made, including Woodward's Reservoir (1916), Melones Dam (1926) and the Tri-Dam Project completed in 1957 after nearly a decade of work. The latter, also a joint project, consisted of three dams, three reservoirs and an equal number of power houses. This was the most ambitious project ever undertaken in the entire United States by an irrigation district. The most recent development is the New Melones Dam, completed in 1978. *(Courtesy South San Joaquin Irrigation District)*

HOTEL WAUKEEN, YOSEMITE AVENUE, c. 1920
This handsome structure was little changed until a 1983 fire. The window openings are trimmed with a light colored brick, creating a striking contrast with the red brick used on the remainder of the masonry. It has now been demolished.

new facilities on Cottage Avenue reached completion and offered forty-nine rooms.

Since the early twentieth century, irrigation has had an overwhelming effect on the growth of Manteca and the productivity of surrounding farm lands. What were once tens of thousands of acres of dry farmed grain became fields of alfalfa, orchards, diversified crops and large scale dairying operations. With the change in crops, the large grain farms were broken into smaller, often forty-acre plots, for intensive agriculture. The increased number of farms brought about a rapidly expanding population. For example, within a short time of completion of the first irrigation system by the Stanislaus and San Joaquin Water Company, the population of Manteca rose from 80 to 500. Further expansion came with the creation of the South San Joaquin Irrigation District in 1909. To further the work, a $1,875,000 bond issue was passed.

Agricultural produce has given distinction to Manteca over the years. For decades, stock yards filled with cattle thriving on beet pulp from a sugar mill made "Manteca fed beef" a household word over a large region. Much more recently, the community has been vying with Half Moon Bay (San Mateo County, California) and Circleville, Ohio, for the distinction of "pumpkin capital of the world." A pumpkin festival has been held continuously since 1974. the 1977 pumpkin seed spitting contest gained recognition in the *Guinness Book of World Records* for a seed cast thirty-six feet and nine inches.

As might be expected, local industry has traditionally been closely associated with the produce of the immediate vicinity. Dairying, responsible

for inspiring the name of the community, was the first such activity. The skimming station in the old box car, mentioned earlier, was a stop for the Bay Area bound trains only when a flag was raised at track side. At this time, it operated as a co-op. In 1906, it was sold to Ed Powers, who leased it to Morgansen and Nielsen, who purchased it in 1914 and opened the business to the public. The proprietors commemorated the event with free ice cream. By 1915, 1,250 pounds of butter were produced each day and the amount was increasing due to the plentiful locally grown alfalfa. By 1920, dairy farming was the largest south county enterprise.

The best known industry in Manteca opened in 1918 and is still in operation, the Spreckels sugar mill, which is one of the largest agri-businesses in San Joaquin County. The firm, now Spreckels-Amstar, processes half of the sugar beets raised in the county plus those brought in by truck from fields located from Sacramento to Chowchilla (Madera County).

Construction was inspired by the sugar shortage of World War I. Spreckels Sugar Company had but a single plant, in Salinas, California, and first became interested in the Manteca area when seed from Germany shipped here in 1915, along with irrigation, encouraged the crop. A year later, fifty farmers had 7,000 acres in beets. All of the production of these fields, however, had to be shipped about one hundred miles to Salinas in Monterey County. Railroad freight rates cut into the profits, and local residents unified to try to convince Spreckels to build in Manteca. An effective inducement was the offer of 440 acres for a plant site. Soon there were plans for a $2 million

YOSEMITE GRAMMAR SCHOOL

On facing page, top, the building as it appeared in the 1920s; bottom, the first class, in 1914.

Upon completion, the school had two teachers, Misses Branson and Alma Locke. Teacher/principal Miss Bowden is shown immediately to the right of the doorway. In 1917, when J. M. Luck was hired as principal, the school trustees provided him with living quarters in this building.

Students are numbered as follows. All those with an asterisk were the first to graduate from the new school, in 1921.

1, 2, 3, 4, 5, and 6. Unknown.
7. Kenneth Graves*
8. Frank Canclini
9. Edward Hale
10. Louis Candini
11. Edward Powers*
12. Robert Olson
13. Unknown
14. Leah McAdams
15. Falice Wise
16. Unknown
17. Ethel Hines*
18. Myrtle Lindenstein*
19. Hilda Walrad
20, 21. Unknown
22. Maggie Warren*
23. Madaline Blake
24. Ruth Johnson*
25. Eulah Newborn
26. Evelyn Olson
27. Ed Shaw
28. Benton Hooper*
29. Raymond Candini
30. Clarence Rennels
31. Wendy Boberg*
32. Bernice Lindenstein
33, 34. Unknown
35. Miss Bowden
36. Earl Sawdon
37. Herbert Whelan*
38. Unknown
39. Carl Blake
40. George Callender
41. Stanley Boberg
42, 43. Unknown

Located on West Yosemite Avenue, this school served until badly damaged by fire in 1948. It was replaced by the present building in 1950. *(Collection of Clarence Rennels)*

plant. Opening was delayed until 1918 because of a steel shortage caused by the war. The plant finally opened with 400 on the payroll at the very end of World War I.

During the thirties, Floyd Richards and Roy Olsen were operating the Manteca Cream and Butter Company. Richards constructed an ice cream parlor in the front of the building which became a favorite local gathering place. Butter and ice cream, ten gallons every six minutes, were the major products. Further expansion, in 1939, made it possible for the firm to obtain government contracts to supply military bases. This creamery was probably the best known business in Manteca to the thousands of motorists traveling between the Sierra and the Bay Area. It was a favorite stop-over, and "Maneto Brand" ice cream was the key to its reputation. All this came to an end in 1965, the year the business closed and the building was torn down.

The population growth of Manteca has been phenomenal, especially since the early 1950s, when the town became established as a bedroom community. Its proximity to Modesto, Tracy and Stockton and industrial plants, especially Libby-Owens-Ford, Sharpe Depot and Best Fertilizer Company, placed Manteca in a somewhat unique position for having population greatly outdistance industrial growth. Its population doubled during each decade since 1940. An unfortunate result was that the lack of industry created a deficient tax base. Nevertheless, progress was made to remedy the situation, and in 1970, a milestone was passed when taxable sales here exceeded those of Tracy, making the community the third most active commercial center in the county, after Stockton and Lodi, a position it still holds. A much improved position in attracting new industry was gained in the early 1970s with sweeping improvement in the sewage system including a new treatment plant and trunk lines.

In recent years, Manteca has become known for the attractive prices of its new homes, the small city atmosphere and a fine school system. Forty-six hundred new homes and apartments were constructed during the 1970s. Also built were a new municipal court building (1971), the City Administration Center (1975), a library expansion creating one of the largest such facilities in the county (1979) and a Boys and Girls Club for 650, built from contributions (1982-83). In addition, there were office complexes, shopping centers and a very successful industrial park that has attracted tenants in the electronics industry described earlier. With growth double that of Stockton, the "City on the Sand Plains" gained distinction as the fastest growing community in San Joaquin County during the 1970s and the first half of the 1980s.

59

MANTECA UNION HIGH SCHOOL, 1923

Before formation of the high school district, local students traveled by Tidewater Southern Railway to Stockton High School or Ripon High School for their studies.

The Spanish Colonial style structure, left, was designed by the Stockton firm of Davis-Heller-Pearce, who also were the architects of the Stockton City Hall.

This building replaced the rough tar paper covered buildings that served as temporary quarters starting in 1920. The school was finished with hardwood floors and trim and boasted a commodious auditorium seating 550. The stage doubled as a gymnasium for decades. A safety net stretched across the edge of the stage kept balls out of the auditorium.

Constructed on a truck chassis, the bus in the photograph below was the first used by the district shortly after it was organized.

LOOKING SOUTH DOWN MAIN STREET TOWARD YOSEMITE AVENUE, 1924
At this time Main Street also served as US 99. On the right is the first bank building in Manteca. Constructed during 1911, it housed the First State Bank of Manteca and remained a bank until 1917 when larger quarters were needed and a second building was erected across Main Street. In this same year the institution was renamed the First National Bank. In 1927, it became the Bank of Italy, and in 1930 was renamed the Bank of America. The building was demolished in 1968 to provide space for parking adjacent to a newly constructed Bank of America.

SPRECKELS SUGAR REFINERY, c. 1965

The view above offers some idea of the dimension of the operation. While a large portion of the original 1917 building is still in use, the equipment is up to date, particularly after extensive modernization in 1967. Below is the main power take-off pulley that was attached to the drive shaft of a Hamilton-Corliss steam engine, retired in that year. This engine operated machinery throughout the plant by an extensive system of pulleys and flat belts.

The role of the plant is to slice sugar beets thinly into "cossettes." Hot water is then run over them, removing the sugar content from the beet slices. Through a complicated process, sugar is extracted from this solution. A typical three-pound beet yields about a quarter pound of sugar.

The plant not only produced granulated sugar and related products but two major and very useful by-products—waste water and beet pulp.

The waste water did not contain anything harmful to crops so it could be used for irrigation. The beet pulp was consumed at the Moffat Feed Yards, adjacent to the plant, where stock was fattened with pulp mixed with molasses, alfalfa and barley. Well remembered by motorists was the odor from the yards filled with "Manteca Fed Beef." The cattle were shipped live to a slaughter house and packing plant in San Francisco until 1966.

While the plant has been in Manteca for more than sixty years, it has not been in continuous operation. A drop in sugar prices and the arrival of insect pests ended the flush times expected for the new mill. It closed in 1922 and was not re-opened until the introduction of more disease resistant seed in 1931. This seed was the result of a joint development by Spreckels and the United States Department of Agriculture. Renewed activity was short lived. During World War II, beet crops were largely abandoned in

(Photograph by Dale Johnson, courtesy Spreckels Sugar Division-Amst

favor of more profitable ones, and the plant was again closed. The navy used its machine shop and filled its warehouses with supplies. Re-opening came in 1946, and production rapidly escalated in the ensuing years. Expansion in 1967 increased capacity to 4,200 tons a day, 25 percent more. Among the facilities was a new lime kiln to reprocess lime used in filtration systems in the plant; this kiln is the largest in the industry. The German-made, lofty diffuser tower where sugar is extracted from the cosettes was also an element of the expansion.

Today, with about 230 employed at peak season, Spreckels slices beets 150 days a year and produces liquid sugar for canners, powdered sugar, brown sugar, 100 pound bags and bulk lots for industrial customers. The Hershey plant in Oakdale is its best customer.

KRAFT-PHENIX CHEESE CORPORATION, MANTECA ROAD AND OAK STREETS, c. 1936
Local dairy farms had a major customer for their cream and milk with this plant, which opened in 1935 and expanded considerably in the early 1960s. The famous Philadelphia brand cream cheese, shipped throughout the West, was one of the most important products. Operations ceased in 1967.

The row of vats shown above are pasteurizers where milk or cream was heated to 145 degrees for thirty minutes through the use of steam. The vats were then chilled to about 90 degrees for the next step, the addition of the culture and rennet to thicken the liquid and start the cheese making process. *(Collection of the Holt-Atherton Center, University of the Pacific, Stockton)*

YOSEMITE AVENUE LOOKING WEST FROM MAIN STREET, c. 1925 and 1982

Of particular interest in this view of the center of town, in the photograph above, are the slender arch spanning the street and a second one that can be faintly seen in the distance. These are two of seven such arches, each holding seven incandescent globes. They were installed in 1916, giving Manteca the reputation of being the "best lighted town in the Valley."

The building at the far right served many purposes over the years, starting as M. B. Hooper's hardware, grocery and dry goods store. From about 1910 to 1913 the Hoopers gave space here for the "Free Library," which contained fifty books, all of which were exchanged for fifty others at the Stockton Public Library each month. With completion of the Odd Fellows Hall next door in 1913, the tiny library was moved there for a few years. This lodge hall was available for the use of other societies, including the Mason's Tryon Lodge, Rebecca Lodge No. 332, Woodmen of the World, Loyal Order of the Moose and Native Daughters of the Golden West, Phoebe A. Hearst Parlor.

This building was almost consumed by the great fire of 1920. The brick west wall acted like a fire wall and contained the fire. It became red hot and was cooled by a bucket brigade. This structure and others along the original business district still stand (see photograph below) and are enhanced by the landscaping of a $500,000 five-block mall completed in 1981.

THE 1927 AMERICAN LA FRANCE PUMPER ON PARADE,
ARMISTICE DAY, c. 1928

Still admirably well preserved by the Manteca Fire Department, this 600 gallon per minute pumper was purchased new for Manteca as its second motorized apparatus. A glimpse of the first such unit can be seen at left. In 1934, financial problems caused by the Depression found the department without funds to make the final payment on the LaFrance. An extension was obtained, and the $275.72 required was raised within about a month through a series of dances, donations solicited door to door, bake sales and an open house at the fire station.

In the early 1920s, there was considerable reorganization of the volunteer department under Elwood Leventon, who was noted for regular drill sessions. Two companies of volunteers were organized: #1 was responsible for fighting fires in town and in the surrounding area; Company #2 was solely responsible for raising funds. With the construction of the Manteca City Hall in 1923-24, the department was provided with substantial quarters, including a clubroom and dormitory. A year later, Company #1 was forbidden to take their apparatus out of the city, following the establishment of a rural fire district. The end of the era of volunteers came in 1958, when a salaried department was organized.

The biggest fires were in 1920, 1939, 1948 and 1952. The first destroyed six businesses, including the restaurant where it started. The huge fire of 1939 was in the Diamond Match Company lumber yard on South Main Street. The Yosemite School was lost in a huge 1948 blaze that brought equipment from Ripon and Tracy. In 1952 a furniture store and adjacent Courtesy Market were destroyed at Main and Center streets.

MASTHEAD OF THE OLDEST NEWSPAPER IN MANTECA, USED FROM 1948 UNTIL REDESIGNED IN 1972
The masthead familiar for many years to citizens of Manteca featured the sugar mill in the center.
National attention has been drawn to Manteca by fine newspaper publishing. The *Manteca Bulletin* has received over thirty state and national awards. Best remembered is the award from the National Editorial Association given to publisher George Murphy, Jr., for his column "Batting the Breeze" that appeared weekly for many years.

This community newspaper can trace its beginnings to 1908 and the campaign to muster support for the irrigation district. The *Irrigation Bulletin*, first published in Ripon, became a useful source of data on the area for state legislators, bond buyers and contractors. It was moved to Manteca in 1912, after the South San Joaquin Irrigation District offices were established there. Two years later, to reflect a new role, it was renamed the *Manteca Bulletin*. The Murphy family, the publisher since 1926, sold the paper to the Morris Newspaper Corporation in 1972. The town has had two newspapers since 1977, when the *Manteca News* was founded to compete with the *Bulletin*. The resulting tug of war for advertisers led to a $4.5 million suit against the *News*, the first anti-trust suit ever tried in San Joaquin County. In 1984 a unanimous verdict was handed down in favor of the *Bulletin*. The *News* forfeited its right of appeal as part of an out of court settlement, other terms of which were not made public. *(Courtesy the* Manteca Bulletin*)*

TROUBLE AT THE DEPOT, 1954
Highways and railroads do not always mix well, and such was the case when a truck loaded with empty wine bottles stalled on the Southern Pacific tracks and was hit by a Southern Pacific train which killed the driver and nearly carried the truck and nearby cars through a wall of the depot.

Railroad connections have been behind much of Manteca's economic growth. It is served today by the Southern Pacific and Tidewater-Southern Railroad plus the Western Pacific Railroad just three miles to the west. Highway 120 runs through the community, and there is ready access to nearby Highway 99 and Interstate 5.

Competition to the Southern Pacific came in 1910 with construction of the Western Pacific. Eight years later a third line came as a freight service branch of an electric interurban system connecting Stockton and Modesto—the Tidewater-Southern. It connected with the main line at Manteca Junction about six and a half miles north of town. Construction was financed by selling stock in the company to owners of property along the route. The company would buy the stock back when the tracks reached the owner's land. This rail service opened a new opportunity to Manteca shoppers. At one time there were twenty-four trains daily between Stockton and Modesto. A round trip between the two communities could be made within about two hours, a great contrast to a day in an automobile, straining over the sometimes hazardous roads. Since passenger service was discontinued in 1932 and the electric lines removed, the line has kept active as a profitable feeder system for the Western Pacific Railroad, which acquired a controlling interest in 1917.

LOOKING NORTHEAST ACROSS THE MANTECA BUSINESS DISTRICT, c. 1960

In the foreground are the Southern Pacific tracks. The complex of buildings between the tracks and the water tower housed the Manteca Canning Company. The intersection of Yosemite Avenue and Main Street appears just to the right of center, a point which is surrounded by buildings composing the commercial center. El Rey Theater, a burned out shell since 1975, can be seen a block east of this intersection. It opened in 1937 with a capacity of 701.

MANTECA BYPASS, A SIX AND A HALF MILE SOLUTION TO A MASSIVE PROBLEM, 1982

Direct highway access to a town is not always advantageous. For Manteca, the relatively narrow main street, Yosemite Avenue, would also serve as State Highway 120. As motor traffic increased, congestion through the center of town became almost unbearable. Finally, in the late 1950s, efforts were made to regain the main street for the local residents.

The idea was to create a bypass between Interstate 5 and Highway 99. Pressure reached the state highway department in the late 1960s, and construction of the $12.4 million, six and a half mile project commenced in

1979. The bypass started diverting 10,000 cars a day from Yosemite Avenue in December 1980. Most local businessmen considered the lessening of traffic a boon. The almost forgotten days of a peaceful central business district returned, through less congestion and far better access, and local people were encouraged to do business in the area much more frequently. Also important in eliminating congestion was the widening of South Main Street to four lanes during 1980, establishing an important connecting link to the southern portion of the city and a major industrial park there. *(Photograph by Glenn Kahl, Manteca)*

A GREAT BOON TO FURTHER INDUSTRIAL GROWTH IN MANTECA, 1982

A recent development is the arrival of industry not related to agriculture. Major electronics firms have located at this industrial park at the southern edge of town, and others are coming. These include Shinko Electric America, lead frame supplier to semi conductor manufacturers, which has expanded its operations since coming here in 1983; Indy, manufacturers of complicated circuits; and Uniphase Corporation, which came during 1985 to start manufacture of laser equipment, including supermarket code bar readers, instruments for the medical profession and instruments for the construction industry. This is one of only twelve such manufacturers in the nation.

RAMPAGE RIDE, OAKWOOD LAKE RESORT, AUGUST 1985

A regionally popular, diversified recreational complex has developed near Manteca since Oakwood Lake Resort opened in 1974. The facilities around the seventy acre lake include waterslides; outdoor roller rink/ dance floor; softball field; the largest RV campground in Northern California; Ski Oakwood, the first cable water skiing facility in California and in the West; and a 6,000 seat amphitheater completed in 1984. During 1985 at least 400,000 visitors were welcomed. Between 350 and 400 employees are kept busy during the summer, making Oakwood one of the most important seasonal employers of youth in San Joaquin County. Barely more than ten years ago this site was just an obscure hole in the ground where sand and gravel had been removed for years on the "Budge" Brown farm.

68

TRACY
OLD "POKER CITY"

Beginning as a dusty, windblown railroad town, this settlement has evolved through a fortunate series of circumstances to a major agricultural and industrial community. Its highway links now overshadow its railroad connections in importance. Such resources may establish Tracy as the second largest community in San Joaquin County by the year 2000.

In 1878 the town plan was laid by the Pacific Improvement Company, a Southern Pacific affiliate. The site on the valley plain was near a point where trains began a tedious, steep two-hour climb over the first ridge of the Coast Range on the line to the San Francisco Bay area. These developments led to the extinction of the nearby railroad center of Ellis, established with the completion of the transcontinental railroad in 1869.

Tracy took shape rapidly in 1878 and 1879, for many buildings from Ellis were hauled three miles by teams of horses to the new townsite. The first newspaper, the *Tracy News*, commenced publication in December 1881. All this development was brought about by construction of the "low level route" to the Bay via Martinez. This reduced dependence upon the steep route to Livermore via the Altamont Pass. The two lines joined at the new town. Lathrop J. Tracy, for whom the town was named, was an Ohio grain merchant who never visited the area, but had his name applied to this point through a good friend, J. H. Stewart, who was a Central Pacific construction official.

Facilities were installed without delay for fuel, water, freight and cattle handling, all of which were expanded to major proportions in the decades to come.

World War II brought railroad activity to its height, and ever since then its influence on the town has been less and less important. A turning point came in 1956, when the last steam locomotive was replaced by a diesel. These engines did not require the sprawling facilities and huge crews of the era of steam. In 1951 the roundhouse crew alone totaled 300. Five years later it was scaled down to fifty-nine. The old yards along 6th Street were too large and antiquated for the new equipment, and a new yard was established at the present location on the east side of town, in 1961. In 1969, 150 of the 220 Tracy trainmen were transferred to Roseville. While railroading is still part of the local economy, Tracy can no longer be thought of as a railroad town.

Before Tracy was founded, risky dry farming of grain was being practiced by pioneer settlers of the "West Side." This was to remain the dominant agricultural activity until the early twentieth century. There was a greater potential for the rich adobe soil if water could be obtained in quantity. Efforts to make Tracy more of an agricultural center did not succeed until a controversial campaign in 1913-14 led to the creation of the West Side Irrigation District. A bond issue approved by an overwhelming majority a year later assured construction of a canal system. A wonderland of new crops then appeared on land that had only been dry farmed. Lima beans, alfalfa, asparagus, orchards and truck crops were thriving. Dairy farming grew rapidly in the late teens and into the twenties.

Profitable World War II crops of baby lima beans were reduced in favor of sugar beets, tomatoes and alfalfa hay. Attention to such produce was a result of influence from local industry, including the Holly Sugar Company, the H. J. Heinz Company, the San Joaquin Valley Hay Growers Association, the dairies and creameries.

Closely related to the food processing industry is Owens-Illinois Glass Container Division, opened in 1962. Starting with just one furnace and 150 employees, the company, now with 500 workers, operates three furnaces twenty-four hours a day. The furnaces produce various colors of glass: clear (or filt) for food products, green for wineries, amber for beer bottling. The glass sand is from Ione in Amador County.

The earliest dairies, the Alaska Dairy and the Blue Bell, were established in the late 1920s. Known from Ukiah to Bakersfield was the Peterson Ice Cream Company, one of the principal ice cream mix suppliers in the 1940s and 1950s.

In 1974 a local cattle breeder introduced "beefalo" after fifteen years of research. "Beefalo," a cross of buffalo, Herford and Charolais cattle, had the advantage of rapid growth and the ability to subsist on low quality grazing land. Interest has become so widespread, there is now a World Beefalo Association.

Not all local industry has been directly related to agriculture. Due to good rail connections, the River Rock and Gravel Company was established in 1914 at the mouth of Corral Hollow Creek. Aggregate needed for such noted construction projects as the Lincoln Highway, the Bay Bridge and the Golden Gate Bridge was provided by the plant. In 1935 another development involving natural resources came with the discovery, near Tracy, of the first commercial gas field in Northern California.

As it did to every American city, World War I brought many changes, some with a lasting effect. Tracy was in an advantageous position because of its major links to rail and truck transportation. It became a locomotive fuel loading center, and huge oil reservoirs were established at the southern edge of the city. Oil was received from Kern County via a Standard Oil of California pipeline. The Southern Pacific yards were greatly improved, with considerable new track and an enlarged turntable for the roundhouse, giving it capacity to handle any locomotive on the sprawling Western Division. Women were hired to do men's work, including roundhouse help. At the airport, the runways were paved and vastly expanded.

The most unusual activity brought about during the war was "Military Intelligence Section No. 1941." There was an air of mystery about the isolated facility in nearby Contra Costa County, which had once been an elaborate resort known since the 1880s as Byron Hot Springs. After the war, it became evident that the resort had been an interrogation center for hundreds of Japanese and German prisoners of war. Many were officers and their stay was usually limited to just a few days

DIRECTORY ADVERTISEMENTS
Just two years after the community was founded, these advertisements appeared in the 1880 Pacific Coast Directory. Note the abbreviation for the railroad company in the hotel ad that stands for the Southern and Central Pacific Railroad, a name created by the merger of the Central Pacific and Southern Pacific Railroad companies. *(Courtesy Stockton Central Library)*

PASSENGER SERVICE, 1883–1971

Built like the stations in Livermore and Bethany, the Tracy depot was designed so that one agent could look after both the freight and passenger compartments. The depot sign reads: "Tracy—83 miles to San Francisco." Originally constructed in 1878 at the nearby town of Ellis, this structure was moved to Tracy in 1882.

Left to right, facing the photographer, are Henry Turner, Dave Welch (Southern Pacific engineer), D. Antius and Southern Pacific passenger director Dave Payne and his son, Charlie. The venerable station was demolished in the early 1960s. Today, Tracy has few reminders of its important role in early railroading—just old #1293, a little noticed switch engine in a park, and the former baggage section from the depot now relocated to Clover Avenue near Tracy Boulevard.

While freight service kept the yards very busy, the pace quickened a bit with the arrival of each passenger train. At the height of activity, twenty-eight passenger trains arrived or originated at Tracy. Most famous were the Owl, a night run between San Francisco and Los Angeles via Tracy, and the San Joaquin Daylight, its counterpart and "flagship" of Southern Pacific passenger transportation. The San Joaquin Daylight is shown in the photo below on its maiden trip, July 4, 1941, as it takes on water at the east tank in the Tracy yards. The cars were painted red and gold. *(Top photograph, Waldo Stevens Collection; bottom photograph, courtesy Herman O. Friedrich)*

SOUTHERN PACIFIC YARDS, 1908

Further significance as a rail center was gained in the summer of 1892 with completion of a line along the West Side of the San Joaquin Valley and across the valley plain to Fresno. Trains were now arriving in Tracy from all four points of the compass, and facilities had to be further expanded. A roundhouse and additional repair shops were built in the early 1890s. It was here that thirty-five to forty steam locomotives were serviced daily. Switch engines were at work twenty-four hours a day. When Tracy became a division point, with establishment of the Stockton division, even larger facilities were required. The most dramatic effect was doubling the size of the roundhouse in 1917. Crews worked out of Tracy to Fresno and Sacramento (later to Roseville), in arrangements that continue to this day. *(Waldo Stevens Collection)*

CENTRAL AVENUE FROM SIXTH STREET, BETWEEN 1905 AND 1911

The intersection is flanked by the Tracy Hotel, built for Charles Slack in 1899 and destroyed in a 1911 fire. The wide verandas had a cooling effect on the building and were especially designed for the hot climate. Across from it is the leading business of the time, the Fabian-Grunauer Company, operated by Phillip Fabian and Abe Grunauer. Fabian, who had been a merchant in Ellis, was the first to establish a business in Tracy. The store, always situated in this prime location, was known not only for its stock of groceries, dry goods, hardware and farm machinery, but also for enterprises in hay, grain and warehousing. *(Waldo Stevens Collection)*

before they were sent to prison camps in Wisconsin and Montana. Much was learned about tactics and equipment that had an incalculable effect on the war. Another prisoner of war detention center was located at the army supply depot south of Tracy. Begun in 1943, the camp had a peak population of 800, mainly from Rommel's Afrika Corps. They were assigned to various projects, including farm labor, and proved to be good workers.

These military centers created an unprecedented demand for housing. Much of the need was quickly met by Wainwright Village, built by the Federal Housing Authority in 1943. It occupied a site, now redeveloped, in part, for the Tracy Civic Center.

State agencies have made Tracy a location for major facilities. Deuel Vocational Institution

A BIT OF HISTORY CAME TO LIGHT, LATE 1960s

During demolition of the Arlington Theater, adjacent to the old Fabian-Grunauer store, this sign, covered since 1911, was exposed to view and remained as seen above until the old store, turned bar and liquor store in more recent years, was demolished in 1985.

CONTRASTS ON SIXTH STREET, c. 1898 AND 1982

Above, the Odd Fellows Hall on Sixth Street as it was rebuilt shortly after the great fire of 1898 that destroyed the original building and every major business in town. The hall became the center for much social and fraternal activity. Aside from the IOOF, the Knights of Pythias, Pythian Sisters and the Native Daughters of the Golden West met here. The structure still stands today and is owned by the Tracy Moose Lodge. Note the unlikely neighbor to the post office. *(Waldo Stevens Collection)*

Below, a 1982 view of the somewhat altered IOOF building. These buildings and others surviving along Sixth Street are reminders of the time local businessmen depended upon railroad employees for much of their patronage. *(Photograph by Raymond W. Hillman)*

opened in 1953 for intermediate security of 1,200 prisoners. It provides rehabilitative training with programs in welding, cabinet work, radio repair, auto mechanics, farming, dairy experience, etc. Starting in the mid-1960s, more serious offenders were sent here, and Deuel now has maximum security facilities. During 1983 inmate population reached 3,179 at Deuel, making it the most over-crowded of the twelve state prisons—95.5 percent over capacity.

Tracy has been the locale for two key units of state water projects: the Tracy Pumping Plant and the Delta Pumping Plant. In 1951, the Tracy Pumping Plant, an integral part of the Federal Central Valley Project, started pumping water into the Delta-Mendota Canal, which extends through farmlands 100 miles to the south. Its sig-nificance was so great that a three day celebration was held.

Of major importance to California was an event that took place in the late summer of 1967, the completion of the Delta Pumping Plant—the "heartbeat" of the California Water Project, which brings surplus Northern California water to the southern portion of the state. It was officially start-ed by Governor Ronald Reagan and, to this day, is pumping water from the Delta to the 444 mile canal and pipeline system to Southern California.

Highway connections have been increasingly important to the growth of Tracy's business and residential districts throughout most of the twen-tieth century. In contrast to the formative days when the Lincoln Highway brought increased demand for roadside service, the emphasis today is upon the ease with which traffic can travel to and from the city. Tracy is situated within a unique triangle of highways constructed between 1965 and 1971: I-5 on the east, 580 on the west and 205, the "Tracy Byapss," on the north. During 1985, through legislative action, Highway 205 was named the Robert Monagan Freeway. Monagan was prominent in Tracy politics before his elec-tion to the California State Assembly. At the same time, Highway 580 became the William E. Brown Freeway, named for another prominent political figure, who was particularly active in the High-way 33 Association.

A world record in concrete paving was made in 1971, when three miles of pavement were laid on Highway 205 in sixteen and a half hours. While the bypass diverted 20,000 cars a day from the main street of Tracy, great benefit was seen by industrial and commercial interests in a vast improvement to the accessibility of Tracy. The eight lanes over Altamont Pass have attracted many new residents wishing to commute to the Bay Area and benefit

FAMILY GATHERING AT THE DUFFY RESIDENCE, 1900
The people are identified from left to right as follows: Mrs. Jesse Parnell, Merton Par-nell, Creighton Duffy, Jesse Parnell (grain farmer near Vernalis), Leslie F. Duffy, Elwyn (Jesse) Duffy, Elizabeth (Bessie) Duffy, Thomas Creighton Duffy (publisher of the *Tracy Press* and justice of the peace), Reu-ben Poling (grain farmer on the West Side), Nella Duffy, Mrs. Reuben Poling, Francis Willard Duffy (Southern Pacific employee, eventually became a locomotive engineer), Jennie Duffy, Leo Parnell. *(Collection of Mrs. Raymond F. (Delma) Bailey)*

from much lower priced real estate; a boom in growth, also experienced by Manteca, has resulted. Aside from eighty-six acres of subdivisions being rapidly sold, 1985 has brought such new commercial/industrial development as Collins Food Service and Gran Trace Shopping Center. Collins ships food over an area from Bakersfield to the Oregon border and Reno to San Francisco. Sixty people are employed by this firm, which moved from Santa Clara. K Mart Corporation has developed Gran Trace, which will employ seventy to eighty.

Transportation attributes and location will be key elements in future growth of this city of 25,000 as one of the most important urban areas within the county.

IN THEIR SUNDAY BEST AT THE FIRST PRESBYTERIAN CHURCH, NINTH AND CENTRAL, c. 1900
The gabled beauty of the belfry was truly an ornament to Tracy when this sanctuary was completed in 1880. The bell not only summoned the faithful to service; it was also Tracy's first fire alarm. T. C. Duffy and his family are in the buggy. (Collection of Mrs. Raymond F. (Delma) Bailey)

TOWN HALL AND JAIL, SHORTLY AFTER COMPLETION IN 1900

Still standing today, this is very likely the oldest government building in the county today. Plans were drawn by noted architects Beasley and Beasley, who designed the facade from a fifteenth century North Italian church, San Francesco di Rimini. The historical and architectural significance of this building has been recognized, and it is now listed on the National Register of Historic Places and has been restored for use as the Tracy Historical Center, incorporated in July 1985.

It is interesting that this building was erected when Tracy had no organized government of its own but was loosely directed by county officials. *(Waldo Stevens Collection)*

TRACY CIVIC CENTER, c. 1920

For many years, this building was known as City Hall, but it also served as the jail and volunteer fire house.

The new City Hall in the Civic Center, first occupied in 1973, was the first built expressly for this purpose since local government was created in 1910. Back in these times, concerns were for things far more basic than an edifice. A lack of a sewer system, poor streets, wooden sidewalks, a water supply concentrated upon private wells and primitive fire protection were factors inspiring incorporation. In spite of the needs, the proposal passed with very few votes to spare.

By 1916, there was more confidence in a local government, and a bond issue passed, leading not only to purchase of fire apparatus but also to construction of the City Hall (above), which was designed by Stockton architects Pater Sala and Frank Mayo. It still stands today on Central Avenue at Ninth Street and serves the fire department.

Buildings originally constructed for other purposes were to serve various city departments, and it was not until the 1970s that especially designed facilities were built, including the aforementioned City Hall as well as police headquarters, occupied in 1978. Other public works projects in 1979 brought a new waste treatment plant and water treatment facility to Tracyites. A $22 million, two year, sewer expansion project commenced in 1985 that will help Tracy realize its goal of doubling its population in seven to ten years.

While most resources have been applied to concerns of the present and future, city government distinguished itself by sponsoring the first architectural/historical building survey in the county. This project, completed in 1978, recognized fifty structures for possible preservation.

CENTRAL SCHOOL, 1912–1961

Perhaps one of the best known older buildings was the Central School, located on Central Avenue immediately south of the Tracy Inn. With eight classrooms and an assembly hall, it served from 1912 to 1938. During World War II, it provided space for air force ground school training as well as for the U.S.O. The City of Tracy purchased and remodeled it during 1946 for use as City Hall; structural failure led to its demolition. The site is now occupied by the Tracy Inn annex. *(Waldo Stevens Collection)*

CENTRAL AVENUE, c. 1920

The expanding main business district turned the corner from Sixth Street between 1910 and 1920. Establishment of businesses all along Central Avenue and a gradual decline of the traditional business center fronting the Southern Pacific yards was the result. Two locally owned banks had substantial buildings on this street by 1920; one of these, with three tall arches, can be seen in the distance at left. This is the West Side Bank, later the Bank of Italy. The Bank of Tracy, not shown, became part of the American Trust Company. Both of these imposing buildings are still standing today, but are banks no longer. *(Waldo Stevens Collection)*

STOPPING FOR LUNCH AT THE TRACY INN, 1928

Shown at the main entrance, about a year after the Tracy Inn opened, are a group of Travel Information Bureau staff members, guests of the California Transit Company for a spring trip to Yosemite and Camp Curry to gather firsthand information. Note the canvas covered baggage rack on top of the bus, which was owned by one of the largest lines in the state. *(From the* Byron Times Booster Edition, *1928-29; Courtesy The Haggin Museum, Stockton)*

HIGHWAY 50, 1946

Major businesses were located here to serve the thousands of travelers passing through town on Highway 50, originally the Lincoln Highway. The tower in the distance is part of the well-known Tracy Inn. Tourists have been dining and staying overnight here since 1927. *(Waldo Stevens Collection)*

AIRPLANE VIEW OF TRACY, 1930s

We are looking southeast across the main business district along Central Avenue to the railroad yards. Near the center is the prominent Tracy Inn, and, immediately behind it, the Central School may be seen. Beyond the tracks is the South Side, where many Hispanic railroad and farm workers lived. In the extreme upper left are the trees of the Tracy Cemetery, which was moved from Banta in 1878. *(Waldo Stevens Collection)*

SERVING THE MOTORIST

Roadside businesses for the motorist started early in Tracy, as the famous Lincoln Highway route went down 11th Street through the community. The Lincoln Highway, the first transcontinental auto route, reached completion in 1925. Garages for auto repair were soon more common than blacksmith shops, and the interior view on this page was typical in many ways. New business opportunities were provided not only by the needs of the automobile but also by the needs of thirsty motorists.

Of particular significance was the Giant Orange stand, the first of which was built in Tracy during 1926. This photo dates from 1934. The founder, Tracy resident Frank Pohl, had similar stands on a franchise basis on highways 40, 50 and 99 from Redding to Bakersfield. These "oases" of the hot valley reached their peak of prosperity in the 1950s. Highway improvements gradually cut off easy access to the stands, and the last closed in 1973.

MAY 29, 1934

80

THE HOLLY SUGAR PLANT, 1932

Sugar beet processing started in 1917, and portions of the first building are still in use as part of the present Holly Sugar Company, which is a unit of the third largest sugar refinery company in the United States. The original plant, financed by East Coast and British investors, was known as the Pacific Sugar Company. Holly purchased the plant after a series of unsuccessful seasons. There were 200 employees at peak and sixty-five year round, processing 700 tons of beets per day.

By 1985 there were 180 seasonal employees plus 160 year round, processing a 4,800 ton daily slice. From the late 1930s into the 1960s, a large cattle feeding operation was maintained to utilize the nutritious beet pulp. A new dimension to the operations, a corn syrup processing plant, was added in 1978 to meet increasing competition to granulated sugar. Unprofitable, it closed in December 1982.

THE H. J. HEINZ FACTORY, 1946

Rice pudding and ketchup required for war rations encouraged construction of this factory. So large was the project that the war was over before production could start, and, while millions of bottles of ketchup have been shipped, not one batch of rice pudding was ever produced.

The Heinz plant started production in 1946. The timing was of great benefit, for it provided hundreds of new jobs for returning veterans. Women forklift drivers, below, have been part of the company work force for decades. Growth of this plant has been phenomenal. Some highlights include a vinegar distillation facility and a tomato paste tank farm. Tomato processing facilities have doubled in size since it opened; this plant has been the West Coast manufacturing headquarters for Heinz.

In 1946, the Tracy factory concentrated on tomato products with some production of canned pears and baby food. Today, while tomato products are predominant, production of soups, baby foods, pickles and vinegar are also important. Five hundred year round employees are increased to 750 during the tomato season. *(Courtesy Heinz U.S.A.)*

TRACY DEFENSE DEPOT, c. 1980

The greatest impact of World War II came in 1942 with what is now known as the Tracy Defense Depot. A 448 acre site was selected, and soon a large portion of it was covered with wooden buildings which were to serve the army's quartermaster depot in Oakland. The initial mission was to supply non-perishable food, clothing and general supplies to installations on the West Coast and in the Pacific. By the end of the year, 1,000 were employed. Since this time, its role has changed and the original depot was greatly expanded, particularly during the Korean War, when the work force reached 1,500 on three shifts. In 1963 it became one of the first facilities of the newly created Defense Supply Agency, which was to supply all branches of the service. Today there are 1,600 civilian employees plus sixteen army, navy, marine corps and air force supervisory personnel. General supplies are provided, as has been done since establishment. Considerable machine shop work was performed for NASA's space shuttle project. Similar work was done for the army M-1 tank project. The depot is the largest year-round employer in San Joaquin County. *(Courtesy Defense Logistics Agency, Defense Depot, Tracy)*

THE CENTENNIAL GAZEBO

A permanent reminder of Tracy's centennial celebration is this gazebo, which was originally located in the center of town and surrounded with about fifty food and entertainment booths. The structure served as a bandstand as well as a centerpiece of the event before being moved to its present location in Lincoln Park.

RIPON
"THE ALMOND CAPITAL OF CALIFORNIA"

Ferries across the Stanislaus River were key to the earliest developments of this southernmost city of San Joaquin County. In 1850, Taylor's Ferry was established at the base of Austin Road. Even earlier than this was Clark's, one mile east. Murphy's, two miles northeast of the present town, was in operation from 1850 to 1870.

The entire townsite and surrounding lands were owned at first by W. H. Hughes, a settler of 1857. Important locales in this sector of the county were, however, ferry crossings until the coming of railroad construction.

This turning point was summarized by pioneer Frank Hutchinson: "They were building the first railroad through the Valley southeast. At this time, 1870, the present site of Ripon was a temporary railhead. A crew of men were building a bridge across the Stanislaus River one mile southeast of the switch. Benjamin and Clara Crederick rigged up a cookhouse out of brush and served meals to the workers . . . The land was all farmed to wheat and barley at the time by Perry Yaple, Isaac Koch, Stoel Cady and Hughes, all pioneers of the locality, each one owning land that is now within the so called city limits of Ripon consisting of one square mile."

While Central Pacific was building down the valley toward Fresno, Ripon—or Stanislaus Station as it was first known—became a temporary railhead town, and the railroad company built corrals here for the shipment of cattle. Considerable grain was also brought to this point, bound

---

OFFICIAL CITY SEAL OF RIPON, ADOPTED IN 1972

Importance of local almond orchards is emphasized by the almond blossom on the seal, complete with a bee, vital to pollination. Each petal is devoted to a basic community theme: industry, religion, education, etc. A local contest was held to select the design; the winning entry was the work of Lori den Dulk (now Mrs. Ed Machado).

Local government, at first, centered around a board of trade until the creation of the Ripon Chamber of Commerce in 1923. Aside from the usual responsibilities of such an organization, it also administered the street lighting district established in 1935. Through the sponsorship of the Ripon Chamber of Commerce, there was a successful movement to incorporate Ripon in 1945.

Hans Madson was elected the first mayor and L. S. Brady city clerk. Along with regular duties, city officers were also to operate the water district established after purchase of the company from the A. J. Nourse estate.

Instrumental in the effort to create a volunteer fire department, first known as the Ripon Fire District, was Judge Sidney W. Reynolds, who continued for decades as fire commissioner. Currently, the Ripon Police Department is staffed with six officers plus a sergeant and a clerk-dispatcher. An interesting anecdote about the department in the 1950s, just a few years after incorporation of Ripon, concerns the way telephone communications to the police department were received when all patrolmen were out on the streets and no one was in the office. Calls would be answered in the home of a local resident, Nellie Van Dyken. If there was need to contact an officer, she would turn on a blue light which would blink from a twenty-five foot pole atop the town's fifty foot water water. An officer would respond by telephoning Mrs. Van Dyken from the base of the tower. *(Courtesy City of Ripon)*

THE FIRST BRICK BUILDING
IOOF HALL, 1886, 1982–84

Photographed shortly after completion (above), this building was the center of early Ripon activity. It was first occupied by pioneer merchants Perry Yaple and E. C. Dickenson. The ground floor housed their general merchandise business (later McKee and Reynolds), and the second floor contained facilities important to the town. In addition to meetings of the Odd Fellows Lodge, church services, Sunday school, dances and first high school classes were also held there.

Still retaining much of its original detailing on the second floor, the structure was occupied by a drapery shop in recent years (above). The single story concrete block building at right was originally built for the post office and telephone exchange and later became the public library.

New life was given the venerable structure in 1983 when new owner Robert Ide renovated both floors for office suites (photo at right).

for Stockton and Port Costa on the Carquinez Straits. This development was encouraged by W. H. Hughes, who had given a right-of-way and a depot site to the Central Pacific.

Shortly thereafter, the first store was established by Amplias B. Crook, late of San Diego. He was originally from Ripon, Wisconsin, and, immediately upon arrival, expressed an interest in renaming the railroad stop, which was still known as Stanislaus Station. The Wisconsin town is famous in American history, as it was here that the present Republican Party was founded in 1854. As he was a partner of Hughes in the enterprise, the re-naming effort was not a difficult task, and the name was officially changed for postal use in 1874.

At this time, the tiny settlement was a trading center for many of the early wheat and barley ranchers dry farming a wide area. By 1884, the town consisted of fourteen houses, a hotel, store, blacksmith shop, two large grain warehouses and a school which was an old cottage with all the partitions removed. A problem confronting further growth was the fact that customers south of the river were, in a large part, discouraged because the only crossing of the river for wagons and foot traffic was a privately operated toll ferry. The town did not have a newspaper until 1912, when the *Ripon Record* was established; it is still published today.

Like neighborhing communities, Ripon took advantage of irrigation to usher in a new era for agriculture. The area was to be benefitted by the South San Joaquin Irrigation District organized in 1909. Water from Goodwin Dam and Woodward Reservoir has served to replace much of the dry farming in the surrounding county with row crops, almond trees and dairies, especially those operated by the Portuguese. The dairymen rented numerous tracts of land. There were sufficient numbers of Portuguese so they could establish a social hall that became the site of colorful celebrations enjoyed by the entire community. A social hall is still maintained, and the Portuguese of Ripon have joined with those in Manteca and share the building under joint ownership.

Dutch families started settling in 1916 as a result of an advertising campaign. Many have been very successful and have encouraged additional countrymen to immigrate. Through the efforts of John de Jong, the Dutch community established their own school. The Society for Christian Instruction was the sponsor, and the school grew from primary grades only in 1924 to all levels through high school.

About the same time as the Dutch, the Swiss were also settling in Ripon in significant numbers and, like the Dutch, were involved in developing the dairy industry.

A fine example of a specialty crop that makes San Joaquin County a remarkable agricultural region is almonds. The first orchards were started in 1900 near Ripon on an experimental basis by J. P. Watkins. Since this time, California has grown to become the world's largest producer of this nut. Its production surpasses that of Italy, Spain, Morocco and Iran. Considerable acreage increase took place in the 1960s. By 1970, there were 11,000 acres of almond trees around Ripon producing more nuts per acre than any other region of the United States. Local producers market their crops at the Regal Almond Growers plant in town, the California Almond Growers Exchange in Sacramento or at Salida in neighboring Stanislaus County where they are sold under the Blue Diamond label. Another marketing center in Salida is the California Almond Orchards, and not far away in the same county is Continental Nut Company of Modesto. Ripon grown nuts travel as far as Russia, Madagascar, Japan, Australia, West Germany and other European and domestic markets.

The significance of this crop led to organizing the Almond Blossom Festival, which has been held annually in late February since 1962. Typical events include ten mile tours of the orchards, an almond bake-off, public dances, competitive sports, an exhibition of almond machinery and the coronation of Miss Almond Blossom and her five princesses.

Most local industries serve the agriculture of the region. Very significant in increasing growth of the dairy industry has been Meyenberg Brothers, local pioneers in milk condensing. Since the 1920s, they have built two plants and upon completion of the second, sold their old plant to the Pet Milk Company, which later became Nestle's Milk Products. In 1974, Meyenberg was acquired by Foster's Freeze to produce flavorings for use in this restaurant chain. This operation has now been suspended in Ripon.

Two local steel fabricators serving the almond industry with specialized equipment are Mid State Manufacturing and Ripon Manufacturing. Well-

PARADE ENTRY AT STOCKTON, OCTOBER 20, 1909

The year 1909 was an important one for both Ripon and Stockton. For Ripon, there was the celebration honoring organization of the irrigation district. This group was sent to Stockton to participate in "The Rush of '49" parade celebrating the sixtieth anniversary of the California Gold Rush.

Alongside the car are Neva McKee Summers, Nita Huntemann, Violet Roberts, Ruby Kuestardt, Evelyn Stuart, Wahneta VanSlyke and Herbie Huntemann.

Seated in the 1909 Cadillac are Gottlob Kuestardt, Vivian Uren, Ella Kuestardt and Fred Huntemann. The Cadillac, purchased at the Hansel and Ortman dealership in Stockton, served the Kuestardt family until 1921. *(Collection of Neva Summers)*

known paving machine manufacturer and general steel fabricator Guntert-Zimmerman relocated its facilities from Stockton to Ripon in 1984.

Industries serving local chicken ranches over the years are Poultry Producers of California, den Dulk Poultry and Nu-Laid Foods, Inc., which processes fresh eggs and maintains a bulk feed operation. In the early 1980s, Nu-Laid headquarters was transferred to Ripon from San Leandro.

Franzia Winery lends significance to Ripon's industries, as it is the third largest producer of California wines. During 1981, it produced 25,000,000 gallons for Taylor California Cellars. Its production is surpassed only by United Vintners of Lodi, producing 48,000,000, and E. & J. Gallo of Modesto, producing 133,000,000. Franzia was family owned until the early 1970s, when it was sold to Coca-Cola.

An industry not related to agriculture that generates significant employment is the Simpson Paper Company, manufacturers of printing paper of considerable variety, including recycled paper products.

The community has had public library services since 1910, and construction of the first library building of its own was facilitated in 1974 by a gift of land by Dr. Gilbert den Dulk and sizable cash donations from private sources to augment city and county contributions.

During 1983 the community embarked on a $2,225,000 redevelopment project that will make considerable improvements on the water and sewer lines as well as bring about residential and commercial rehabilitation.

A *Stockton Record* correspondent, Joan Ennis, pleasantly summarized the spirit of the "almond capital" in 1978: "Merchants know their customers' names, sidewalks and alleys are swept and there is always room for a planter of flowers in a corner." Not only is there a fine spirit but there is always a nice aroma about town. During much of the year it is coffee from the Nestlé plant. However, this delight is "upstaged" for a brief week or two by the blossoming of thousands of surrounding acres of almond trees. Their perfume enters the town, and white petals swirl in the streets like snowflakes.

MAIN STREET LOOKING WEST,
c. 1905 and 1982

Serving as a landmark in both pictures is the two-story brick IOOF Hall. The first building across from the IOOF Hall in the historic view (above) is the brick Thomson Bros. Cash Grocers. Next to it, in the two-story, wooden building, is Monroe DeVee's hotel and saloon. Behind this structure was a large dance hall where the town's Christmas parties and New Year's masquerade balls were held.

For the present day view (to the right), we have the same general location the photographer used some eighty years earlier. This vantage point is Highway 99. Note the sharp angle to the south that Main Street now takes. This is a result of the bisection of the community that resulted from the highway construction in 1967–68. This drastic change was necessitated by a series of tragic accidents at the highway crossing.

RIPON CONCERT BAND, 1913
Posed before the Ripon Elementary School, this group holds several silver plated brass instruments no longer used in bands today. Of particular interest are the cornets at the far right in each row.

Front row: George Chipman, tuba; Robert Low, tuba; Fred Huntemann, bass drum; Bob Chadwick, snare drum; Alton VanSlyke, cornet; Frank Thorpe, cornet.

Back row: Art Stewart, alto horn; Frank Hutchison, alto horn; Stuart Thompson, trombone; Frank McKee, baritone; Sydney Reynolds, clarinet; Jim Garrison, clarinet; Irving Goodwin, cornet; Professor Schwartz, band director. *(Collection of Neva Summers)*

THEATRICAL AND INSTRUMENTAL PERFORMERS AT SWISS HALL, c. 1943

The San Joaquin Swiss Echo Society has been particularly important in maintaining Swiss culture and tradition in this region. This view was taken just after the large social hall was built on grounds owned by the society.

Annual gatherings have been held featuring authentic alpine songs, yodeling, instrumental performances and dancing. A highlight for the group was in 1978 when the society hosted the sixteenth Pacific Coast Swiss Singing and Yodeling Festival. The four day event, held in Ripon and Stockton, was attended by 3,000 including the Swiss Consul General from San Francisco.

Shown from left to right are: Babette Rupf, Nita Kaiser, Julie Blattler, Mrs. Gusler, Agatha Ott, Mary Bach, Florence Sieber, Eda Mae Kaiser, (Vater) Joe Imfeld, Walter Imfeld (with accordian), Bill Scheuber, Hans Wagner, Lovie Blattler, Fred Fillinger, Al Wagner, and Emil Ott. *(Collection of the San Joaquin Swiss Echo Society)*

THE NESTLÉ COMPANY, 230 INDUSTRIAL AVENE

Originally operated in the 1930s as a milk condensing plant by Nestlé Milk Products, the plant still remains a major employer for Ripon today. Now as the Nestlé Company, Inc., its production is considerably different. In the 1950s, it became the first instant coffee operation on the West Coast. Today it is the only Nestlé instant coffee plant west of the Mississippi. Production centers upon Nescafe and Sunrise instant regular and decaffeinated coffees. Other products include decaffeinated green beans. For fourteen years prior to 1978, instant tea was produced. Shipments from the operation, which employs 125 people, are made throughout the West Coast and some overseas markets.

The tallest building shown houses the spray driers where coffee in liquid form is sprayed into chambers of hot air, creating the crystals. To the right of this are the smoke stacks of the boiler house; the small, tall tank farther to the right holds spent coffee grounds. The pair of light colored tanks in the foreground are fuel tanks.

The interior view shows the capping machine in the Nescafe operation. *(Courtesy The Nestlé Company)*

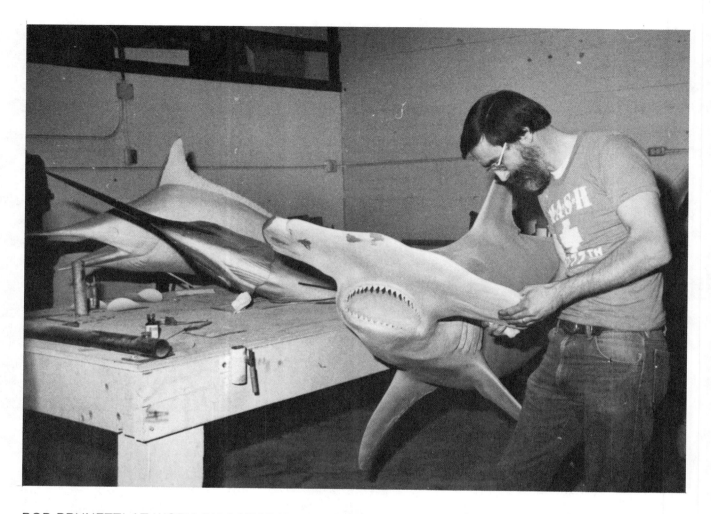

BOB BRUNETTI AT WORK ON A HAMMER HEAD SHARK IN BRUNETTI BROTHERS TAXIDERMY, 1982
　　When Bob and Richard Brunetti relocated their shop from Modesto to Ripon in 1975, they brought a measure of distinction to this community. This firm is one of very few on the West Coast that mounts fish. Frozen specimens are brought in from all over the West. The only part of the fish that can be used is the skin, which is mounted on a carved styrofoam form created from exact measurements of the specimen received. After mounting on the form, it must dry for one to two months. When the curing time is completed, the colorful markings are then painted on the skin.
　　Orders are regularly received for work on large and small mouth bass, crappie, bluegill, grayling, striper, salmon, trout, catfish and salt water varieties.
　　The firm also mounts birds and mammals, which are done by Richard Brunetti.

TILE WORK ABOVE THE ENTRANCE TO BETHANY HOME, 1983

Christian residence facilities for active seniors as well as nursing care were first provided by the Reformed and Christian Reformed churches of Central California in 1958. This was a pioneering project in the field of convalescent homes. Their Bethany Home was built in 1963 to serve the elderly of Ripon with a seventy-four bed facility. Aside from twenty-four hour skilled nursing care, there are pharmaceutical service, landscaped grounds, activity programs, etc. Statewide attention has been attracted by the excellence of the facility.

Starting in 1968, the Bethany Manor Apartments were developed and there are now thirty-three garden units, most of which have two bedrooms. More recently, fifty-six apartments with kitchens were added.

SPRING CREEK GOLF AND COUNTRY CLUB, 1983
A newly completed bar/lounge and locker facility appears in the center distance. A part of the eighteen hole course is in the foreground. There are about 430 members in this club, which was established in 1966.
(Photograph by Raymond W. Hillman)

ESCALON
"THE LAND OF PEACHES AND CREAM"

Few communities in the United States had as auspicious a beginning as the one achieved by the founding family of Escalon. This was a huge, two-story brick house known as "the brick mansion of the plains." Built in 1867, it was the first substantial structure erected on what was to become the Escalon townsite. John Wheeler Jones, former plantation overseer in South Carolina, first settled here in 1855 after working as a teamster during the gold rush. He planted the first grain crops here by hand and used a harrow made of sage brush. His crop was successful and soon he was building his fortune and expanding his land holdings.

As his ranch was close to the famous Big Oak Flat Road to the mines, the house was not only the Jones family residence but also provided lodging to teamsters. Jones also operated the Blue Tent Tavern at a point on present Highway 120 about one and a quarter miles east of the present town. His food was well known and featured locally hunted antelope. Eventually he owned over 45,000 acres; upon this land were planted the first vineyard and fruit and nut orchards in the region. Much of this land was devoted to raising cattle in the 1850s, and in an effort to improve the breed, he traveled east in 1857, buying cattle and driving them overland.

Unlike most land developers of today, the Jones family sunk its roots deeply into the region. It was the role of the second generation to actually develop the town. The opportunity came in the spring of 1896 when the San Francisco-San Joaquin Valley Railroad was completed. It soon became part of the second transcontinental railroad to serve California, the Atkinson-Topeka and Santa Fe. The Santa Fe depot was one of the first buildings erected in the new town. Within a few years it became a shipping point for dairy products, fruit and alfalfa. The railroad also maintained a pumping plant here for filling the tenders of steam locomotives. By 1915 a second line connected Escalon with the surrounding communities, the Tidewater-Southern, which at one time had hourly trains between Stockton and Modesto. These developments in transportation eclipsed the role of nearby Farmington as the trading center for this portion of the county. This was a logical development, as the Big Oak Flat Road was to become State Highway 120 and grow in importance as a main entry to Yosemite National Park.

The first paved route to Stockton was the Mariposa Road, surfaced for twenty-one miles in 1910 and 1911. Just a short time later, the French Camp Road was also paved. In the early 1930s, passenger service of two railroads was augmented by Pacific Lines. These good transportation resources encouraged the region's growing importance in

OFFICIAL CITY SEAL OF ESCALON

In official use since 1974, the seal features the Stanislaus River flowing past orchards on its way from the snowy Sierra Nevada Mountains. Representing the name of the community are three "stepping stones" drawn symbolically in the river.

The year the seal was adopted, construction of the new City Hall commenced on donated land at Third and Coley streets. *(Courtesy City of Escalon)*

dairying and peach orchards, a combination that inspired local boosters to call Escalon "The Land of Peaches and Cream." It was also well known for vineyards, alfalfa and field crops, especially tomatoes. Alfalfa was particularly significant in the area during the 1930s.

The rapid growth of dairying was significantly influenced by Swedish immigrants. By 1914, 40 percent of the population of 650 was from Sweden. This was the result of efforts by the Swedish Colonization Society organized in 1907 with Charles M. Carson, president, and Otto Peterson, secretary.

The sons of John Wheeler Jones, especially James, who inherited 1,000 acres of what was to become the townsite of Escalon, were behind much of the activity in founding the community. James selected the name Escalon himself while reading *Overland Monthly* magazine at the Stockton Public Library. It means "stepping stone" in Spanish.

He built the first commercial structure, a large, temporary hotel to accommodate potential investors. Much of his work in promoting the new town was done in partnership with John A. Coley.

Coley invested the profits from extensive farming and grain buying activities in the construction of additional commercial property. He built one of the first stores, which was occupied not only by a grocery concern owned by Mrs. Charles Jordan, wife of the station agent, but eventually by the post office and telephone exchange. The telephone system, the first extensive one to be installed, was another Coley project. He also worked closely in bringing the Tidewater-Southern Railroad through the area and as vice-president personally assisted in the sale of stock. Near the depot Bert Lamasnay opened the first merchandise store in Escalon; he was also the first postmaster. The post office was located in the hotel at Second and Jackson streets. In 1898 there was daily mail service at the post office. Before long, the office was the base for a twenty-one mile rural route. By the 1980s, this had expanded to 188 miles.

A great boost to the commercial district came in 1912, when the Escalon State Bank was established in the front portion of the Escalon Hotel, its temporary quarters during construction of its own building. By 1914 the town had a business district composed of the bank, three hotels, three general

GATHERING AT JACKSON'S SALOON, MAIN STREET, 1897
Proprietor J. H. Jackson is comfortably seated with a pair of greyhounds nearby. Standing next to the door is a local laborer, Charlie Lancaster. In the distance is the first hotel in Escalon built for the convenience of potential investors in the new community. *(Collection of Angelo Dugo)*

SANTA FE DEPOT, c. 1910
Just opposite the business center, this facility was a familiar sight from the early twentieth century until it was demolished about 1970. There were some remodeling and additions over the years, but it was, basically, the original depot until the end. *(Collection of Angelo Dugo)*

MAIN STREET LOOKING TOWARD SECOND STREET OPPOSITE THE DEPOT, 1911

The two-story masonry building at right not only served as the telephone exchange but also as St. John and Thornton's real estate office and the public library. Dr. Avery's office was one flight up. Between this building and the McPherson General Merchandise, a lad is playing amongst the empty boxes and barrels.

H. Lester McPherson operated an exceptionally well known business in the center-most building, completed in 1909. Credit at McPherson's store kept farms and businesses going until bills could be paid after the crops were sold. For the convenience of customers, the post office was located in the same building. When this photo was taken, there were ten clerks. Mr. McPherson was very civic minded, raising funds for celebrations, donating the first hose cart to the fire department and financing development of a park next to the depot.

The two-story false front wooden building on the next corner was the Escalon Hotel. The gable roofed building down the street from it was J. N. Leighton's general merchandise store, with a dance hall on the second floor. *(Collection of Angelo Dugo)*

"THE BRICK MANSION OF THE PLAINS,"
PARK AND PIONEER STREETS

Left, the home as it appeared about 1915. By this time, a cupola had been removed from the center of the roof and the veranda shortened at both ends. *(Courtesy Mr. and Mrs. Stan Holtz)*

The bottom photo shows the original staircase between the second and third floors as it appears today.

Of all the older structures in Escalon, none is more deeply instilled with the history of the community than this one. Not only did this mansion serve the family and weary travelers, but it also was used as a school. For a time, the pioneer school was held in a room above the kitchen. However, the scuffling feet of restless children were too much for the householders and inspired construction of a school building in 1878.

John Wheeler Jones hired the teacher, who not only instructed his children but other children in the area, who were invited to attend provided they help pay the teacher's salary. In these very early days, there was only one other non-residential building in the vicinity, the Lone Tree Methodist Church at the northeast corner of Lone Tree and Escalon-Bellota roads. This church was constructed in 1893; a circuit preacher held services there and also at Farmington, Atlanta, Riverbank and Oakdale.

The Jones house was again a school from 1919 to 1922 when it was headquarters for the newly formed high school district. In 1944, after use by the Escalon Women's Club, the property was given by Alice Deliah Jones, daughter of J. W. Jones, to Dr. Phillip von Hunger for a hospital. Known as the Pioneer Hospital, the old home served into the 1960s and became the hospital offices after construction of a twenty bed facility on adjacent land in 1959. It has since been extensively restored and is the residence of Mr. and Mrs. Stan Holtz. Stan, an expert potter, maintains a shop and kiln on the grounds.

POSSIBLY THE EARLIEST PANORAMA OF ESCALON, c. 1908
Shown at the extreme right are the freight sheds that were important facilities in making the town a railroad shipping point. The Santa Fe depot is the isolated structure to the right of the tracks. Beyond this are the wood frame buildings of the business district. The photographer was perched atop the town water tower. *(Collection of Josephine Hall)*

stores, a drug store, two hardware firms, two lumber yards, two plumbing shops, three restaurants, a clothing store and two blacksmiths. There were also four churches.

A year later, the town was to have its first newspaper, the *Escalon Tribune*. At first a financially faltering enterprise centering around an army surplus press, the newspaper became much better established by 1913 under the ownership of Frank S. Thornton. By 1925 the *Tribune* had been sold and moved to Modesto to become the *Modesto Tribune*. The *Escalon Times*, which is still published today, has been operated by the Stickles family since 1927 and was started with equipment from a defunct operation in Newman, California.

With irrigation and the resulting smaller farms, there was a great increase in population over a very short time. Many of the newcomers settled in and around Escalon, and there was increased concern for fire protection. A series of hydrants with a water pressure of sixty-five pounds were placed in operation. The volunteer fire department, organized in 1912, was further equipped with a hose cart and a steel triangle that was hung on Second Street to serve as the alarm. The first motorized apparatus was purchased eight years later with the formation of the Escalon Fire District, encompassing a square mile including the town. The apparatus was an American LaFrance pumper and chemical unit. With the establishment of a rural fire district in 1939, a new apparatus, a Van Pelt built in nearby Oakdale, was financed through funds raised from the citizens.

In the 1920s a hose company and a chemical company were formed by a rather disorganized group of volunteers, probably inspired by the fire of 1920, which burned the heart of the commercial district. Total losses in this fire were the newly refurnished hotel, post office, restaurant, pool hall, drug store, Bender's Bakery with a great deal of modern equipment, and other businesses. Low water pressure and inadequate equipment were blamed as contributing to the great loss. Apparatus responding from Oakdale, Riverbank and Modesto were of little help in the fire that quickly spread over a large area by means of burning shingles and embers.

Another great fire was in 1962 when four warehouse buildings along the tracks were burned in a spectacular blaze punctuated with explosions. Since this time there have been no major fires, and to this day the fire department is still manned by thirty volunteers on a twenty-four hour dispatch system. In 1982 the rural district and Escalon's were consolidated into one organization.

Until about 1906 improvements to the town were at a very rudimentary stage. Mules running loose on the streets were a common sight. Between the plowing and harvesting season, they were allowed to forage for themselves. This custom ceased with the increased number of fences that resulted from the subdivision of the once great expanse of surrounding grain fields.

The Board of Trade, established in 1911, was behind numerous city projects including the irrigation district, street lighting and paving, a Fourth of July celebration in 1913 and a community fair in 1917. This fair was so successful it inspired reactivation of the San Joaquin County Fair, which had not been held since a fire de-

WORLD WAR I SERVICE FLAG, MAIN STREET NEAR SECOND STREET, 1918
It was with great local pride that this huge red, white and blue banner was displayed over the street. Each of the seventy blue stars represented a local boy serving in the armed forces. *(Collection of Angelo Dugo)*

stroyed its spectacular wooden exhibition pavilion in Stockton during 1902.

The Escalon Commercial Club was an important supporter of the community fair as well as the raising of finances for street improvements which were accomplished in 1917. The Escalon Women's Club also worked toward civic progress including construction of the first fire house in 1914, road improvement and beautification projects. Well remembered is the park they developed and maintained for decades north of the depot in an area that had long been an eyesore. After Prohibition was enacted, the Women's Club was behind the removal of a series of large liquor signs that had been attached to several buildings for years. The Escalon Community Movies financed civic improvements by donating the profits from ticket sales for at least a decade, starting in 1920.

The first water system was a stockholders proposition, the Escalon Water Company. Only those buying stock at ten dollars a share could obtain a connection to the water main. This was reincor-

porated in 1912 as the Escalon Water and Light Company, which made many improvements including an electric pump, a 30,000-gallon steel tank tower and an expanded system of water mains and fire hydrants. This utility also brought the first electricty into town, obtained from the trunk line of the San Francisco Light and Power Company. The Escalon Water and Light Company served the town until purchase by the City. Telephones were in service by 1908, but as there were as many as fifteen parties on one line, they were not convenient to use. Each subscriber purchased his own telephone and was responsible for installing his own wire to the contact line; the usual route selected was along a series of fence posts. In 1927 the original, very imperfect system was rebuilt and there were no more than eight to a party line. This took place shortly after Pacific Telephone acquired the company. In 1955 a dial system was installed, replacing the switchboard.

The beginnings of the Escalon Police Department can be traced to shortly after World War I when local merchants collectively financed the services of a night watchman who continued his rounds until the late 1940s, when a police district was established by popular vote. At first there were two men on the force, and one patrol car. In 1985 the force consisted of six sworn and fourteen reserve officers.

Escalon is the youngest of the incorporated cities in San Joaquin County. With incorporation and the initial organization of city government in 1957, there was no longer an elected board of trustees to oversee the street, light and police district. The sanitary sewer district was also soon incorporated into the duties of city officials. The first mayor was Francis E. Blixt, one of five elected city councilmen who in turn hire a city administrator and other officials.

There has been a public library in town since 1910. The first librarian, Albert St. John, offered space in the telephone exchange he owned. Later local druggist E. W. Bidwell assumed the duties and gave the collection space in his store. Escalon now has a building expressly for a library.

At about the same time the library was first established, irrigation water first became available. Large grain farms were divided into smaller tracts for dairy farms, orchards and vineyards.

Local industry responded to the new crops and wineries—dehydrators for alfalfa, fruit drying yards and a large cannery were established. A local vineyard and small winery had a major role in the very beginnings of the huge Petri Wine Company, now of world wide proportions. Rafaele Petri and his partner, Dante Foresti, were operating the Cosmopolitan Hotel in San Francisco. Foresti visited Escalon and purchased a vineyard and winery on Sexton Road about 1914. A 4,000-gallon capacity winery was operated on the property, and much of the product was sent East. Their success was quickly ended by Prohibition, but after its repeal, the partnership was re-established as the Petri Wine Company, which continued later as Allied Grape Growers. This organization, the largest wine producers' cooperative in the world, maintained a bottling plant in Escalon which has since been moved to Asti, California.

ESCALON ELEMENTARY SCHOOL, FIRST STREET AND PRESENT HIGHWAY 120, c. 1904
Containing two classrooms, this building served for a decade after completion in 1904. Later the school and yard were sold to the Presbyterian Church for their sanctuary. It served for many years, with the second floor rented to the Masonic Lodge. After completion of the present Escalon Presbyterian Church, over twenty-five years ago, the old building was demolished.

MAIN AND FIRST STREETS, c. 1920 and 1982
About sixty years separate these two photographs, and little has changed aside from awnings and signs. the sturdy building on the corner was built in 1912 for the Escalon State Bank. By 1943 it had become the Central Valley National Bank, one of twenty-six branches of this Richmond, California, based institution. Today it is the Central Bank. It remained the only bank in town until 1967, when Center State Bank located in Escalon. *(Collection of Angelo Dugo)*

Another very important agriculturally oriented industry is Escalon Packers Incorporated. During 1944, it started its operations with the canning of cherries, apricots, peaches, artichokes, chick peas, and a full line of tomato products. Since the late 1960s, the firm has been specializing exclusively in tomatoes and tomato products which are well established and well known throughout the United States. These products include 6 in 1 tomatoes, Bonta Pizza Sauce, Emma Bella Marinara Sauce and Christina Pizza Sauce. The efforts of the company are directed toward large size cans and the institutional trade.

The plant encompasses fifteen acres of buildings and equipment and employs about 300 at peak season. The management is proud to have had financial backing from the Bank of America since its inception. The corporation is owned by Christopher and Emma Colombo, husband and wife.

Local cattle and poultry operations have gained international significance. Outstanding Berkshire hogs and Guernsey cows bred by Anthony Bird Humphrey won major prizes at the Panama-Pacific Exposition held in San Francisco during 1915. In ensuing years, many breeding Berkshires and Guernseys were sent all over the eastern United States as well as to China, the Philippines and Hawaii. Humphrey was also noted for planting the first Lady Finger grapes in this part of California.

The poultry operations established by a naturalized citizen from Iran have been the pride of Escalon. Operating in the early 1960s with 100,000 birds, Hashem Naraghi developed innovative techniques including four-deck cages. These, along with other equipment, have been patented in Western Europe as well as in this country.

In the early 1960s Frank S. Thornton wrote in his *History of the Escalon Community* that local growth was never affected by a building boom; growth had always been very steady. However, at the time Escalon was on the verge of its first boom. By 1970 the population reached 2,400, an increase of 800 over a decade; there were 3,200 residents by the mid-1980s. While the residential districts have expanded, the commercial/industrial center has not experienced significant growth. A considerable number of local wage earners commute to jobs in outlying areas. As in many communities, new or expanded industry will contribute greatly to the course of its future growth.

THE UNION HIGH SCHOOL
ON YOSEMITE AVENUE

Particularly important to Escalon's social and educational advancement was the formation of the Escalon Union High School District, which was made possible in 1919 through the combined efforts of six elementary school districts. The first classes were held in the old John Wheeler Jones house, but attendance rapidly grew from thirty-five to seventy-nine, and the need for a school building was evident.

An eight and a half acre campus site was purchased, and construction of the initial buildings was completed in 1922. Most of the furniture, including the tablet arm chairs, was a product of the state prison at San Quentin. The principal speaker at the opening exercises was Dr. Tully Knoles, president of the College of the Pacific, which was then making plans to relocate from San Jose, California, to Stockton.

Students were brought to school at first by jitney service. Then, in 1923, a new thirty passenger Reo bus and two smaller Stockton-built Graham Brothers buses were on routes to neighboring elementary school districts. Most of the early additions to the original building were sports orientated facilities, including a 57 by 100 foot swimming pool which was to be enjoyed not only by students but local residents as well. Between 1949 and 1955, twenty-six new classrooms were added to the campus, which expanded to nearly thirty-nine acres. With the completion of the new facilities, the original school was torn down.

RUNSTEN'S SHOE AND HARNESS REPAIR SHOP, FIRST STREET BETWEEN MAIN AND COLEY, 1921
    At left, A. E. Runsten has paused in his work on a shoe as his son, Eric, looks on. Originally a harness maker by trade, Mr. Runsten had to make the transition dictated by the automobile age and devote the greater part of his business to boot and shoe repair. If one looks closely, there is some harness hanging in back of the shop. Harness makers across the United States were making this gradual shift in their trade between about 1910 and the 1920s. *(Collection of Ruth Runsten)*

ESCALON HOME BAKERY, FIRST AND MAIN STREETS, 1948
    Arno Bender, behind counter, was widely known for service and a friendly manner. His German apprenticeship as a baker lent a special style which was appreciated by local residents for forty years, starting in 1919. During his first year, four bread routes were started over an extensive territory. Operations were moved to First and Main in 1931 with completion of a new building. The next year a fountain was added, and, during 1941, a restaurant. Bender's successors continue to operate the bakery. *(Collection of Angelo Dugo)*

THE LAST OF THE PONY EXPRESS RIDERS, WILLIAM CAMPBELL, 1841-1934

An occupation that lasted less than a year was to give William Campbell the experience of a lifetime. Born to Scotch parents in Ireland, he immigrated to the United States at age nineteen. Shortly after his arrival, he carried mail over about one hundred miles of the Pony Express route along the Platte River in Nebraska. This was part of the 1,980 mile route between Saint Joseph, Missouri, and Sacramento, California. Campbell and about eighty other riders lost their jobs in 1861, when the transcontinental telegraph was completed.

Campbell settled in Escalon during 1893 on what had been part of John Wheeler Jones' old Blue Tent Ranch and lived there for several decades. *(Courtesy Mrs. C. G. Wakefield)*

AN EARLY BOTTLE FILLING MACHINE WAS DECOR AT "THE OLD WINERY" SHOPPING AND DINING COMPLEX, FIRST STREET AND McHENRY BOULEVARD

In 1977 Escalon gained a distinctive attraction with the opening of the first of three phases of development centering upon a long abandoned winery. Three years later, the third phase reached completion. There were twenty-eight shops, including a restaurant and bar as well as several antique and boutique shops. Progress came to a halt, and all businesses except the bar closed. In the summer of 1985 the City of Escalon became involved in two lawsuits filed by the owner of the complex, Robert Wilford, and the former operator of the restaurant. Their suits, totalling $4 million, claimed the city forced them out of business. City Hall representatives claimed earthquake safety and other engineering reports were not properly filed and the building was operated with threatening situations to public safety. A lengthy litigation was predicted.

SLIP FORM PIPE MACHINE BUILT BY HOGAN MANUFACTURING, INC. FOR THE MX TEST MISSILE PROGRAM AT YUMA, ARIZONA, 1979

Hogan Manufacturing, Inc., formerly known as California Blowpipe and Steel Company, Inc., has its headquarters at First and Coley streets. This facility, with extensive modern equipment for cutting, bending and welding heavy steel, was established in 1944 by Walter F. Hogan.

Over the years, it has assisted in the construction of oil refineries, copper smelters, glass plants, canneries, etc. Conveying equipment, air pollution control units and office and mill buildings are among its products. It is said there is not a place in California where you can drive a hundred miles without passing something that Hogan Manufacturing has constructed. While the majority of their work is in California, products are shipped to the seven Western states and overseas to Chile, Saudi Arabia, the Philippines, Africa, India and Iran.

The company is still managed by the Hogan family, and the third generation is now looking after the day to day operations. *(Courtesy Hogan Manufacturing, Inc.)*

COMMUNITY SERVICE CENTER, ESCALON-BELLOTA ROAD AT ARTHUR ROAD

Through a federally supported JOBS program, the community was fortunate to obtain this facility in 1976. The $200,000 construction project reached completion with only $50,000 of the cost derived from local sources. The center, which contains three meeting rooms, was the first constructed in the county through the Economic Development Act. *(Photograph by Angelo Dugo)*

PART II
THE UNINCORPORATED TOWNS

ACAMPO
BANTA
CLEMENTS
FARMINGTON
FRENCH CAMP
LATHROP
LINDEN
LOCKEFORD
SAN JOAQUIN CITY
SAN JOAQUIN RIVER CLUB
THORNTON
VERNALIS
VICTOR
WOODBRIDGE

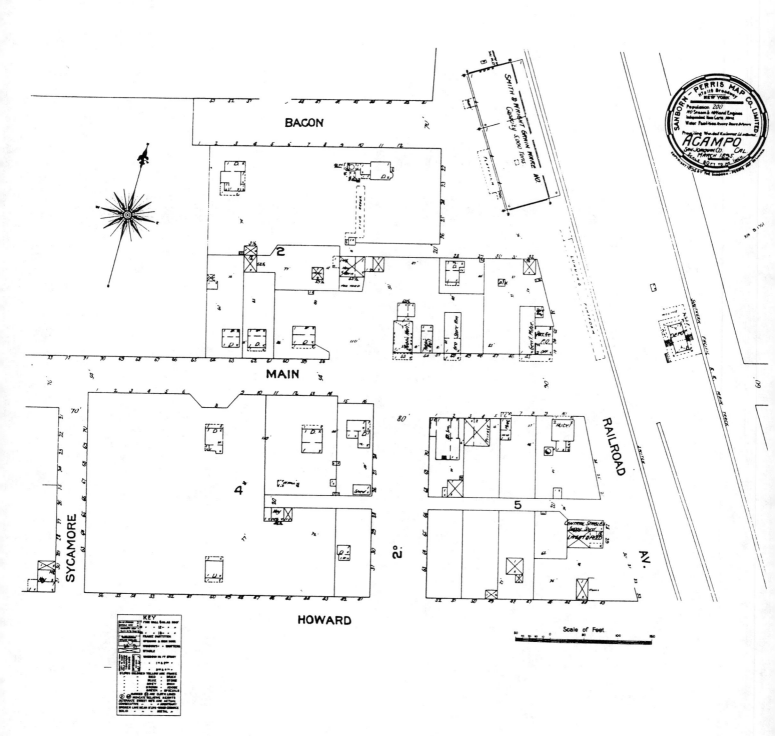

CENTER OF ACAMPO, MARCH 1895

This detailed record of the nature and extent of the business district was recorded by the Sanborn-Perris Map Company. Such maps were prepared to assist in the determination of insurance premiums.

At the upper right is the largest building in town, now the Barengo Winery. On the north side of Main Street starting at the corner opposite the Southern Pacific depot are a general store and post office, grocery and two public halls side by side. The south side frontage is composed of a hotel, meat market, private residence and blacksmith shop. *(Collection of California State University, Northridge, Geography Map Library)*

ACAMPO
GRAIN FIELDS, WATERMELON PATCHES, ORCHARDS AND VINEYARDS

Settlement of the Acampo area traces its beginnings to a town about one and a half miles to the north. This was Liberty, which existed from 1852 to 1870. With completion of the Central Pacific Railroad in 1869, Galt in nearby Sacramento County was favored over Liberty as a railroad stop. A year earlier, part of Liberty was relocated to the right of way to make a bid for a depot. This point, named New Liberty, became known in 1872 as Acampo, which means grazing land in Spanish.

John N. Woods, a teamster and a relative to the founder of Woodbridge, laid out the first town lots, which were on his 320 acre ranch. Moving the town did not bring the hoped for results. It was never an important stop, the honor going to Galt. In 1876, however, a substantial freight and passenger depot was constructed that would be an asset to a larger community. It was operated by Garvin Kirkland, who had been running the general store and post office for years. About this time, there were ten buildings in the town and there were four blacksmiths (one a hardware dealer) plus a saloon and the Houston District School.

Benjamin F. Langford, pioneer orchardist in this region and later state senator, used his influence to establish and maintain Acampo as a railroad stop and shipping point for produce.

In the late 1880s, the town consisted of a hotel, large general store/post office, saloon, grain warehouse, brick yard, feed stable, two blacksmiths, two harness makers, a large wagon shop and Isaac Hill's barley and corn mill. The Houston District School was attended by all forty-eight children in the area. The population was fast approaching 100. By 1915, the business section consisted of only a general store, small hotel, blacksmith, stable and a fruit packing shed. Before long, the stable and hotel would close. The post office rural route was particularly extensive.

During the 1880s, watermelons were an important crop, but these were replaced by apricot, almond and prune orchards. Vineyards were also being planted along with the orchards, and some of the earliest Japanese residents of this part of California worked at the Langford Ranch, planting vines at the north end of present Orchard Road. Some of these Japanese farmers were to purchase land and make a significant contribution to agriculture around Acampo.

The most prominent winery in the town was started in 1934 as Acampo Winery & Distillers, Inc., with Frank L. Murphy as president. The operation prospered so that, by 1940, the cooperage capacity was over two million gallons—brandy, table wine and sweet wine were produced. Dino Barengo purchased the property in 1944 and about twenty years later renamed the operation Barengo Vineyards. The operation, now Lost Hills/Barengo Winery, is now owned by Herb Benham. Considerable modernization has been undertaken and grapes are processed from their vineyards here. Cooperage capacity includes 265,000 gallons in stainless steel.

Over the decades, many progressive families have resided in Acampo. Particularly distinguished are Senator Benjamin F. Langford, who is identified prominently with formulating agricultural policies for the State of California, and Mr. and Mrs. John N. Ballantyne, owners of vineyards and orchards, who contributed substantially in 1964 to the University of the Pacific cluster college, Covell College. One of the dormitories, Ballantyne Hall, is named in their honor.

While vineyards are an important part of Acampo economy, orchards and dairies as well as horse breeding and training ranches are very much a part of today's activities in this region.

EAST OF ACAMPO, 1983

Travelers approaching this community from Highway 99 are treated to the grandeur of an avenue of California fan palms extending more than a mile between the highway and the Southern Pacific tracks on the edge of town. These palms, native to Southern California deserts, were planted in 1887 by nurseryman Morris Van Gelder, who moved here from Sacramento. Many local orchardists became established through his nursery stock. the Capital Nursery, owned by W. R. Strong, was also prominent at about this time. A nursery is still active in Acampo. *(Photograph by Raymond W. Hillman)*

ENTRANCE TO THE BARENGO WINERY TASTING ROOM, 1983

This large winery has incorporated into its facility what may well be the oldest building in Acampo. Originally built in 1868 as D. M. Denahay's grain warehouse, it became the Acampo Fruit Growers facility in 1911 and now houses an attractive tasting room. *(Photograph by Raymond W. Hillman)*

DISPLAY ADVERTISEMENT FROM AN 1883 COUNTY DIRECTORY

This is the earliest illustration relating to Acampo that could be found. It was published in the J. W. Smith & Company *City and County Directory of Stockton City and San Joaquin County, 1883–1884. (Courtesy Stockton Public Library)*

110

BANTA
WEST SIDE SUPPLY CENTER AND STAGE STOP

Originally the location of a gold rush stage stop known as the Elk Horn Inn, the future site of Banta was familiar to travelers as the last sign of civilization before crossing the sand plains on the Stockton-San Jose stage road. This roadhouse saw the beginnings of the present community and was located at the starting point of the West Side-River Road extending through Los Banos to the present site of Tranquillity. The inn gained importance, and in 1853 Ransom Chamberlain bought the facility and built a pretentious two-story hotel, restaurant and saloon that became known as the White House. It was a station for stage lines, including the McCloud Stage Company, providing the San Jose service.

The man for whom the community was named, Henry C. Banta, purchased Chamberlain's White House in 1863. Banta had a pioneer spirit about him. He was born in a covered wagon in 1835 while his parents were traveling into the Missouri frontier from Kentucky. Nineteen years later, he was on a similar journey across the plains to California. He finally settled at this point seventeen miles southwest of Stockton, where the locale seemed to hold promise. The transcontinental railroad main line was to cross a portion of the property, and it was anticipated that this would be a major shipping point for the West Side of the San Joaquin Valley.

Several buildings and corrals were constructed a half mile south of the old roadhouse. Teamsters soon looked at "San Joaquin Valley," as the settlement was known in the 1860s, as a terminal for shipping cattle and sheep by rail. Hay and grain were also loaded on freight trains here. The West Side-River Road was also heavily used by freight wagons carrying grain bound for Mohr's Landing on Old River, and Banta's property was a halfway point in these travels.

In 1867 and 1868, after the White House burned, Banta tried to focus the attention of railroad officials upon this point on their line. He gave one-half of the townsite to the Central Pacific with the understanding that the Antioch Branch, or the low level route, would be built through this point. This would place Banta, as it became known in 1870, at a major railroad junction. Anticipating this development, Banta borrowed all the capital he could and built a twelve room, $6,000 hotel, a $3,000 livery stable and a $2,000 store, plus a few houses. The tragic result was that the railroad decided not to run the line through this portion of the county, ruining Banta's town. Banta sold out for what he could get and became a sheep raiser. Unfortunately, these efforts, too, were plagued by hard luck.

At the height of development in the 1870s, before the establishment of Tracy, Banta had, aside from the hotel, four general stores, two blacksmiths, a livery stable, five saloons, a harness and saddle maker, the Banta and Hill's Ferry stage line, a Wells-Fargo agency, a jeweler and a hair dresser.

At this time, Banta was the chief town of the West Side, but with the establishment of Tracy in 1878, surrounding towns were to fade in importance. With their roles ended as railroad or river transportation points, San Joaquin City, Ellis and Wickland dwindled to obscurity. However, in spite of losing considerable importance and losing its big hotel to fire in 1882, Banta was to survive as a small shipping and supply center. The best known businessmen of the nineteenth and early twentieth centuries were G. Brichetto and Nicolas Canale, who opened a grocery store in 1886 that was to be patronized for decades by customers from over a wide area, including sheepherders from the far off foothills of the West Side.

Staple goods were the stock in trade: sides of bacon, sacks of beans and potatoes, cases of tomatoes, prunes, etc. It was understood that the grocery bills of most customers were paid only once a year, at harvest time—if there was a harvest.

The operation changed in the early twentieth century; the two partners established separate businesses. Brichetto built a large brick store, and Canale constructed a wooden building close by, in partnership with August Steinmetz. The business remained in the Canale family and was operated by his daughter, Irene Bittner, until 1978. The store is now the only grocery in town, but is no longer a Canale family business. It is little changed and much of the old shelving and old showcases are still in use.

As early as 1880, irrigation was recognized as a requirement for fully developing the agricultural potential of the area. Such development was not to take place until the early 1920s. California Irrigated Farms subdivided about 13,000 acres owned by A. O. Stewart into 40 to 100 acre parcels, greatly assisting the population growth. They would sell the parcels, often complete with house and barn, to Americans as well as immigrants from Germany, Switzerland, Italy and Portugal. Many established dairy farms; others became fruit growers, truck gardeners and vineyardists. Much of the produce found a ready market.

The Banta-Carbona Irrigation District was organized in 1922 and, with water from the San Joaquin River, established a system to serve the region, extending to a point south of Tracy. By 1985, Delta Mendota Canal water was being purchased due to the lack of water from the San Joaquin and its poor quality. Also important was the Pescadero Reclamation District, bringing water from Tom Paine Slough.

In recent years, the population reached 150, about one-third more than the town had in the mid 1880s. It is no longer an important rail point; it has even lost its position on Highway 50 as a result of re-routing.

There are still many dairies, and the local producers sell to Foremost or another major marketer or contract with the cooperative which operates the Laprina Cheese Company in Tracy. A well-known Banta firm is Haley's Flying Service, with five pilots and six planes spraying fertilizer and pesticides on crops in four counties.

As much of the growth of this region is around Tracy, little expansion is expected for Banta. Two or three homes are being constructed each year. Efforts by county officials to generate local interest in a community water system and sewage plant have been unsuccessful. One local resident summed up the feelings of many: "The place doesn't change much and I'd like to keep it that way."

BILLHEAD FOR AN EARLY BANTA INDUSTRY, 1881
When this apparently short-lived brick works was established, the community was tiny and struggling. Such works were in various parts of the county where rivers had deposited commercial quality clay. (Collection of the Haggin Museum, Stockton)

BUSINESS CENTER OF BANTA, c. 1915

The large building in the center was built by John N. Brichetto in 1911 as a general merchandise store which also housed the post office and library. A few years later, it became Raspo's Store, operated until 1968 by Brichetto's son-in-law and unofficial "Mayor of Banta," Joe Sanguinetti. The structure is still in good condition and is an electrical supply shop.

The little shed in front of Louis Steinmetz's billiard hall and soft drink counter housed a gasoline pump.

At the far right stands a bar, hotel and restaurant known for years as the Cool Corner. At the time this picture was taken, it was the property of Frank Gallego, who bought it in 1899. It was condemned and replaced by the present Banta Inn in 1937. Gallego's daughter, Jenny, was still operating the bar with her daughter, "Sis," at age eighty-seven in 1978. *(Collection of Mrs. L. Waller)*

THE WEST SIDE HOTEL AND SALOON ON THE EAST SIDE OF THE SOUTHERN PACIFIC TRACKS, c. 1907
    Barkeep Charlie Dreyer was a photographer and recorded this interior himself while standing behind the bar, with a cable release. He moved the saloon about 1888 from San Joaquin City, which was rapidly becoming a ghost town. Note the landscapes hand painted by Dreyer onto panels of the bar.
    The placard, upper right, "honoring" Prohibitionist Carrie Nation is a document of the times and is another example of his handiwork. It bears the wording, "We Welcome All Nations, Carrie." Another, just below it, gracefully declines credit:

> "To trust you to Whiskey
> Oh no, it's too riskey
> So pay, for your Booze
> Then I can't refuse"

(Collection of Waldo Stevens)

THE WEST SIDE HOTEL ON THE EAST SIDE OF THE SOUTHERN PACIFIC TRACKS, c. 1900
Once the principal hotel, restaurant and livery stable in town, this business was operated for many years by Benjamin F. Prather. "Valley Brew," made in Stockton, was obviously a featured beverage served in Charlie Dreyer's West Side Saloon. (See saloon interior, facing page.) *(Collection of Minnie Brichetto)*

A PORTION OF THE BANTA BUSINESS DISTRICT ON THE EAST SIDE OF THE TRACKS, c. 1905
The two buildings in the center are the Commercial Restaurant, R. C. Banta, proprietor, and the Exchange Saloon. The restaurant staff, including a waitress, is seen prominently in white. The tank tower at the far right is unusual, for it has apparently been expanded with the second exposed tank to supplement the tank already enclosed in the tank house. Water use in the immediate vicinity must have been high. *(Collection of Mrs. Raymond F. Bailey)*

BANTA ELEMENTARY SCHOOLS

Even after years of disuse, this fine building (above) is still an asset to the community. It was replaced by the new school, in the distance, in 1970. The future of the old building, which is under private ownership, is uncertain.

The old school received a flurry of attention in 1982, when a grand reunion was held at both the new and old Banta elementary schools for fifty years of classes between 1926 and 1976. The school was built in 1925–26 and donated to the community by California Irrigated Farms. In the first year, 108 children were in attendance. Just five years earlier, there were only five students attending the old Valley School (left), a 1901 structure that still stands on 7th Street near F, 200 feet south of its original location. It is now the clubhouse of the Western Horse and Trailer Club. The first Valley School was erected in 1878 and it may have been the earliest in the area, but there is evidence of an effort to finance a schoolhouse for Banta as early as 1869. *(Photograph c. 1916, Collection of Minnie Brichetto)*

CLEMENTS
FREIGHT LINES, STAGE LINES, RAILROAD LINES

A controversial political figure, a flour mill and a stampede have each had a part in providing a bit of distinction to this tiny community at the base of the oak studded foothills of the Sierra Nevada.

One of the earliest residents, David S. Terry, hot tempered Stockton attorney and state supreme court justice, was a prisoner of the San Francisco Vigilantes, dueled with Senator David Broderick near San Francisco, fatally shooting him, and was a Confederate colonel during the Civil War. While Terry's residence for his family was at Center and Fremont streets in Stockton, his 1,400 acres along the south bank of the Mokelumne River seemed to be a retreat. Here pro-slavery sympathizers congregated from time to time, and Terry, who was usually well armed, practiced pistol shooting at this property.

A particularly well-known enterprise here was the Lone Star Mill, established in 1854 and rebuilt after a fire two years later by Terry and Hodge. This was the only flour mill operating over a wide area and was an important facility.

The town of Clements was yet to be established, and the only settlement was Poland, a road house a quarter mile east of present Clements on Highway 88 that served teamsters and travelers. The beginnings of Clements can be traced to 1871, when Thomas Clements, a native of Northern Ireland, purchased all of Terry's interests in the river bottom lands as well as the present town site. Clements was eventually to become owner of extensive agricultural land totaling nearly 10,000 acres, about three-quarters of which was in Tulare County. On his land in San Joaquin County, he dry farmed grain, raised stock and later planted vineyards and orchards.

The opportunity to establish a town was presented when the San Joaquin-Sierra Nevada Railroad reached this point in 1882 from the Lodi area.

Clements had already constructed substantial buildings here. One of the first businesses was Bruml & Bamert, general merchandise. The partners came from Lockeford, and Bamert became the first postmaster in 1881. It is interesting to note that the town's third postal official was Miss Cecilia Gillies, who served from 1893 to 1933. She also had an insurance business. The post office department authorized a new post office building for the town in 1984.

The town site was laid out in 1882 on land owned by Clements and Magee. It was in this year that Clements completed the third two-story brick commercial building in the center of town. Also adding stature to the community center were four blacksmith shops, the first of which was Lukin's.

The railroad did much to foster regional agriculture. The two large brick warehouses that still stand alongside the tracks were originally built by the Farmers Mutual Warehouse Company in 1883. S. L. Magee was the principal figure behind their construction, and the financiers were from Clements, Lockeford and Elliott. Grain was stored here by local farmers and grain buyers until the market price was right. The salmon red bricks in these sturdy warehouses were made by Chinese who lived in a group of shacks on a nearby hillside. Others were launderers and farm laborers, and a few also mined for gold a few miles to the east. For decades, well into the twentieth century, there were large corrals where the Feed Lot Restaurant now stands, next to the right of way, on the eastern edge of town. Local cattlemen and sheepmen drove their animals to these corrals and shipped them to market by rail. It was not unusual to see thirty cars of sheep and cattle leaving town. A feed mill also operated in this location, starting in about 1907 under the ownership of Chrisman and Clements. The building burned in recent years.

By 1915, the narrow gauge railroad had long

LONE STAR FLOUR MILL, ONE MILE NORTH OF TOWN ON THE OLD CLEMENTS-IONE ROAD

The stone building shown here was erected in 1856 on the site of the original mill that burned a year earlier. Initially owned by political figure David S. Terry, it was sold to S. L. Magee when Terry left California to fight for the Confederacy. During the Civil War and later, a million pounds of wheat and 900,000 pounds of barley were processed annually. Magee's operation continued to serve a large area until the railroad reached Clements. Starting in the early 1880s, the new line provided access to more modern and efficient mills in Stockton, and the Lone Star became silent.

The mill is shown here about 1910 when it was serving as a warehouse. It was one of the first early structures in the county to become a California State Historical Landmark. It eventually fell into ruinous condition and the walls were taken down in 1950. The Stillman L. Magee County Park occupies the site today.

The main road to the Mother Lode once ran directly in front of the mill and crossed the Mokelumne River a short distance north. Several bridges have occupied the site, dating back to a covered bridge built in 1850. The present span was dedicated in 1977 and replaced the antique iron truss Mackville bridge of 1906. (Collection of the Haggin Museum, Stockton)

since been acquired by Southern Pacific and converted to standard gauge as the Valley Springs line. At this time, two passenger trains arrived daily; passenger service continued for another nine years. The depot and freight office closed in 1938.

Aside from the railroad, the town had other forms of communication. The first newspaper, the *Weekly Tidings*, was published in 1893; the *Lockeford-Clements News*, published since 1961, continues to this day. Telephone service from the Farmers Telephone Line started in 1906; "central" was in the Clements Hotel. The service was acquired by the Clements Mutual Telephone Association during 1944. A dial system was introduced in 1955. Clements and Linden are now served by the Continental Telephone Company. Just six years after the telephone arrived, electric power was supplied by the Western States Electric Company, a firm absorbed by Pacific Gas and Electric in 1915.

While the fire district was established in 1931, and the railroad was still making stops for freight, the town was entering a period of decline. Many of the businesses gradually closed, and a particularly crushing blow was the construction of Camanche Dam and reservoir in the 1960s. Numerous old ranches, with vast pasture lands, were condemned for the project, and Clements was no longer to be a supply center for these sprawling operations. There is a small privately owned water system, no sewer treatment service, and, as a result of these factors, home construction is limited to parcels one and a quarter acres or larger.

As Clements is on Highway 88, one of the main routes to recreational areas in the Sierra, a tremendous number of travelers pass through the community. The opportunities for roadside business have long been recognized, especially in the establishment of the "88 Inn" in 1963.

Another very ambitious project has been undertaken in recent years with the complex of old buildings that were once part of a feed mill and grain warehouse. Presently, the Clements Corporation, composed of local residents, is operating the Feed Lot Restaurant and proposes to operate a shop complex in the 18,000 square foot, century old, brick warehouse, the largest building ever constructed in Clements.

For many years prior to 1905, Clements distinguished itself by a May Day picnic held at an idyllic setting in a grove by the river. Participants came by rail in large numbers; these trains often had ten cars. There was a baseball game, merry-go-round, racing and dancing in a covered pavilion. The evening dance was held in the big brick warehouse that still stands opposite the business center. Of course, there was plenty of food, including pies and cakes home baked in Clements the preceding day. The tradition is continued by the Snowflake Rebekah Lodge #276 of the I.O.O.F.

The settlement's greatest distinction in recent decades has been the Clements Stampede, known as the biggest one day rodeo in California. It is held in April of each year in special grounds near the eastern edge of town. Recently there were 300 entries for the saddle bronc, bareback Brahma bull riding, all girl goat tying, wild cow milking contest, jeep roping, stock horse competition and other events. The stampede is sponsored by the Clements Buckaroos.

A CLEMENTS FIRM OF 1884–1885
L. M. McKinney and Company published this page as part of their directory for San Joaquin County. *(Courtesy Stockton Central Library)*

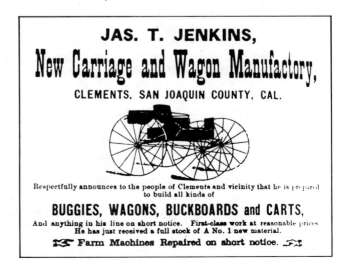

BEHIND THE ATHEARN SCHOOL, ABOUT A QUARTER MILE EAST OF TOWN, 1907
Students are identified, left to right, as follows: Sitting (front row), Leo Friedberger, Roy Russell, Beatrice Bryant, Stevens (first name unknown), unidentified. Second row, Pearl Anglum, Danny Anglum, Ella Smith, Doris Moran, Florence Miller, May Steely, Luella Linn, Athearn Stevens, Adelbert Anderson, Annie Sullivan, Rita Clasen, Sidney Moran, Lester Raines. Third row, Velma Raines, Della Smith, Bernice Weber, Malarky Smith, Clements Brown, Joe Christy, Roy Steely, Lawrence Putnam, Oscar Swett, Charles Lee Bryant, principal-teacher. Fourth row, unidentified, Mamie A. Taft, primary teacher, Harry Fenton, Helen Clasen, Smith (first name unknown), Mamie Weber, Alta Fenton, Elsie Westfal, Berenice Bryant, Reba Staples, Ruth Chrisman, William Clasen, Lawrence Schmitt, Clinton Miller. On roof of woodshed, Clarence Fenton, Marshall Atkins, Arthur Raines, George Fenton, Smith (first name unknown), Winford Linn, Bob White. *(Collection of San Joaquin County Historical Museum)*

IN THE ATHEARN SCHOOL, c. 1905
In the center photo on the facing page is the classroom on the lower floor of the two-story brick building constructed in 1877. The students here are from primary to fifth grade.
Students are identified as follows: desks on left, 1. Beatrice Bryant and Luella Linn; 2. Elmer Mahin; 3. Roy Steely; 4. Winford Linn; 5. unidentified. Desks on right, 1. George Fenton; 2. Jessie Blaine and Bernice Weber*; 3. Annie Sullivan; 4. Velma Raines; 5. Jimmy Anderson and Lester Raines. The teacher is Miss Taft; the time is 3:15. Grades six through nine were taught in the upstairs classroom. *(Collection of San Joaquin County Historical Museum)*
*Bernice Weber Clifford was eighty-eight years old in 1985. She was a Lockeford teacher for many years.

FRIEDBERGER'S GENERAL MERCHANDISE, c. 1905

In the true spirit of a general store, there is a tremendous variety of merchandise on display. The firm had a shoe department and this special interest is emphasized by the boots so prominently exhibited among the seed packets and Cleveland Baking Powder. Below these items on the left is a display of specimens of lacquer finished boards illustrating the qualities of Lacqueret products. To the right can be seen part of an ornate pattern lithographed on the sheet metal covering of a stove board used to insulate a wooden floor from the heat of a stove.

Shown in the store from left to right are: Cecilia Gillies, Leo Friedberger, Jr., Leo Friedberger, Sr. and Ed Whipple, helper. *(Collection of Leo Friedberger, Jr.)*

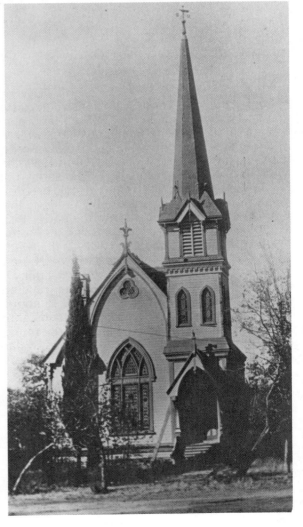

PRESBYTERIAN CHURCH, c. 1900

Right, the town gained a very cosmopolitan asset when this sanctuary was constructed about 1890. It was located on the north side of Highway 88 at the western edge of the community. The decline in population during the early twentieth century reduced the size of the congregation so that they could no longer maintain their own sanctuary. Rather than have the attractive structure deteriorate, it was torn down in 1919 and the property sold. Two houses now occupy the site. Lumber from the old structure was taken to Manteca to build a new church. *(Collection of the San Joaquin County Historical Museum)*

BUSINESS CENTER, CLEMENTS CAL.

TOWN CENTER ABOUT 1918

All of these buildings were constructed at various times between 1872 and 1882 by Thomas Clements. The brick was locally made by Chinese laborers using kilns to fire their product. The building with the bay windows housed the principal business, which was operated by George Chrisman and George Clements, son of Thomas, starting in 1907. Their stock of groceries, notions, hardware, dry goods, feed and grain was one of the largest outside of Stockton. Until 1929, the post office was located here, and the business was the only food market in town until 1947. The second floor was used as a lodge hall and also had two apartments.

Parked at left is what appears to be the grocery delivery truck, two tank wagons for delivery of oil products are in front of the store, and at the far right, the "Clements, Waterloo and Stockton Stage" is ready to start its run. Operations continued into the early 1920s, when the stage from Jackson started running to Stockton.

The second floor of the building in the center had a dance floor and was also used as a community hall. The lower floor was occupied early in the twentieth century by a candy and ice cream store, butcher shop and saloon. A saddle and harness shop was here at an earlier date.

The candy store front became the Lucky Thrifty Market in the 1950s and was also the locale of the post office and library. The library was later transferred to the Chrisman and Clements store, which became a Red and White store operating from 1941 to about 1970.

Time has not been kind to these substantial buildings. The Clements Hotel (far right behind trees), built by Young and Ringer in 1882 and still operating in the 1950s, burned during remodeling about 1959; the upper stories of the other buildings, weakened by earthquake damage and age, were removed by 1950. (Collection of the Haggin Museum, Stockton)

GOLD DREDGING ON THE MOKELUMNE RIVER NEAR CLEMENTS, 1949

The only gold mining area of San Joaquin County was on the Mokelumne River between Clements and the Amador County border at the western edge of the Camanche-Lancha Plana Mining District. Starting in the early twentieth century, dredges have been at work, principally those of the American Dredging Company and later the one shown above, operated by the Gold Hill Dredging Company. Several of the dredgermen made their home in Clements.

This bucket line dredge worked river gravels up to thirty feet below the surface at the Lawrence Putnam Ranch and finally, between 1949 and 1951, on the Featherstone Ranch. The huge dredge is shown here on its way between the two ranches in January 1949. It literally cut its way around the southern approach to the old Mackville Bridge. Traffic on Highway 88, which once used this bridge, was routed around the dredge via a "shoofly." The D7 Caterpillar is clearing away topsoil overburden. High operating costs and low gold prices forced the dredge to cease operations in 1951. Vandalism and thievery were so extensive that the remains were sold for scrap metal and there is not a trace of it left today.

The huge piles of gravel and rock left by this dredge were useful and led to the creation of the Claude C. Wood Company, a gravel plant, founded in 1941. This firm is the largest employer in the Clements area, providing two full time and up to thirteen hourly jobs. It was given a great impetus in 1944 when awarded the contract to supply aggregate to the navy annex being constructed on Rough and Ready Island on the San Joaquin River west of Stockton. One hundred twenty-five trucks, driven by 123 men and two women, were at work along with thirty to forty railroad cars hauling rock to the site where the largest concrete wharf in the world was being constructed. Over the years, the firm has been involved with a multitude of construction projects, providing gravel and aggregate for state and county highway projects, including Highway 99 from the Mokelumne River to Dry Creek, the Kettleman Lane underpass and six lane road west of it through Lodi, the Pacific Avenue widening project in Stockton from Alpine Avenue to March Lane, the Alameda Naval Station, and ready mix for all the structures on Interstate 5 between Highway 12 and Lambert Road.

These and numerous other projects have vastly expanded the Claude C. Wood operation so that it now has six quarries from Coalinga to Marysville. In 1981 the firm was sold to the Al Johnson Construction Company, a nationwide conglomerate with home offices in Minneapolis, Minnesota.

Teichert Construction also operated a gravel plant a short distance east of these operations in another section of old dredge tailings. *(Collection of Claude C. Wood Company)*

JEEP ROPING AT THE CLEMENTS STAMPEDE, c. 1981

Attendance of 12,000 is not unusual at this annual April event that is now known as the largest amateur rodeo in the world and the biggest one-day rodeo in California. There is considerable competition for entries in the various riding and roping events, one of which is the unique jeep roping, shown above.

A "bull session" in George Clements' General Store back in 1940 inspired this event that has brought considerable attention to this tiny community. The Clements Buckaroos was organized during a subsequent meeting at the schoolhouse. Art Berger was the first president.

The beginnings of the Stampede came in 1942 as a non-professional roundup event with a horse show plus riding and roping. Lee Black was the first general chairman and 300 horses and riders participated before an audience of 1,500. The Stockton Marine Corps League was the sponsor during World War II, and 20 percent of the gate fees were given to this organization. Patriotism ran high; during the 1943 event alone $190,000 for war bonds was raised through the auction of horses. Since 1944, the Buckaroos have been affiliated with the California State Horsemen's Association.

Over the years, the events have grown in number and variety and include not only saddle broncos and bareback riding but also Brahma bull riding, girls' goat tying, team roping, stock horse competition and a host of others. *(Courtesy Lodi News-Sentinel)*

TWO FAMILIAR LANDMARKS ON HIGHWAY 88, 1983

The bar at left, named "The Old Corner" since at least 1947, was originally constructed as a general store. Known as Schmitt's store, the proprietor had an interesting sideline, taxidermy. He kept his specimens in an upstairs room; particularly remembered by the children and other visitors was the wildcat that seemed ready to jump on you as you opened the door.

On the right is one of the old brick buildings in town, the Odd Fellows Hall. Under construction from March to September 1917, this structure was the first owned by IOOF Lodge No. 355, established in 1889. For many years it met above a blacksmith shop and later over the Chrisman and Clements store, where the Good Templars and Knights of Pythias also held meetings. The sturdy 1917 hall and the Athearn School, a short distance east, were badly damaged in the "small hurricane" of 1938. The hall lost its roof and the school had to be torn down.

The lodge has now given up its charter due to its small membership and has consolidated with Lockeford. The building is now owned by Snowflake Rebekah Lodge No. 276, IOOF; the Lone Star Encampment No. 133 and the Ladies Encampment Auxiliary 133 also hold meetings here.

FARMINGTON
TEAMSTERS' STOP ON THE SONORA ROAD

During the great California Gold Rush, the stage and freight wagon road between Stockton and Sonora was as busy as any thoroughfare one could find in the United States of the 1850s. Lodging houses and saloons were established along the road about a day's travel from each other to serve teamsters and travelers.

Perhaps the earliest of these roadside enterprises was the Oregon Tent. It was nothing more than a tule thatched hut when erected by George Thayer and David Wells in 1848. The place was named after Oregon, as Wells hailed from that territory before settling on the bank of Little John Creek and forming the beginnings of what is now Farmington. The partners also planted the first grain in Douglas Township, which extends to Linden.

Development of the town started when Nathaniel Harrold bought the 320 acres owned by the proprietors of Oregon Tent in 1852. Grain farming and cattle comprised the economy, and Harrold, who owned half the present townsite, decided to rename the place Farmington in 1858.

Another very important landowner was W. P. Stamper, who owned the other half of the present townsite. Harrold had the town surveyed into blocks, with individual lots priced at $150. This was a high figure for the time but was intended to discourage speculators and encourage those who purchased lots to develop them.

One of the first commercial buildings was a hotel constructed by Stamper along with a blacksmith shop and saloon he also financed. A second hotel in town, known as the Farmington Hotel, was operated by the John A. Campbell family. Originally a gold rush roadhouse, it was acquired by Charles M. Alders and was known for years as the Central Hotel. With ten rooms, parlor, dining room and saloon, it operated until 1918 as the last hotel in town.

In the early 1870s, the Stockton and Visalia Railroad was to spur development of the town by construction of a branch to Oakdale in Stanislaus County from the main line of the Stockton and Copperopolis Railroad at Peters. The project was controversial and before long, Southern Pacific acquired the line. By 1915, there were three passenter trains daily each way.

Aside from the train, there was also the Southern Pacific Motor Car Service, which took high school students to Stockton. These gasoline driven cars had special flanged wheels that could run on the tracks.

The business district was to grow considerably as a result of the railroad. By 1880, there were two saloons, two blacksmiths, a meat market, a boot and shoe maker and a harness shop, in addition to the hotels already mentioned. At about this time, there were also two Chinese laundries, a pharmacy, doctor's office and livery stable.

The close of the 1890s was a turning point, with the completion of the Santa Fe Railroad through Escalon in 1896. Farmington lost its role as a regional trading center to this new community. In 1902, the day after Independence Day, a fire caused by a firecracker destroyed eleven commercial buildings in Farmington's business district. While some were rebuilt, the town was never to recover.

Cultural, social and sports activities have been varied and ambitious. In the late nineteenth century, there were two bands, the Farmington Independent Cornet Band, with fifteen musicians, and a five piece string band under the direction of Professor James Martin.

A great sensation for the sports minded came when a skating rink was opened in an old blacksmith shop during 1885. It was so successful that the building was expanded and refreshment booths installed. Skaters were attracted from Linden and other localities. The rink, operated for years, was so popular that the saloon keepers were complain-

ONE OF THE OLDEST FARMHOUSES IN THE COUNTY—THE NATHANIEL S. HARROLD HOUSE

The house as it appeared originally was recorded in the 1879 Thompson and West *History of San Joaquin County*. The artist was likely F. J. Howell. In the background of this lithograph, a typical grain harvesting operation is underway without the use of combined harvesters, which had not yet become popular. A threshing machine powered by a steam tractor is in the center of the circle; the cutting of the crop is underway with headers and header bed wagons.

THE HARROLD HOUSE IN 1982

Built in 1868, this nine room house has five fireplaces and outside walls eighteen inches thick. This was home for the eight children of Mr. and Mrs. Harrold, owners of a huge stock ranch and general farming operations that extended almost to Escalon. By the late 1870s, the family owned 15,000 acres.

Harrold had his start in this area during the gold rush, working as a cook in a roadhouse just four miles west of town known as the Texas Tent. He later operated extensive cattle interests, sometimes driving about a thousand head of cattle to market in the mining country.

The Harrold home became the residence of the Thomas Jefferson Drais family in about 1900. Drais cultivated 743 acres, 300 in vineyard. The house remained in the family until the mid 1940s.

ing that their young customers had been lost.

The first organized fire department was the result of efforts by the J. F. Goodwin Company, a cattle ranch. Much of the organizational effort and funds bringing the service were contributed by Goodwin. The first piece of equipment was a new Chevrolet truck. Six years later, the Farmington Fire District was established through tax funds. There was a paid chief, and a one and a half ton Diamond "T" fire truck was especially built for Farmington. It was equipped to fight grain fires. Floods, like fires, were also anticipated, as nearby Little John, Rock and Duck creeks posed a constant threat of flooding until a federally financed project, the Farmington Dam, was completed in 1955.

The citizens of Farmington, as well as those who had moved away years before, were united in a special project during the 1970s. The old Farmington Cemetery, established in 1888, had become badly run down. Since a takeover was allowed by private enterprise in the 1950s, the operation passed through a series of speculative ownerships and the burial plots suffered severe neglect. In 1976, a non-profit Farmington Cemetery Association took over operation and restored the grounds with the help of volunteers and young men from Peterson Hall, a juvenile home in French Camp.

In recent times, the social life has centered around the Farmington Elementary School P.T.A., 4-H Club, Methodist Church, volunteer fire department and the Chamber of Commerce. All participate in an annual Community Day held every June since 1952. The event features a parade, barbecue and other activities, providing funds for community improvement projects. Also starting in the same year was a unique celebration of Groundhog Day. Using numerous interpretations of the observance, the 4-H Club serves a dinner featuring pork sausage, a bingo game with "piggy" items for prizes, etc.

The movie industry has added excitement in recent years. In 1957, "The Big Country," with Gregory Peck, Charlton Heston, Charles Bickford and Jean Simmons, was filmed at the old Drais Ranch east of town. In 1980, a segment of "Coast to Coast" was filmed, starring Robert Blake and Dyan Cannon. Segments of other productions also have been filmed here.

Future growth of Farmington is not expected to take place soon. A local bartender, Walter Riggs, summed up the situation: "... the big ranches own all the land around the town and they're not selling; they don't want to see it get any bigger." As in its earliest days, cattle are still run and grain is dry farmed on the broad agricultural lands surrounding Farmington. Only in the twentieth century has the look of the land changed; it has become a bit greener year around with irrigated row crops and orchards.

NORTH SIDE OF THE MAIN STREET, LATE 1890s
Note how the front porches have been extended into the streets to offer winter/summer protection to customers and their animals. To the right of the restaurant is a saloon, possibly the Avon. The last building is the Farmington Stable, operated by C. M. Alders and Joseph Sharpe. The windmills in back of the buildings pumped water for domestic use.

Just a few years after this photograph was taken, all of these buildings were destroyed by fire, in 1902. (Collection of the San Joaquin County Historical Museum)

THE SHADY GROVE SCHOOL, OCTOBER 1896, PHOTO BY SLOAN

Since the mid 1850s there has always been a school here. For generations it was known as the Shady Grove School. At first, classes were held only in March, April and May. In the early 1880s, the school was relocated to a lot just east of the Odd Fellows Hall. In 1889, this huge two-story, two classroom wooden building with a belfry was completed on the main street, just west of the railroad tracks, adding greatly to the appearance of the town. Grades one through eight were taught there. It was replaced by a brick school in 1923; the old school was reduced to one story and moved to become a residence, a purpose it serves to this day.

Facilities were supplemented by four more classrooms in the early 1950s. There was no school bus for the 114 pupils until 1951. The brick school served until condemned, after becoming part of the Escalon School District in the early 1970s. *(Collection of the San Joaquin County Historical Museum)*

ODD FELLOWS HALL AND OGILVIE'S STORE, HIGHWAY 4 AND ESCALON-BELLOTA ROAD, 1982

Constructed by the Farmington Hall Association in 1882, this is the principal building in town. Within a year after its completion, the IOOF Lodge purchased the structure and has held meetings there ever since. At one time, it had its own band and hosted grand balls here.

During the early twentieth century, this was the store of R. M. Buckman, and for decades, starting in 1911, was the Toda Brothers General Merchandise. L.A. and J. D. Toda served customers from ten miles in every direction.

There has always been a store on the ground floor of this building. The fifth owner, Howard J. Ogilvie, was at this location for over thirty years, until the fall of 1982. Ogilvie's store was the best example of an old time general store in the county. Gasoline was dispensed from a single pump. There was a wooden bench outside, near the town bulletin board, and tradition established the front porch as a genuine gathering place for row croppers, farm hands and the kids. The business was successful, expanding its stock and store area vastly over the years. It was purchased by a Manteca businessman and has re-opened as Cross' General Store.

C. A. "DOC" ALDERS' WHEELWRIGHTING AND CARRIAGE BUILDING SHOP, 1982

"Doc" is at work on one of dozens of wheels brought to his shop for repair. Alders has done work on wheels from stage coaches used at the History Center in Yosemite National Park and from San Francisco's oldest hand pump fire engine. The stout wheels of steam fire engines preserved at Woodland and Concord, California, have also received his expert attention. His work has been viewed by millions on the television series, "Little House on the Prairie" and "Father Murphy."

Such is the trade at Alders' Service, which started as a hobby twenty years ago when he found the iron for a Miller Carriage Works buggy and undertook the project of making it a buggy once again. In the background is a stage coach he built from original iron from such a vehicle, found under an oak tree at Angels Camp.

"Doc" has completely abandoned automobile servicing except for filling gas tanks and repairing tires. Customers come to him from all over the West to order his Petaluma carts, single seat buggies and Phaeton carts or to have old carriages renewed.

130

FRENCH CAMP
HUDSON'S BAY COMPANY POST

French Camp has a longer history than any other town in the county. The first homes built by white men in San Joaquin County were located here. While these were only the temporary shelters of a trappers' camp, they were the advance guard of permanent settlement. Trappers came after the 1827 discovery of vast numbers of beaver in this area by Jedediah Smith, well-known mountain man and the first white traveler over the Sierra. Smith's party met disaster after reaching Oregon, and only three, including Smith, survived to report their findings at Fort Vancouver on the Columbia River. At first, only a survey party was sent back along Smith's route to gather lost belongings and to verify the new beaver resource. Trapping began in earnest about 1832 when men and their families, a group of sixty-five including women and children, were led to what is now French Camp by Michel La Framboise, a well known figure along the Oregon, Washington and California frontiers.

The party built tule and willow huts and soon the men were establishing extensive trap lines throughout the nearby waterways, trapping and skinning beaver. This was solely a winter time activity, when furs were thickest; during the remainder of the year the camp was deserted. The annual overland party from Fort Vancouver, which grew to 400 men, women and children at one point, was to continue until 1845.

An outbreak of smallpox, a decrease in the number of pelts and mounting political unrest in California ended these annual treks.

Nonetheless, this point in the Valley was already well-known among Mexican-Californians as El Campo de los Franceses (The French Camp). The name was to be applied to the second largest land grant ever given by the Mexican government. Awarded in 1844, it totaled 48,747 acres and was surpassed only by John Sutter's grant in the Sacramento Valley, which was only eighty acres larger. El Rancho del Campo de los Franceses belonged to Guillermo Gulnac and Charles M. Weber, who was later to found the city of Stockton.

Their first efforts to settle the grant involved the David Kelsey family and Thomas Lindsay. Lindsay settled in what is now Stockton, and Kelsey, who had been offered a square mile of land by Gulnac if he stayed a year, settled in French Camp. Here he built a tule hut for his wife and daughter, America. This was a lonely place and reception from Indians was uncertain. As a precaution, a swivel gun was given to him by Gulnac, who had obtained it from Sutter. The gun was fired nightly to frighten the Indians. However, the danger they were to face was disease contracted during a visit to San Jose. Kelsey died of smallpox; the rest of the family narrowly escaped death, and after their rescue did not return to French Camp. Successful, permanent settlement of the grant lands was accomplished in 1847, two years after Weber had become sole owner. Thousands of cattle were herded onto the land, small plots were cultivated and five corrals were established, one of which was located in French Camp.

The beginnings of commercial activity can be traced to August 1849 and the work of Colonel P. W. Noble and A. Stevenson. They built a store, saloon and freight depot, at first intended mainly for shipment of supplies to their store in Mariposa.

Belding and Atwood were also here in 1849 to establish a winter freight depot. By 1850 there were two hotels, Noble and Stevenson's and LeBarron's. These and other Stockton businessmen took an interest in the good, high banks and navigable depths of French Camp Slough because of a miserable situation developing in Stockton during each rainy season. The roads became so muddy that it was impossible to approach within four miles of Stockton. The only route was through French

131

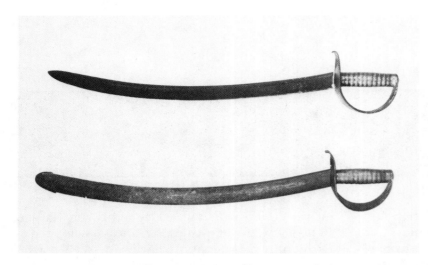

CUTLASSES FROM THE FAMOUS
FRENCH CAMP CACHE

These are just two of the forty cutlasses, swords and muskets found in 1856 by school boys Eldredge, Edward and James Reynolds. The cache was buried in a wood lined pit under a lofty oak tree in what is now the school yard. Their origin is still one of the great mysteries of San Joaquin County. Apparently, a local businessman, Col. P. W. Noble, knew something about it, as he encouraged the boys to dig in this certain spot when they seemed to need some excitement. The weapons might have been left by French Canadian trappers or by one of the expeditions organized to subdue Indians in the Sierra, or perhaps this was a forgotten cache from the Bear Flag Revolt. The two cutlasses, with twenty-five inch blades, are both United States Navy issue of about 1840. This pair plus a sword are the only known items still surviving from the cache. *(Collection of the Haggin Museum, Stockton)*

Camp, easily reached by water from Stockton. Stage coaches and freight wagons could travel from this point year round because the road east passed through sandy soil.

French Camp Slough soon became a major transportation artery. E. W. Atwood was its pioneer navigator, sailing a yawl with a capacity of four passengers and 1,500 pounds of freight. This freight service made $3,000 in one winter. Soon the yawl was replaced by the *Mint*, a small paddle wheel steamer. Two other steamers regularly seen during the early 1850s in French Camp Slough were the *Fairy* and the *Game Cock*, twenty-four tons gross. There was much activity these winter months; countless teams and five stage lines had their rendezvous at French Camp, meeting the river boats. One observer tallied seventy freight wagons enroute to Sonora on the French Camp Road in a single day. Many thought French Camp's role as a transportation center might overshadow Stockton's. By 1853, there were two hotels doing big business providing lodging and meals to stage passengers, as many as 100 at a time.

These boom times were not to last. Dry years, plus plans to build an all-year toll road between Stockton and French Camp, worked to Stockton's advantage. Completion of the French Camp Turnpike in 1865 eclipsed the town's significance.

French Camp would continue as a regional supply center for the ever-increasing agricultural activity as well as to provide services to travelers. It was linked by rail in 1869 by the Central Pacific

and was located at a major fork of wagon roads through the region. One could continue on down through the San Joaquin Valley by the French Camp Road or the route via Mossdale and Altamont Pass to the San Francisco Bay area.

In 1879, the population reached about 200 and there were two hotels, W. S. Belden's and W. F. McLeland's, two blacksmith and wagon shops, two saloons, a boot and shoemaker, livery stable, post office and school. Maps from the seventies to the early twentieth century do not always use the name French Camp but, instead, Castoria, the Spanish word for beaver.

By 1916 the town was on the famous transcontinental auto route, the Lincoln Highway. A guide for the highway described the businesses, which included a hotel, garage, Southern Pacific and Western Pacific service, six stores and a school. The town was listed as being 3,257 miles from New York City.

Since 1895, the settlement has gained greater significance, as several county facilities have been established here, including the county hospital, relocated from Stockton after an 1895 fire, and the county honor farm, first occupied in 1946. A noteworthy program here was "work furlough" for groups of inmates who worked outside the compound. In the 1960s, the largest work furlough program in the world was operated here under the administration of Sheriff "Mike" Canlis. Crews of inmates worked at the metropolitan airport, Micke Grove Park and the county hospital and on litter patrol as well as in private industry. Peterson Hall was completed in 1949 to serve juvenile cases. A $3 million addition to these facilities was dedicated in July 1983.

The women's jail was established in the mid-1950s with a major program involving laundry operations and production of uniforms, blankets and similar goods. With the closure of the county jail at San Joaquin and Channel streets in Stockton, the maximum security section was added to county facilities in 1959, all flanking the north

SAN JOAQUIN COUNTY HOSPITAL

The San Joaquin County General Hosptial can trace its history in French Camp to the buildings shown below, constructed in 1895 on a 430 acre site just three years after a fire destroyed the hospital in Stockton. In the early twentieth century, a school of nursing was established here. Most of the old structures have been replaced and the site is now dominated by the present brick building dating from 1932 with a major addition in 1943. The hospital cares for more than 8,000 patients annually, plus nearly 80,000 outpatients and 32,000 emergency cases. It celebrated its 125th anniversary during June 1983.

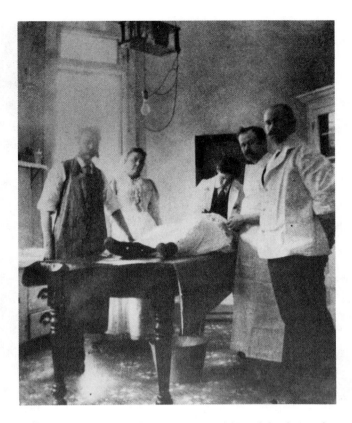

The rare view of the operating room, above, is a marvelous record of what was once considered the latest in hospital facilities. Note the bare, single light globe and the bucket under the wooden table. The photograph was taken in the Admissions Building. (Above, Collection of the San Joaquin County Historical Museum. Below, Collection of the Holt-Atherton Center for Western Studies, University of the Pacific, Stockton)

134

FRENCH CAMP ELEMENTARY SCHOOL

This lacy structure enhanced the community for many years starting in the 1890s. The exterior view was taken in 1907; the interior view, above, dates from about the same time. The building was demolished in the late 1920s just after completion of the present school. Its site is now the play yard. A school has been part of French Camp since 1851, when the second school established in the county was funded through public subscription. The pioneering building was also used for public assemblies. A second story was later added for a Sons of Temperance meeting hall. (*Collection of Maradah Seegers*)

135

side of Matthews Road. By 1985 there were 536 in the men's and women's jails, the men's facility 23 percent beyond capacity and the women's 55 percent. Today, the county is the largest employer in French Camp. Jail improvement has first priority among county construction plans, and $54 million will be spent here over the next twenty years.

The French Camp Fire District was established in 1946 to serve twenty-five square miles with a paid chief and five volunteers. Now there are sixteen square miles served by ten employees and fifteen reserves. No successful effort has been made to further organize the community beyond a municipal advisory council. French Camp just grew when there was need, with little formal planning. A domestic water system should replace wells which have an uncertain future due to the decline in ground water quality. A sewage system and street lights would also be of great benefit. The old Lincoln Highway, Highway 50, passed through the business district, but with the construction of Interstate 5, the town has been bypassed and several gas stations and other roadside businesses have closed. The route through town, however, has become a much used connecting link between Interstate 5 and Highway 99. Proximity to major highways plus rail transportation by Western

Pacific and Southern Pacific are ideal resources for encouraging industrial development.

Among the major firms in French Camp are Ace Tomato; J. B. Beaiard Company, steel tank fabricators; Carnation Company Milling Division, Continental Grain and Stockton Hay and Grain, all producing animal feed; Granite Construction Company; Monray Roof Tile; and Poly Cal Plastics, Inc., manufacturers of polyethelene tanks. The Stockton Livestock Auction Yard brings activity to the town every Saturday for this Stagi Brothers enterprise.

Since the 1920s, a significant Japanese population has become established, particularly through truck gardening. Turnips, green onions, beets, parsley and lettuce were grown by about seventy-five families just before World War II. During the thirties, a marketing co-op was founded which operated alongside the Southern Pacific tracks. These activities gave French Camp a reputation as the "Salad Bowl of the Valley."

Starting in 1926, a temple and language school was founded in an old Grange Hall, which served until replaced by a new community hall in 1964. Japanese language studies always took place after the daily session in public school.

During World War II, all of these families were

BUSINESS CENTER OF FRENCH CAMP, 1962

On the left is the Lincoln Station, built to serve motorists traveling on the Lincoln Highway, which passed in front of the building and turned west. The station was operated by James and Cleveland Beattie for many years.

Part of the ground floor was occupied by a bar, and the second floor was the Beattie residence before they built a substantial brick house among the trees just north of the Beattie General Merchandise on the opposite side of the street. In the late 1920s, this structure replaced the old store James Beattie had operated since the early twentieth century across from the school one block east. A portion of the post office building can be seen at the far right.

136

relocated from their farms by order of the federal government. First they were sent to an assembly center in Turlock, Stanislaus County, and then to Gila, Arizona. Many did not return to French Camp after the war. Today there are still about forty Japanese families residing in and around this community.

Of ethnic interest, too, is the only Chinese cemetery in the region, at Matthews Road and Interstate 5. Stockton's Chinese Benevolent Association purchased the grounds early in the twentieth century, and it is still well maintained and important today.

The unusually long and varied history of this small community gained state recognition in 1959, when a plaque recognizing French Camp as California State Historical Landmark #668 was unveiled by representatives of the pioneer Reynolds family, Native Daughters, Ladies Auxiliary to the California Pioneers and the French Camp District Chamber of Commerce.

IN THE CENTER OF TOWN, FRENCH CAMP ROAD AND ASH STREET, 1923
It looks as if this serious looking group of young people is about to be taken somewhere. The boys are dressed in knickerbockers, "knickers" for short. This popular garment was a must for boys from coast to coast; the stockings had to reach above the knees.
By this time, the feed stable in the distance had seen its most prosperous days; this was the era of the automobile, truck and gasoline tractor. *(Collection of Maradah Seegers)*

GENERAL MILLS FEED PLANT UNDER CONSTRUCTION ON THE NORTH EDGE OF FRENCH CAMP, 1956

Completed for General Mills in 1957, this highly automated facility was designed to produce 350 to 400 tons of dairy cattle, poultry and specialty feeds a day. The ten sixty-four foot high storage tanks in the foreground were for storage of grain and soft feeds.

This mill and warehouse were built to serve California from the Tehachapi Mountains to the Oregon border. Modeled after a company operation in Iowa, it replaced a facility in Vallejo, California. It has been sold by General Mills and is now operated by Carnation Company Milling Division. Livestock and poultry feed continue to be produced, including Calf-Manna, for a service area extending from Merced to Red Bluff.

POLY CAL PLASTICS INC., SOUTH ASH STREET AND WESTERN PACIFIC TRACKS, 1983

French Camp is an important, ever growing community. One of the newer firms, shown above, builds tanks of durable cross-linked polyethelene. Poly Cal Plastics moved to this area from Stockton in 1981 to occupy the plant where Magnus Metals formerly produced rail car bearings.

The lightweight, low maintenance tanks have found many industrial applications, particularly in the handling of liquid fertilizers for farming operations. Only one other firm, in Los Angeles, is manufacturing this product. Poly Cal, serving fourteen western states and markets in Hawaii, Saudi Arabia, Venezuela and other countries, has hired a staff of thirty-five. *(Photograph by Raymond W. Hillman)*

LATHROP
LELAND STANFORD'S "SPITE TOWN"

Before significant growth with the coming of the Central Pacific Railroad, this place was known as Wilson's Station and was composed of a store and a school house. Thomas A. Wilson, a pioneer merchant in nearby French Camp, was a principal land owner in what was to become Lathrop. His land was once part of the extreme southern edge of the Weber grant.

There may never have been a Lathrop if the Central Pacific had had its way in Stockton. A controversy developed between the city council and railroad officials regarding which street would become the right-of-way. There were delays that infuriated Stanford, who ordered construction outside the eastern city limits and emphasis upon little Wilson Station for many of the services that were to have been located in Stockton.

The settlement was renamed in honor of Stanford's brother-in-law, Charles Lathrop, and Stanford proclaimed that grass would grow on the streets of Stockton as the new town drew away significant commerce. However, he underestimated the importance of riverboat service to Stockton. Nevertheless, in order to make his "spite town" successful, he gave special freight rates and passenger fares to Lathrop. The machine shops and roundhouse were constructed here, and the town became an important division point and major stop starting in 1871. By this time, the Visalia Division of Southern Pacific Railroad, serving the length of the San Joaquin Valley, was completed.

As Lathrop was a division point, a "wye," the largest in California and still in use, was built there for the switching and making up of trains. In its center stood the roundhouse. Lathrop rapidly became a shipping point for valley produce bound for the Bay area. Wheat and fruit were typical shipments.

The principal building in Lathrop, the Central Pacific Railroad restaurant, was completed May 10, 1871. Before dining cars were common, trains would make meal stops. All trains bound for San Joaquin Valley points as well as to the Bay area from Sacramento would stop here, creating a beehive of activity at meal time.

Without doubt, the most historically important event in Lathrop history occurred in 1889, inside the railroad dining room. A feud between David S. Terry and United States Supreme Court Justice Stephen Field came to a tragic end here. Attorney Terry, infuriated by a decision made against his client, Sarah Althea Hill, in the case involving Senator William Sharon's fortune, struck Field. Terry was shot by Field's body guard, U.S. Marshal Neagle. Under California law, Neagle could have been held for murder, but the case was heard by the United States Supreme Court and the result was a landmark case in federal-state relations. The ruling supported the hiring of a body guard for a justice on the basis the action was "fairly and properly inferable" from the Constitution. This was one of the broadest interpretations yet given the implied powers of the United States government.

Lathrop reached the peak of its growth in 1879. There were twenty-four buildings, including three hotels, the Central, the Lathrop House and the Shannon House; seven saloons, two restaurants, two general merchandise stores, a bakery, two blacksmith shops, several freighting companies and a school. Six hundred people resided here.

Over the years, three newspapers have been published. During the nineteenth century, there were the *Lathrop Junction* and the *Railroad Journal*, the latter appearing in the late 1880s. About 1912, the third and last, the *Lathrop Sun*, was being published.

There was a busy Wells-Fargo office next to the depot and there was a post office that had an extensive rural route, part of which included what is

THE MEAL STOP AT LATHROP

Above, this was a familiar setting to those traveling across the United States in the latter part of the nineteenth century. This particular engraving accompanied a series, "Overland Rail Travel," that was published in *Frank Leslie's Illustrated* newspaper, May 11, 1878. Aside from the dining room, the principal attraction at this time was "Suzie," a caged grizzly bear. The 2,100 pound bear eventually became fed up with the prodding masses looking at her and became dangerous. She was sold to a San Francisco butcher who turned quite a Christmas time profit on her at ten cents a pound.

The large hotel and restaurant building in the distance was completed in 1871 and between then and 1892 was replaced twice as a result of fire. It was in the second building (facing page), completed in 1889, that the shooting of David S. Terry took place and forever assured Lathrop a niche in California political history. When this structure burned after just three years, it was not replaced by a new building but by the old, single story wooden passenger depot from Stockton, cut into sections and moved in six flat cars.

Left, a handbill distributed throughout the passenger cars in about 1890 announced the dining facilities in Lathrop. Fifty cents was a high price for dinner in those days. There were usually no dining cars and you either brought your own food or stepped off the train for the scheduled meal stop. *(Above, Courtesy of Sacramento Public Library; left, Collection of the Haggin Museum, Stockton)*

140

now Manteca. The post office lost its significance in 1908, when much of its rural service was transferred to the new town of Manteca.

By the early twentieth century, there were still two hotels, a grocery, Geraty's general merchandise, a hardware store, restaurant, barber shop, blacksmith, butcher shop and a Chinese laundry. An ambitious addition to the business center was W. H. Miller's Hardware Store, completed in 1917 of concrete block, with apartments on the second floor. There were two major meeting places. The school was used by various religious groups, including the Methodists, German Baptists and Dunkards. The Woodmen of the World had a reputation for having one of the best dance floors in the valley, and their hall was a favorite gathering spot for families.

In 1890, Lathrop was still very much a railroad town, with its 500 residents mainly "railroad hands," a natural development as this was the terminus of two railroad divisions. At this time, switching operations continued day and night, and each day twelve passenger and forty-four freight trains passed through. The freight business was on an increase with the completion of rail service down the West Side. However, its days of importance were numbered with the growth of Tracy. The machine shop and roundhouse were transferred there in the early 1890s, and the only major facility to remain in Lathrop was the railroad restaurant.

It was here that passengers bound for Los Angeles and San Joaquin Valley points would always change trains. Western Pacific, as a rival line after 1909, did not have any great effect, as the station was three-quarters of a mile from town. However, there was a major fire in the business district during 1911 from which the town never recovered.

By the early 1920s, George Tinkham recorded in his *History of San Joaquin County*, "Lathrop is a town of the past, a silent reminder of the time when Stanford and Company endeavored to found a town as a rival to Stockton...." By 1935, the town had one store, a barber shop, blacksmith and hardware business.

A very important war industry was operated in Lathrop between August 1942 and June 1944, Permanente Metals Corporation, managed by Henry J. Kaiser of Kaiser Industries. This became the most important source of magnesium in California, and the metal, which had been in short supply, was used to make aircraft parts (being a third lighter than aluminum) and "goop bombs"

A PORTION OF THE CENTRAL PACIFIC ROUNDHOUSE, SPRING 1891
A major role in serving the railroad was held by this community from 1869 to the early 1890s. This twelve compartment roundhouse was one of the primary facilities along with a large dining room serving passenger trains. Note the unlikely location for a young tree in the doorway of the second compartment from the left. *(Collection of Dr. Howard Letcher)*

(containing magnesium in oil, they were very destructive and helped shorten the war).

The plant was located here because a pipeline from the Kettleman Hills in the Southern San Joaquin Valley passed under Lathrop and was a ready supplier of natural gas, which was needed in astronomical quantities to maintain 2200 degrees Farenheit in sixty-four furnaces, twenty-four hours a day, seven days a week. The process used had never been tried before, but within six months the plant was in full operation, producing 65,000 pounds a day. The process involved shipping quartz from Turlock which yielded silicon (for ferro silicon) and shipping dolomite from Natividad in Monterey County, which, after processing, yielded magnesium oxide and calcium oxide. During retorting of these combined powders, the magnesium vented away as a gas and when reaching the water jacket around the furnace condensed into beautiful, nearly pure crystals of magnesium.

The tremendously successful operation employed 600 and closed only because there was a huge stockpile of ingots in the basement and the production cost of sixty-five cents per pound was undercut by plants elsewhere producing at twenty cents per pound.

The greatest twentieth century development was Sharpe Army Depot, established in 1942 and destined to become one of the major army supply depots in the western United States. It was named for Major General Henry Granville Sharpe, who gave innovative service to the Quartermaster Corps during his forty year career. The depot is two miles long and a half mile wide, has 2.5 million square feet of warehouses, its own 3,200 foot air strip and a fleet of about thirty watercraft in its Watercraft Storage Division on the Stockton Channel at Rough and Ready Island.

Currently it is one of the major employers of the entire county. During 1985, there were about 1,400 civilians and forty-five military personnel on the staff.

When first established during World War II, it was named Lathrop Holding and Reconsignment Point. It was here that supplies were held for shipment through ports of embarkation in the San Francisco Bay Area. It became a principal installation at this time. It was not unusual for 450 rail cars to be loaded and unloaded in twenty-four hours. During the Korean War, operations were expanded and buildings modernized. This was one of a series of upgrading and expansion projects that has kept Sharpe in a leading position able to meet its "Can Do" motto.

During the Vietnam War, Sharpe's mission again expanded and the depot became the army's "Gateway to the Pacific," moving supplies to Southeast Asia and readying helicopters and other aircraft for combat. About 3,400 civilian and military personnel were employed.

Presently, the installation is the army's western distribution center for repair and spare parts for military units throughout the western United States, Alaska, Hawaii and the entire Pacific Basin. More than 2,500 orders a day are processed, and more than three-quarters of a million materiel release orders have been processed annually. The depot is presently on the threshold of a major modernization and expansion project which will vastly increase its capacity. The $100 million, two-

FRONT STREET (NOW SEVENTH STREET) LOOKING NORTH, ABOUT 1900–1907

Reproduced from a post card, this view shows the Southwell and Sutton General Store at left. The tower in the distance is part of the Dario Sanguinetti residence built above one of the most prominent general stores in town, operated by Sanguinetti and Joseph Geraty. This store and other businesses were destroyed in May 1927 by the last large fire in town, a loss from which this commercial center never entirely recovered. Several of the present day firms operating in Lathrop are occupying newer buildings on the site of the old business district. The railroad tracks are directly across the street.

CARE AND PRESERVATION HANGAR
AT SHARPE DEPOT, FEBRUARY 1969
Part of the depot's aircraft maintenance
mission was carried out in this newly built
facility during the Vietnam War and up to
June 1976. A crew of women as well as
men is at work on the helicopters.

year project will result in twenty acres under one roof plus state of the art computer and materiel handling systems. Ground breaking is planned for the fall of 1985. These facilities will be a prototype for larger centers to be constructed in Pennsylvania and Texas.

Weekend and annual training exercises are hosted at the depot for army reserve and National Guard units; during 1983 there were more than 6,000 such trainees. An $800,000 barracks for their use was completed the following year.

In the 1940s, Lathrop expanded from its original townsite into five square miles east of Interstate 5. This became Lathrop Acres, Lathrop Village and a shopping center extending to Louise Avenue. The region was still primarily agricultural, and in the late 1940s, there was considerable shipment of milk to condensing plants and cheese factories. The raising of poultry and rabbits and the operation of hatcheries have been important.

The Filipino population is significant, with about fifty families residing here. In 1981 the Filipino Association of Lathrop was organized, providing a social club and hosting occasional special events.

In 1953, Best Fertilizer built its main chemical plant here, which was sold ten years later to Occi-dental Petroleum. The firm, acquired in January 1983 by J. R. Simplot of Boise, Idaho, has employed as many as 450 people in its production, marketing and distribution of fertilizers, pesticides and other agricultural chemicals. In 1982, considerable attention was directed to the plant when a massive suit was brought against Occidental over its exposure of the now banned pesticide, D.B.C.P., to area residents and employees.

Another major plant is Libby-Owens, Ford, one of eleven plants operated across the nation by this firm. It has had as many as 1,200 hourly employees, working three shifts, producing window glass for General Motors automobiles and the construction industry. The auto glass was shipped to General Motors plants in Fremont and Los Angeles. Currently glass is being supplied to the General Motors-Toyota cooperative venture in Fremont.

Lathrop, with only an elected municipal advisory council and water board, has considerable resources for further industrial expansion. Its newest industrial subdivision of seventy-eight lots was approved by the county supervisors in 1982. Residential growth also was booming, and the *Stockton Record* identified Lathrop as the fastest growing community in the county during the early 1980s.

A SPECIAL CEREMONY AT SHARPE DEPOT
A ceremony was held for the 100th helicopter processed by the facility, May 2, 1969. *(Courtesy Public Affairs Officer, U.S. Army photograph, Sharpe Army Depot, Lathrop)*

These men are working in the auto glass department. At the table to the left, glass is being cut with the aid of a templet, while at right, edges are being ground smooth. *(Courtesy Rich Turner, Stockton Record)*

LIBBY-OWENS-FORD PLANT, c. 1980
Freshly poured glass 130 inches wide rolls toward the cutting machine. In the manufacture of these sheets of glass, the molten material is poured into a tank of liquid tin and allowed to float to the surface. The tin provides perfectly smooth support, making both sides ready for use without time consuming polishing of one uneven surface as was the case with older methods.

LINDEN
THE CHERRY AND WALNUT CENTER OF SAN JOAQUIN COUNTY

Original settlements in this vicinity were the 14 Mile House and Foreman's Ranch, also known as the 15 Mile House in 1849. The inn, owned by William T. Treblecock, served numerous teamsters and travelers on what is now known as Highway 26, formerly the Mokelumne Hill Road, once a major gold rush route between Stockton and the mining country of the Sierra foothills.

A Foreman's Ranch post office was established in 1855. Samuel Foreman was an early settler. The following year a general merchandise store was opened by Thomas McCarter.

In 1863 the Foreman's Ranch post office was relocated about a mile to the southwest, and through the influence of James Wasley, Foreman's Ranch was renamed Linden after his birthplace in Linden, Ohio. He helped plan the community with a survey plotting six streets, the principal one being the Mokelumne Hill Road, which was paralleled by Union and Foreman streets; running north and south were Mill, Market and Hunter streets.

A writer for the *Stockton Weekly Independent* in May 1868 described the town: "Linden is a progressive little town and will continue to grow with the rich country surrounding it.... There are in the place two stores, two blacksmith shops, one wheelwright, a flour mill, two churches, a school house and a hotel." At this time, there was daily stage service to Stockton, and the coach would stop anywhere along the route for passengers. The roads, though busy, were not good. One writer summed up the situation: "In summer, the dust was six inches deep, and the mud was twice as deep in winter. It was a big day's trip to Stockton and return."

The roads were traversed by numerous wagons laden with sacks of grain. Dry farming had become firmly established over a wide territory, and during the summer and fall, the road was busy with farmers hauling the harvest in wagons hitched to one or two trailers. Many would start for Stockton at 2:00 A.M. to avoid a return trip in the heat of the day. Another crop was alfalfa, which could be grown without irrigation due to the high water table.

A very ambitious development in the transportation system came with construction of the Stockton Terminal and Eastern Railroad, which was completed in 1910. Aside from Stockton, the principal town reached was Linden, but the actual terminus was the hamlet of Bellota, about four miles to the east. By 1915, according to a Sunset Home Seekers Bureau publication, the railroad was serving Linden with two passenger trains daily. The line soon experienced financial difficulty but was always operational. During its languishing era, it became known as the "Slow, Tired and Easy." Today, the company is more prosperous than ever before through diversification, especially in warehousing, and is one of the few short line railroads operating in the black.

An additional improvement in transportation by 1915 was a twelve mile paved highway to Stockton, present Highway 26.

Another unusual development came through the interest of a local resident, Sam Finerty, in airplanes. He was associated with radio professionals in Stockton and had a set installed in his airplane in the 1920s. This is believed to be one of the first radio equipped aircraft.

While much of the early agriculture centered upon grain, especially wheat, some small orchards and fields of vegetables were planted. Cattle, horses, sheep, chickens, beef and hogs were also raised. Area prominence in fruit production did not materialize until David W. Miller, Sr., proved the locale's potential by successfully planting forty acres to prunes, apricots and peaches in 1895. Such crops require an abundance of water, and the region's beginnings in the not always suc-

147

cessful and often controversial promotions for water projects can be traced to a private dam built across Mormon Slough about the turn of the century. This and other efforts led to the establishment of the Linden Irrigation District in 1929, just two weeks before the Great Crash. Since then, this district and the Stockton East San Joaquin Conservation District have centered their work upon improving and maintaining the water table.

Of all the crops grown around Linden today, cherries are best known. The local cherry orchards have now reached a total of 8,000 acres from which 2.5 million eighteen-pound boxes are shipped. The Linden Cherry Festival, held annually in May, has done much to draw attention to Linden. It was first started as a Future Farmers of America Fair barbecue. Since the Linden-Peters Chamber of Commerce has become a sponsor, the event has become quite extensive.

What was once the largest walnut orchard in the world under one management is operated here by the Anderson Barngrover Ranch Company. Five hundred acres were planted in 1917 and 1918.

The very first industry, a flour mill, was established in 1854 to serve scattered local settlers raising grain. Over the years, the operation has been known as the Calaveras Mills, the State Mills and Linden Mills. Before construction of the brick building, which still stands, in 1871, the mill was destroyed twice by fire. It supplies both flour and feed not only to points throughout San Joaquin County but also to the adjacent Mother Lode. It was always run by steam generated in boilers stoked with wood abundantly available through the extensive clearing of groves of valley oak trees by farmers. The mill was closed by the 1890s but after idleness of many years, new activity came when the building became part of the Stockton District Kidney Bean Growers Association.

This firm was started as a co-op of local kidney bean growers who were providing seed beans to farmers in New York State who needed disease-free California beans. The early shipments of 20,000 100-pound bags have increased to more than 200,000. Eighty-five percent of the present shipments of dry beans is for consumption; only about 15 percent are seed beans.

The bean growers adaptive use of the old mill is typical of twentieth century industry locating here to serve crops made possible through irrigation. One of the earliest was the Linden Walnut Growers Association, which built a large plant on the

THE GUERNSEY GENERAL MERCHANDISE STORE, c. 1890

This was one of the first substantial buildings constructed in the business district. Note the iron shutters which are typical of buildings constructed during the 1850s and 1860s. In the late 1880s, when Fred Guernsey was proprietor, his billheads proclaimed that butter and eggs could be exchanged for goods.

This store was a focal point of the community for many years, as it was headquarters for the post office and also had the first and only telephone in the area for many years. During the winter, when flooding was threatened by the nearby Calaveras River, the store was a clearing house for flood information between Linden and Stockton. All this came to an end in 1906, when the building burned. Its ruins stood until the late 1930s, when the old bricks found new usefulness in the walls of the home built on Main Street by Mr. and Mrs. George d'Carlo.

STOCKTON DISTRICT KIDNEY BEAN GROWERS INC., FORMER LINDEN FLOURING MILLS, 1982

One of the oldest industrial structures in the county is the three-story brick building (left), presently a part of the bean growers plant. It was constructed for milling flour in 1871 and had a capacity of 120 barrels a day. When Williams, Bingham & Company were operators in the late 1870s, extra and super fine flour were produced along with graham flour, ground barley, corn meal and other products. At the right is an 1875 billhead from the mill.

After the mill closed, the second floor became a comfortable four bedroom home for the Fanning family. Their daughter, Mary Jane, used the top floor for a play house. A former warehouse on the west side of the mill became a roller skating rink which also doubled occasionally as a fine dance floor. The floor was polished for the event by having a horse drag a bale of hay over it.

In 1946 the old mill again became an industrial plant, which is now sending over 10,000 tons of dark and light red kidney beans to customers all over the United States plus Puerto Rico, South America, Canada, England, Switzerland, Germany and Sweden. Fifteen seasonal employees are at work in the facility, which covers nearly an entire block in the center of Linden.

eastern edge of town in 1928 on land donated by the Stockton Terminal and Eastern Railroad. Here walnuts from surrounding orchards are still sorted, bleached and cracked and the meats graded and packaged. This important operation was sold in 1953 to Diamond Walnut Growers Association, which soon relocated its headquarters from Los Angeles to Stockton. Today, Sun-Diamond, Inc. operates the plant.

Two other local firms serving agriculture are Ramacher Manufacturing and Hul-It, both producing equipment for processing orchard produce. Ramacher, first located in Linden in 1952, initially developed nut harvesting equipment through encouragement from Barney Anderson of Anderson Barngrover fame. Its products presently include three models of sweepers which are used to gather nuts shaken from the trees into "wind rows" so the harvesting equipment can pick up the crop. Development of this equipment has led to five United States patents, all issued from 1953

to 1976. Hul-It manufactures cherry sizing machinery as well as hulling equipment for walnuts and pecans, an automatic dehydrator and graders for peaches, pears and bell peppers. In recent years the walnut hullers have found customers in Australia. As a sideline, a calf roping machine for indoor amusement has been developed.

Hul-It has been a family business since it was first established by William Charles Anderson in 1934. It was purchased by Percy and Bernice Brown in 1947, who sold it to a long-time employee, Ron Kaiser, and his wife, Julia, in 1972. At present, there are thirteen full time employees.

While there is some well established industry in Linden, the town is still unincorporated. Efforts to organize a local government can be traced back to 1893, when a successful election for incorporation was overturned by the failure of the county board of supervisors to file proper documents in Sacramento. The controversy reached the state supreme court. Revival of such efforts has oc-

LINDEN ELEMENTARY SCHOOL, c. 1901

Shown shortly after completion, this building, as large and imposing as it appeared, had only two classrooms, both on the ground floor. The upper story was devoted to an auditorium. In 1910, the bell, it is remembered, rang a long, merry greeting for the arrival of the first train, the Stockton Terminal and Eastern.

This wooden building remained in use until a three room brick school was completed in 1921. The brick school remains standing today and is one of the most attractive structures on the main highway through town.

Upon completion of the new elementary school, the newly organized high school district obtained the old wooden building for its use. It was furnished with desks and other items made at San Quentin Prison and shipped via riverboat and trucked from Stockton. The school was finally dismantled after replacement by extensive new construction.

HOLY CROSS CATHOLIC CHURCH, c. 1900

Until this thirty by fifty foot sanctuary was constructed in 1882, those of the Catholic faith had to travel to services in Stockton or Lockeford. It served until 1953, when it was replaced by a new building. The old church was moved during preparations for the new building and has been turned to the west from its original position facing south. It has served as a classroom and social hall and is one of the oldest buildings in Linden.

A favorite story about this sanctuary was how a "hell fire and brimstone" sermon delivered by a visiting missionary seemed to affect the front door, which would not open until a youngster climbed out a window and opened it from the outside.

curred several times over the years without success, the last being in 1972. Interest for incorporation was generated from time to time because of the impetus this would give businesses wishing to relocate here. Increased activity for the business district has been a concern. At one time, there were four hardware and building supply firms. All but one are gone now due to competition from shopping centers in Stockton and Modesto. There is no question, however, that the town still retains its role as a regional supply center. The usually quiet commercial district was enlivened in the late 1970s when Randy Sparks of New Christy Minstrels fame operated a very popular tavern known as the "Lloyds of Linden." His new group, the internationally known Back Porch Majority, rehearsed and performed here when not on tour, attracting huge crowds.

A real highlight of recent years was the town's 1963 centennial celebration, with 140 sponsors. The biggest crowd ever was attracted; over 7,000 joined residents in the event. A lasting benefit of the 100th anniversary was the centennial edition of the *Linden Herald* newspaper, which comprised the first substantial history of the town. This work was enlarged and republished in hard cover form by the Linden Scio Odd Fellows Lodge in 1976 under the appropriate title of *From Stage Stop to Friendly Community*.

FOURTH OF JULY ON MAIN STREET, c. 1900

At the far left is a structure that was actually out in the middle of the street, the Linden Water Works tankhouse. Behind it is one of the most prominent buildings of the business district, the Masonic/Odd Fellows Hall, which had a grocery and post office on the ground floor. The long, single story brick building to the right was known for years as the Guernsey General Merchandise store. The last building at right is the Linden Hotel, expanded to eleven rooms when the old Moore School was attached to the rear.

The property on the other side of the street was owned by the Santos family, operators of a large dairy farm in the San Joaquin Delta. At the time of this photo, the only building on that side of the street was a house. It was not until the 1930s that the Santos family developed this land and made it part of the business district.

To the right is a 1982 photo taken from the approximate spot selected by the earlier photographer. All of the early buildings have been torn down or burned. The most prominent building in this view, originally built in 1940 as the Toggery shoe and clothing store and apartments, is now Linden Publications. Here the *Linden Herald* and other newspapers are printed, including the *Lockeford-Clements News,* California Odd Fellow, Rebekah and International Rebekah news. The *Herald*, published continuously since 1959, succeeded the *Linden Diamond* (1953–58), a paper first published by the Reverend Richard Walsh. A predecessor of the Diamond, the *Linden Light*, first appearing in 1918, was established by another community religious leader, W. F. Coffin.

STOCKTON TERMINAL AND EASTERN RAILROAD EQUIPMENT

Below is the Stockton Terminal and Eastern Locomotive #1 as currently displayed in Travel Town, Griffith Park, Hollywood, California. At the top of the facing page is a Hall-Scott gasoline motor coach, c. 1915. Particularly noteworthy among the rolling stock of the ST&E was this 1912 self-propelled coach which was the only new piece of equipment owned by the company. This is a still from a c. 1915 real estate promotion film.

The remarkable career of Locomotive #1, a thirty-one ton, Morris-Lancaster built 4-4-0, started in 1864 when she was Central Pacific Railroad's "Klamath" and ended ninety years later. Acquired by the ST&E in 1914, she was the only steam power on the line until replaced by a 1922 Baldwin in 1953, which the company still owns but no longer operates. When old #1 was retired, she had more years of service than any other ICC inspected locomotive.

Completion of the railroad from Stockton to Linden and Bellota, its near neighbor to the east, was celebrated in 1910. A gold spike ceremony was held near the present bean plant, and a free barbecue and rodeo followed.

In its heyday, the line had nine loading stations between Jack Tone Road and Bellota for use by fruit growers hauling produce to these points by wagon and motor truck. The lug boxes of fruit were usually carried in cattle cars. During the peak season, there would be two trains daily from Linden to canneries in Stockton.

With road improvements and increased use of motor trucks, the line lost lucrative business and had a struggling existence for decades. The first change was discontinuance of passenger service in 1918. In 1956, the ST&E was sold to Dr. Martin M. Hiss, a Los Angeles chiropodist, who came from Los Angeles every Thursday to run the locomotive through Saturday and then return home. He operated it as a full scale model railroad. After two years of being run as a hobby, the line was sold to its present owner, Tom Beard and his father.

To this day, there is no regular schedule. As tracks run through the center of Linden, there are never any trains when school children might be on the streets, and on Sundays, autos are often parked on the tracks by churchgoers who know that if a rare Sunday run is made, the locomotive will blow its whistle in time for them to move their cars.

A 1909 Mitchell Autocar was a familiar sight on the tracks of the ST&E for about ten years. It was among the first "rolling stock" purchased by the company. During construction of the line, it operated on conventional tires, but starting in 1910, it spent the rest of its days on flanged wheels, running as many as six round trips daily. It was known to many as "The Milk Train," for aside from carrying up to seven passengers, it also provided freight service by pulling a trailer that was often loaded with milk cans, bread and baggage. During 1911, it was involved in the first accident on the line, a rail crossing collision with a Central California Traction Company water car. When the ST&E was going into receivership in 1916–17, the Mitchell was the only equipment operating on the line. *(From an original drawing by Stockton Record illustrator Ralph Yardley. Collection of the Haggin Museum, Stockton, gift of the Stockton Record.)*

153

MAIN STREET, c. 1920

The substantial brick building at left, which served for years as the Masonic/IOOF Hall with a grocery and post office on the ground floor, was originally constructed as a warehouse for the Linden Flour Mill, located one block north. Next to it is the weathered gable roof of a long-closed barley mill. The large two-story building in the distance is the Linden Hotel and Bar.

DIAMOND WALNUT GROWERS PLANT, c. 1928

Still standing today amidst a greatly expanded facility, this is the largest building ever constructed in Linden. Dried and hulled walnuts were received here from the growers. Inside, the nuts would be bleached, stamped with the firm's mark and packaged. At the time this photograph was taken, the headquarters of the company were located in Los Angeles. *(Photograph by Ralph O. Yardley from original glass plate)*

A TOWN GATHERING PLACE—THE LINDEN CLUB AT THE LINDEN HOTEL, c. 1935
Behind the bar are Walter Snow and owner George diCarlo. Sitting at the counter are George Drunsfield (a plumber), John Costa (farmer), Bert Smith (butcher) and another Drunsfield (farmer). The woman standing in the center is Pietra diCarlo; she was surprised by the photographer's flash. The cabinet at the right is a juke box. *(Collection of Mrs. George diCarlo)*

FIRE APPARATUS ON REVIEW, FEBRUARY 1962

At this time, the well-equipped department had three pumpers, shown in the main building, plus a civil defense tank truck and the chief's pickup. The intake hose on the White pumper parked on the far right can be plainly seen.

Fire protection was first organized when a hand-pulled chemical cart was purchased and stationed at a blacksmith shop at Bonham and Front streets in 1921. This unit was supplemented by thirty-six soda-acid fire extinguishers on various ranches. The next development came with the organization of the Linden-Peters Fire Protection Association in 1930. Its work was financed by assessments of ten cents an acre plus donations. A Reo truck with a pump and 400 gallon tank was purchased the following year as the first motor driven apparatus. It remained a familiar sight until 1955.

This fire house remained in use until the facility moved to a new building a short distance away in early 1984.

RAMACHER HARVESTER AT WORK IN THE DE BENEDETTI WALNUT ORCHARD, 1977

Machines such as this one are manufactured at the five acre facility of Ramacher Manufacturing, Inc. Both self propelled and tractor attached models of harvesters, like this one, and sweepers are manufactured. The equipment is sent to almond and walnut growers in California, filbert ranches in Oregon and the pecan country of the southeastern United States. Macadamia nut growers in Australia and Hawaii also have purchased this Linden-built equipment. *(Courtesy Ramacher Manufacturing)*

LOCKEFORD AND STAPLES FERRY
RIVER TOWNS OF THE MOKELUMNE

A famous explorer of the American West, John C. Fremont was the first to leave a written record of the picturesque Mokelumne River Valley above which the town of Lockeford is now situated. He recognized it as a good stopping point, and, in view of his extensive travels, his compliments regarding the region have considerable merit. His party of forty camped in the valley northwest of Lockeford on March 25, 1844. No doubt the Miwok Indians, who occupied this region for thousands of years, also found this place desirable, particularly as a place to gather acorns.

There was a six mile wide belt of timber roughly bisected by the Mokelumne River. This remained largely intact until about 1880, but is now cut down except for a few isolated trees that were spared when the land was cleared for agriculture.

The necessity for ferry crossings was to direct some of the earliest activity to this region of San Joaquin County. The second ferry operation in the county commenced here in 1849 just a mile or so northwest of Lockeford. It was originally established by John Laird and later sold to Weston and Staples,* who maintained this ferry on the San Jose-Sutter's Fort Trail. It was soon on the route of J. Smith's stage between Stockton and Sacramento. During 1850, this ferry was replaced by a wooden bridge, the first across the Mokelumne. Dedication ceremonies were enlivened by the first traveler across the span, a grizzly bear. Just two years later, flood waters carried away the bridge and the point again became a ferry crossing.

Another less frequently used ferry was operated immediately north of Lockeford when the water was high. When the river became shallow, a ford was maintained there. This crossing, safe from

*It is interesting to note that David J. Staples later became prominent in San Francisco; in 1867 he became president of the Fireman's Fund Insurance Company, a famous firm, and served in this position for thirty-two years.

quicksand, was known as Locke's Ford, and its name was eventually applied to the community.

The very first settlers came in 1849. David Staples was among them and was owner of 1,000 acres, formerly part of the Andres Pico Grant. About one-third of this property, including the Mokelumne River bottom land, was sold in 1851 to Dr. Dean Jewett Locke. Locke's brother, Elmer, first located here and invited his brother, who had been mining at Mokelumne Hill, to join him along with a colony of people from Mississippi Bar. Dr. Locke's original purchase of 360 acres was made at a cost of one dollar per acre. Unfortunately, the seller's claim was based upon a Mexican grant that was later proven invalid, and Locke had to repurchase the land from the United States government at $1.25 per acre. Some of this land was hilly and particularly desirable, as it offered refuge during periodic, extensive flooding that covered much of the valley.

The Lockes first settled on what is now known as Pioneer Hill and built a log cabin beneath three huge oak trees; this was the beginning of the first town in northeastern San Joaquin County. Lockeford has always been an agriculturally orientated community. The first crops were vegetables grown where oak trees had been cleared to provide space for patches of cucumbers, corn, tomatoes, onions, squash and melons. During the gold rush, this produce, including watermelons, was sold from an iron wheeled cart. The founder of Lockeford, Dr. Dean Jewett Locke, was the traveling merchant. He also conducted a medical practice along with the produce sales.

Cattle and dairy operations were soon started but were dealt a severe blow by the drought of 1863-64, from which the area never completely recovered. After the drought, wheat raising was encouraged by Central Pacific Railroad connections just ten miles away. Initially, the early grain farmers were raising as much as twenty bushels to the acre. The product gradually declined, and by the late 1880s, the local boom in wheat production was over. Now what grain is produced is largely barley and oats. Other crops became increasingly important after 1900. As far as acreage and value are concerned, vineyards were prominent and profitable until the problems of statewide overproduction and imports.

Recent agricultural trends have been turned toward development of permanent irrigated pastures of Ladino clover, alfalfa and rye grass. Climate and soil conditions have encouraged the Soil Conservation Service, a federal agency, to plant experimental ground cover on 106 acres here, starting in 1971. Plants passing their tests are eventually certified and their seed distributed through the California Crop Improvement As-

FOUNDER, DR. DEAN JEWETT LOCKE, 1823–1887
This remarkable man was born in Langdon, New Hampshire, and received his medical degree at Harvard. He came to California as a wagon train physician in 1849. Like the founder of Stockton, Captain Charles M. Weber, Locke gave generously of his own assets for the betterment of the town. Lots were given for the school and several churches, funds were donated for school construction, levee work, street improvement, etc. He even planted the numerous eucalyptus trees with his own hands.

Aside from his constant effort in the development of the community, he was also a merchant, postmaster, rancher, physician and member of the school board almost steadily from 1854 to 1887.

Today his town is a registered California State Historic Landmark; in the early 1970s, he was further honored by having a building named for him at San Joaquin Delta College.

By 1915, the fabulous river bottom lands were devoted largely to raising cattle and hogs as well as fruit trees of a wide variety, including oranges. At this time, the growth and future of the Mokelumne River Valley depended upon a collective effort for flood control. Considerable progress had been made since 1905 through the formation of an organization to direct the straightening of the river and improvement of the levee.

By the early 1920s, there were several successful dairy farms. One drawing an unusual amount of attention for its Jersey cows was owned by Nathaniel Howard Locke, a leading California stockman. His Jerseys won a prize at the Alaska-Yukon-Pacific Exposition in Seattle during 1909. He also exported dairy stock to Hawaii, Mexico and to many parts of the western United States.

sociation. The results are erosion control on farms, forest fire sites, roadwork, etc.

The agriculture of the area is regularly hampered by lack of water. The river flow is controlled by the East Bay Municipal Utility District, which has vast rights to the waters of the Mokelumne for the Oakland-Berkeley-Richmond region of the San Francisco Bay area. This has been a particular concern since Pardee Dam was completed in 1929.

With the establishment of agriculture and the position of the settlement on a major route to the mines, it was practical to establish a commercial center. The first store building was known as the White House. It was founded by Luther Locke in the summer of 1856 and also served as the post office. With the arrival of a large shipment of dry goods in early 1862, the structure was moved from

LOCKE HOME AND FAMILY

The Locke home was on Elliott Road, immediately north of the business district. Dr. and Mrs. Locke are shown in this daguerreotype, c. 1875, with nine of their children. The photo to the right shows a 1982 view.

The twenty-two rooms of this residence were put to good service. Dr. and Mrs. Locke raised thirteen children here. Of these, eleven went to college; two graduated from MIT and a third received a degree in medicine from Harvard.

The home was built of locally made brick in 1865. The brick tower at the rear, added in 1880, contains a tank and once served the entire community. For decades, this home, one of the largest in the area, was the center of Lockeford social life. It has remained in the Locke family to this day. The last surviving daughter of Dr. and Mrs. Locke, Mrs. Theresa Thorp, resided here until her death in 1969 at age eighty-nine.

In 1972 the house and adjacent granary were the first structures in San Joaquin County to be listed on the National Register.

the Locke Ranch to what is now the corner of Main and Locust streets. By this time there were two hotels nearby—the Megerle House and the Locke Hotel.

These early developments prompted Dr. D. J. Locke to formally establish a town, which was done by surveying and platting a townsite in June of 1862. In this year, two blacksmiths and a wagon shop were also opened. The greatest disaster in Lockeford was an incendiary fire started by a drunken farm hand who had been denied whiskey in Caldwell and Starkey's saloon. The fire he started in a stack of straw spread to a livery stable, the saloon and the extensive Steacy Carriage Works and paint shops. At one point, it looked as if the entire town would be consumed, but the bucket brigade was effective. A hotel continued to operate until well into the twentieth century.

Three newspapers have served the area since the turn of the century. The first two, the *Lockeford Eagle* (1898) and the *Reporter* (1914) were very short-lived. The present newspaper, the *Lockeford-Clements News*, has been published weekly since 1949.

The wagon road was not the only advantage the town had as a trading center. The founder of the

FLAG RAISING AT THE HARMONY GROVE CHURCH, 1982

Left to right are James H. Hammond, Shannon Dalley (age sixteen) and Jason Farris (age nine). During this event the building was dedicated as a point of historic interest by the Native Daughters of the Golden West.

The greatest local effort in preserving an historic structure in San Joaquin County centered around this Methodist Church from 1966 to 1973. Built on part of the Staples Ferry townsite between 1859 and 1863, it originally had a flat roof and Greek Revival style. The brick pediment and Gothic appearance were added in 1868. With completion of the new Methodist Church in nearby Lockeford fifteen years later, most of the congregation was drawn away. A small group continued meeting here until 1918. The building then passed into obscurity as a warehouse for nearly half a century until sold by the Methodist Conference in San Francisco.

A Lodi developer, Lloyd Dawson, purchased the building and surrounding acreage in 1965 and planned to clear the site and build homes. When demolition started on the church, a local outcry immediately began that

resulted in the developer's giving the building and nearly an acre of land to the county board of supervisors. Prime mover in the restoration was the Lockeford-Clements Women's Club, which made it a major project. The club's efforts plus numerous donations from private sources made it possible to add a substantial local contribution to county funds. Restoration work was extensive, involving considerable restructuring, masonry and foundation work. The time capsule sealed in the cornerstone in 1859 was removed during the work. It yielded coins, a roster of church members and officers, three religious books and newspapers from Boston, Stockton and Sacramento. These items are now in the care of the county museum.

The name Harmony Grove was inspired by New Harmony, Indiana, from which one of the original church members, Edward Tretheway, came. The oak grove on the ten acres donated by David Staples gave inspiration for the remainder of the name. The church, cemetery and a rectory, long ago destroyed by fire, occupied part of this land.

The church was originally intended to serve as a community house of worship, but it soon became apparent it would be Methodist, resulting in a division among the people and construction of Grace Church in Lockeford.

Today, interdenominational services are occasionally held in fulfillment of the wishes of long-ago early residents. The building may be rented for day use through the county parks and recreation department, not only for services but for club meetings and other activities. *(Collection of the San Joaquin County Historical Museum)*

OLD TOWN HALL, GRANARY AND ARMORY, 1982

This is one of the most remarkable early buildings in the county. Attached to the rear of this 1862 brick addition is a rammed earth granary erected in 1858. The granary was designed with a second floor that was used extensively as a meeting hall. Several organizations were founded there, including the Lockeford Good Templar Society, the Congregational Church, Ladies Home Library Association, the Dashaways and Sons of Temperance.

There was strong Union sentiment in Lockeford during the Civil War. During one rally, Jeff Davis was burned in effigy. There was some concern about Confederate sympathizers who congregated in nearby Clements. As the building was situated on a bluff above the Mokelumne, it was considered a good idea to fortify it by cutting loopholes in the adobe walls for rifles, should there be trouble (see picture to the right). Early in the war, the Mokelumne Light Dragons were organized and met here for drills. They were sanctioned by the State of California and received swords and pistols from Sacramento. They were never called to military duty and their services were confined to participation in parades and escorting children to the picnic grounds on holidays. The organization disbanded in 1867 and the state property returned to Sacramento. Since this time, the wooden staircase to the main entrance on the second floor has been removed.

While the brick addition has been recently restored, the historically and architecturally important granary suffered major structural failure and has fallen into ruin over the last decade.

community looked upon the Mokelumne River as a resource for additional growth. In 1862, he made plans to establish Lockeford as the head of navigation on the Mokelumne. Woodbridge, a few miles to the west, had already assumed this position, and Locke's plan met with considerable opposition. Despite this, the steamer *Pert*, which had been purchased by Locke, reached his landing in 1862. It operated successfully along with another river boat, the *O.K.* The service was maintained by the Mokelumne River Steam Navigation Company for fifteen years. Even though considerable improvement of the waterway was undertaken by the removal of snags and sandbars, service was eventually abandoned as freight to the Mother Lode declined and increased silt and debris in the river were a constant problem.

Rail connections were established in 1882, when the town became a major stop on the San Joaquin and Sierra Nevada Railroad, which connected Brack's Landing in the Delta with Valley Springs. Construction was encouraged through the sale of stock. Those wishing to exchange labor for shares in the company did so by grading the right of way through their land. Dr. D. J. Locke supported the project by donating a depot site and financing the purchase of railroad cars. While the line provided a useful service, it did not make a profit, and soon a controlling interest was bought by Southern Pacific for twenty-five cents on the dollar. Freight and passenger service continued; in 1915 four trains ran daily. Special excursions were planned for the popular Lockeford picnic, attended by many in the Lodi-Stockton area. Railroad passen-

THE ONLY STORE IN TOWN, 1862–1870
Originally established by Luther Locke and his father, the Locke store at Elliott Road and Main Street (Highway 88) remained the post office from its beginnings, with just brief interruptions, to 1919. Dr. D. J. Locke is at the far left in this daguerreotype. In 1870, this dry goods business was supplemented by two other stores. The building shown here burned in 1882 and the Lockes replaced it with another wooden store building.

ger service was supplemented by two auto stages operating over a newly paved road to Stockton. The tracks, though little used, are still in place today.

Brick making, the first extensive industrial enterprise, was started in 1855 by Dr. Locke. There were eventually six kilns by five clay pits around town. A Chinese contractor and crew were hired to quarry the clay, make the bricks and fire them. Locke felt that providing a ready source of brick would encourage construction of substantial buildings within his town, several of which are still standing along the main street. The largest, dating from 1883, was known as Locke's Store and in later years was Goehring Hardware. For twenty years, the top floor was a roller skating rink, and at one time water tanks, part of the domestic system, were mounted on the northeast corner of this building.

Wagon manufacture became important, and by 1881, three such businesses were in operation: Tretheway & Daly, James P. Grant and the largest, employing nine, Benjamin Steacy.

The Lockeford Creamery, founded in 1898 as another Locke family enterprise, was supervised by Howard Locke. It served and encouraged dairy operations in the region. A year later, it was producing 300 pounds of butter per day. Early in the twentieth century, business declined through competition from similar operations in Stockton and Lodi with established markets for bottled milk. The creamery closed and soon was transformed into a winery.

Situation of the town on a major route to the resorts, reservoirs and lakes of the Sierra has benefitted local businesses. With the completion of a shopping center, the opening of antique shops and other commercial developments, business volume increased considerably between 1970 and 1975, 25 percent in one year alone. At this time, a consolidation of local utility services has taken place that is expected to be a key to larger state and federal grants.

Recently about 60 percent of the work force has been employed in Stockton and Lodi with the remainder employed on local farms, ranches and businesses. Industrial firms that have become important in recent years are Andersen Steel Buildings, Elkins Equestrian Facilities, Inc. and Sumiden Wire Products.

Andersen Steel Buildings was originally established in Lodi by Bob Andersen and moved to Lockeford in 1976. It produces all-steel buildings for agricultural, industrial and commercial as well as institutional use. Buildings with clear spans up to 200 feet have been shipped all over the western United States and to Alaska and Hawaii. Orders have been received from Japan, Australia, Argentina, Israel, Saudi Arabia and other foreign countries. The plant consists of 140,000 square feet of buildings on twenty-four acres. When it is operating at capacity, 170 people are employed.

SURVEYING INSTRUMENT, 1862

Known as a surveyor's compass, this instrument was purchased by Dr. D. J. Locke in San Francisco and used in various surveying projects around Lockeford, including laying out present Waterloo Road (Highway 88). It was mounted on a stout wooden tripod when in use. The vertical parts at the edges are sighting vanes.

Such an instrument is rare, as it has long since been replaced by the transit. Such compasses represent the type of instrument available for surveying in George Washington's time.

The instrument and tripod were donated to the Haggin Museum in Stockton by Niel Locke.

THE LOCKEFORD SCHOOL, 1879

Thompson and West included the above monochrome lithograph in their *History of San Joaquin County*. Of particular interest is the little octagon building at the far right. Known as "The Octagon School," it was erected in 1856 to replace "The Rag School House," a tent supported by willow poles located near the river. The octagon was largely financed by Dr. D. J. Locke, who was always ready to try something innovative for the benefit of the community. He was an experienced teacher, having taught before studying medicine, and encouraged the founding of the first school.

The building was later moved to the present grounds of the Lockeford Elementary School and was replaced in 1874 by a much larger building (shown at left), which still stands among other, much more modern structures.

SAINT JOACHIM CHURCH AND IOOF TEMPLE, 1982

Located on Highway 88, these buildings are just two of the remarkable number of early buildings in the town. Saint Joachim's is one of the oldest non-residential structures in the county. Originally a store on the Locke Ranch in the 1850s, it later became a sanctuary. The United Brethren Church of Christ moved the building to its present site in 1872 and undertook extensive remodeling. The Catholic Church bought the building in 1876. It has been in continuous use since this time except for a few months in 1981, after the venerable structure had been buffeted by severe winds and county inspectors declared it unsafe. The sum of $27,000 was spent on its restoration, which included a new foundation and additional framing. Restrooms were added, finally eliminating the necessity of using facilities at the neighboring service station.

In the distance is the IOOF Hall, occupied by the first of the town's fraternal organizations, Progressive Lodge No. 134, established in 1867. It has been meeting in the building since 1879. In the late nineteenth century, most of the structure was used by Steacy's Wagon and Carriage Shop.

LUTHER LOCKE BUTCHER SHOP, 1981

One of the most outstanding late nineteenth century commercial buildings anywhere in the Valley reached the "century mark" in 1983. Designed in Queen Anne style by noted Stockton architect Charles Beasley, it looks much the same as it did when completed. Only the flag pole on the cupola and a balustraded canopy over the ground floor windows have been removed. It is listed on the National Register for its architectural importance.

This business was established after Luther J. Locke III had been engaged as a partner in the family's far-flung cattle business that centered upon large acreage in Nevada from which cattle were driven overland to various parts of California. Luther operated the market on the ground floor and shipped supplies of beef and mutton from the Locke ranches to the Mother Lode. Luther's wife, Alice, operated a dressmaking shop here. The family home was upstairs.

Slaughtering for this market was done in a separate building located on the bluffs overlooking the Mokelumne River. The six foot diameter wooden wheel (see the 1977 photo below) was used as a windlass to hoist the carcasses for butchering.

SOME LOCKEFORD FIRMS OF 1884–85

This is a page reproduced from L. M. McKenney & Company's directory for San Joaquin County. The cut illustrating the hotel is identical to that used for other hotels in various parts of the county. The brick building shown is much too metropolitan for Lockeford, which never had any three-story commercial structures. (Courtesy Stockton Central Library)

THE POST OFFICE IN AMBROSE'S GENERAL MERCHANDISE, 1915
Lockeford has maintained a post office since 1861; in earlier days, it was always in one of the general stores. Shown in the post office cubicle are W. B. Ambrose and Bernice Weber. *(Collection of the San Joaquin County Historical Museum)*

BASEBALL TEAM ENROUTE TO A GAME IN LOCKEFORD
This baseball team from Stockton was on its way to a game in Lockeford in about 1900, in "uniforms" that were not very uniform. *(Collection of the Haggin Museum, Stockton)*

THE SNOW OF JANUARY 1, 1916

Snowfall in the Valley is a rare sight, and that of 1916 not only blanketed Lockeford but also Stockton and other surrounding communities. Another spectacular snowfall occurred when about a foot fell on the area December 3, 1893. Above, ancient oaks on Elliott Road just north of the Locke home display their frosty patterns.

Below, a rather chilled-looking delivery truck driver awaits the arrival of the Southern Pacific passenger train, one of two that passed through the town daily at this time. The station, originally constructed in the early 1880s for the San Joaquin-Sierra Nevada Railroad, remained standing at the Tully Road crossing until the early 1970s.

(Collection of the San Joaquin County Historical Museum)

166

Elkins builds steel and wooden buildings to customer specifications, specializing in horse facilities, the largest being covered riding arenas with 250-foot clear span. Elkins, started at Lockeford in 1971, now has offices in Southern California at Ontario and in the Santa Ynez Valley. As many as thirty have been employed, and nearly all the buildings have been made for use throughout California.

Sumiden is a Maryland-based firm with plants in Australia and Mexico. It moved its West Coast manufacturing and warehousing operations from Escondido, California, to Lockeford in 1975. The local manufacturing and marketing operation deals with a variety of industries, particularly those that handle food on conveyor belts. Most of the food processors in Central California use woven wire and plastic belting produced by this firm. These include, for example, H. J. Heinz, Del Monte and Tri Valley Growers in this region, as well as more distant operations such as California Canners and Growers in San Jose. Other customers are the Owens-Illinois glass plant near Tracy and the White Sands Missile Range in New Mexico. Sixteen to twenty people are employed in the plant and three in the office.

The history of Lockeford has been rich and varied, and the above firms are certainly broadening its horizons.

SULKY RACING ON THE LOCKEFORD TRACK, c. 1900

Taken during one of the popular Lockeford picnics, this photograph shows a race nearing an exciting end. Sulky racing, also known as harness racing, was the most common form of horse racing in this region during the nineteenth and early twentieth centuries. The track was located near the southwest portion of town and has long ago gone back to pasture.

So popular were the Lockeford picnics, there were special railroad excursion trains from Stockton and Lodi to carry the crowds. A raffle was part of the events and one year, the grand prize was a surrey with a fringe on top. This surrey is now on view at the San Joaquin County Historical Museum. *(Collection of the San Joaquin County Historical Museum)*

THE "LANDMARK" GASOLINE PUMPS
OF HIGHWAY 12/88, 1972

These early gravity feed pumps have been alongside the highway through town so long they are now in the right of way. They were originally installed about 1920 by Lloyd Russell, Lockeford area native, who also financed construction of the large garage building adjacent to the nine and a half foot high pumps and old-style "oil island." Russell is well remembered as a "good, old-style mechanic." He and his wife, Naomi, lived upstairs.

After Russell operated the business for years, it was sold to Alfred E. James, originally from Baton Rouge, Louisiana, where he was a glass blower. He operated these pumps into the 1950s. In his later years, pumping more than five gallons into the glass bowl by hand became quite an effort so if more than this was needed, he would see to this after giving his arm a rest while the first five gallons drained into the tank.

About a block east on the main street is a corrugated iron building that housed another well-known garage. It was operated by Fred Figge and his partner, remembered only as Votaw, and was known as the Central Garage. (*Photograph by Raymond W. Hillman*)

U.S. GASOHOL PLANT, LOCKE ROAD

An old winery was renovated with considerable specialized equipment to produce an up-to-the-moment product, gasohol. Activities in this 1946 winery complex, which was originally the Lockeford Winery, then a co-op and later Lodi Vintners, produced alcohol from cull fruit, corn, grain and molasses. The alcohol was added to gasoline to become gasohol. Operations started in April 1981 and about 60,000 gallons were produced before the plant closed five months later. The plant was not large enough and there was too much fruit handling expense to make the operation cost effective.

SAN JOAQUIN CITY
INDIAN VILLAGE, GHOST TOWN

Long before the beginning of pioneer settlement, Yokuts Indians recognized this site as a good place to settle. The high ground here was vital when the San Joaquin was at flood stage. When pioneer settlers came here in the late 1840s, there was evidence of Indian presence including arrowheads, other stone artifacts and human skeletons which had been exposed during earth moving or erosion. The first Caucasian settler on what became known as the West Side was Captain Charles M. Imus, who arrived in the fall of 1846 and built a cabin of pine logs cut at the mouth of Corral Hollow Canyon. This temporary dwelling, erected on land that was to become part of San Joaquin City, was to serve until a pre-fabricated wood frame house arrived from Boston. It was erected by Mexican vaqueros and when painted white was named La Casa Blanca. Imus' first enterprise was to capture and sell wild horses.

A town was to grow because this was the intersection of two principal wagon and stage roads, and it was here that a ferry was established in 1850. Those crossing the San Joaquin River continued on to mining districts in the Sierra. Because of this role, the village, for a short time, offered significant competition to Stockton as a gold rush transportation center. The steamer *Mint* was a familiar sight at this time.

Titus and Manley established the ferry, which later became well known as Durham Ferry. There was plenty of travel, especially in the winter, as this route followed high ground. The ferry operators were genuine entrepreneurs. A tiny hostelry was part of their living quarters. They sold from a small stock of groceries and liquor and even had second hand mining tools, received in trade from luckless miners returning to San Francisco. These would be re-sold to hopefuls traveling in the opposite direction. The ferry remained in operation until replaced by a bridge in 1902.

San Joaquin City took the semblance of a town by 1850 when six wooden houses and several tents stood there. Initial growth soon ceased, when Stockton became firmly established as a transportation center. Further development was to come with purchase of the townsite by Larry B. Holt from John McMullins, starting in 1861. The following year, nine streets, eighty feet wide, were surveyed, creating a dozen city blocks. Development reached its height in the late 1860s and early 1870s. There were about twelve saloons, half as many stores, a stage station, three hotels, a laundry, livery stable, blacksmith, bakery and barber. It is well remembered that the livery stable kept many beautiful rigs owned by local German families.

When the settlement became a river landing, a row of oak trees along Durham's Levee served as moorings. The first river boats and barges came for grain and cord wood.

The nineteenth century role of San Joaquin City was well summarized by *San Joaquin Historian* magazine: "The development of large-scale grain farming all along the West Side Plains from Tracy to Patterson made San Joaquin City an important inland shipping point for the area's farmers." At this time, river travel had been encouraged by a government project involving the side wheel, coal burning snag boat *Marion*. With its work completed, regular and extensive travel commenced, not only on this portion of the San Joaquin River but on the Tuolumne and Stanislaus as well. In 1878 alone, 120,000 tons of grain were shipped from the area; the largest of the steamers carrying this cargo was the 155-foot long sternwheeler *Centennial*.

The decline of San Joaquin City extended from 1887 to 1911. While long in service, the ferry crossing did not maintain importance after the gold rush. In 1887, with construction of the Southern Pacific line down the West Side of the San Joaquin Valley to Fresno, the River Road running through the town was no longer the central transportation artery. During the following year, the post office was moved to Vernalis, a new town created by the railroad.

Steamboat traffic became sporadic as a result of changes in the river course and shallow water, which was due to increased diversion for irrigation. The greatest blow was in 1911, when the main channel of the San Joaquin moved a considerable distance east from the town, isolating it from what little river traffic remained. Shortly after this, the town was largely depopulated and buildings that were not torn down deteriorated. Today none of the original buildings remains, and the site, at the intersection of Kasson Road and Durham Ferry Road, is marked by a monument. Since 1962, it has been a registered State Historical Landmark, one of twenty-two presently in the county.

DREYER SALOON AND HOTEL, c. 1900
This establishment, owned by Charlie Dreyer, was the last to operate in San Joaquin City. Dreyer also maintained a boarding house at the San Joaquin River levee for the crews loading steamboats and barges. The vacant shell of the building shown above marked the site of the old business district for years until it was torn down in about 1920.

THE SAN JOAQUIN RIVER CLUB
RENEWED ACTIVITY ON AN OLD SITE

Barely a stone's throw from the site of old San Joaquin City is a much newer settlement, the San Joaquin River Club, originally planned as an outdoor recreational club. The present site was selected in 1938, after a two year search from Santa Cruz to Humboldt counties. The land was once the John Ohm Ranch and the principal building was the old ranch house, still standing. In the early days, the ranch well was the only source of water.

The 450 acre site was particularly desirable because it had three miles of winding frontage on the San Joaquin River. This section of the river was well-known among sport fishermen long before the San Joaquin River Club was established. The river remained a "hot shot" salmon stream into the 1940s.

The settlement has been described as a "do it yourself recreational subdivision." It is operated as a non-profit corporation, and its articles of incorporation were filed with the secretary of state in 1939. In several ways, it is like a small town. It has a one-man, one patrol car police force and there was a volunteer fire department for a time. Its government is by a nine-member board of directors. The first directors were Edwin F. Hillendahl and Gertrude E. Hillendahl of Oakland, Murray and Mary Lundy of Berkeley and N. J. Osborne.

The club is a membership organization and the cost of membership has varied, depending upon the location of the property to be leased. The most expensive land fronts either Keystone, Rainbow or Crescent lakes, which cover nearly forty-five acres in all. Each member receives 5,000 square feet of land plus utilities. Aside from construction of a permanent residence, members are required to plant at least two trees. It is here that one might obtain a hint of the tremendous amount of volunteer help and donations that have made the club what it is today.

One member, Mrs. Jerry C. Lewis, donated truckloads of trees and shrubs from her home in Oakland, where they were grown as a hobby. A hundred shade trees were also donated nearly forty years ago from the nursery of Floyd and Dorothy Hughes. Typical of the spirit of development, a volunteer crew dug pits for 1,000 trees and laid pipe lines from fourteen well heads. Some materials and services could not be donated, and various fund raising events provided funds to finance such projects.

Not all went smoothly for the club. The biggest threat was floods, three in six years. The worst were caused by levee breaks in 1950 and 1955 that resulted in the evacuation of some members.

With the decline of the San Joaquin River as an anglers' paradise, the members became more inclined to sail and fish in the stocked lakes. The fishermen's shacks built for weekend use in the formative days were gradually replaced with permanent homes.

By 1964 the club's statement of purposes as a non-profit organization had to be changed. Originally concerned with the conservation of fish and game, waterways and natural resources, as well as with the enforcement and clarification of fish and game laws, the members of the club had to draft a new statement of purposes. The basic purposes were to become the erection of homes as rural residences and the maintenance of levees, utilities and other improvements. Membership was to grow rapidly from the original thirty-seven in 1939. The mortgage on the land was burned by the club in 1941, so successful was the response to membership. By 1958 there were 555. By 1979 there were 820 permanent and part time residents in 323 homes. The goal to have a maximum of 1,000 memberships is hampered, at the present time, by poor drinking water, but there is such vitality about the club that this problem will surely be overcome.

A PARADE OF 259 MAIL BOXES AND THE CLUBHOUSE, 1982

The huge clubhouse has been a community focal point since it first opened with a formal dedication and Halloween costume jamboree in 1949, attended by about 2,000.

There is a large dance floor and lounge as well as outdoor facilities for barbecues, swimming area and a beach. During major events, it is not unusual to have 1,500 in attendance.

Parts of the clubhouse were originally a gymnasium at Camp Shoemaker. After the material was removed from this World War II navy training camp, it was re-erected largely through the efforts of volunteers. *(Photograph by Raymond W. Hillman)*

FISHERMAN'S SHACK ON THE SAN JOAQUIN RIVER, c. 1946

This was a familiar scene during the formative days of the club. The shack on the war surplus float offered just enough space to warm up after a session of fishing. Many prized specimens of salmon were caught in this particular section of the river.

In 1930, a twenty-pound bass was caught. One member caught forty salmon weighing a total of 800 pounds in 1946. An abundance of fish was not uncommon, and as one long-time member stated, "We salted it, canned it, smoked it and just gave it away." While the salmon are gone, there is still some good fishing; a twenty-four pound striped bass was brought in during 1981. *(Collection of Christine Peterman)*

A "CATCH" AT THE SAN JOAQUIN RIVER CLUB, c. 1948

Dick Harris and "Bud" Peterman pose with a huge beaver that was caught on the club grounds. These mammals still abound in the San Joaquin Delta and are particularly destructive. In addition to chewing down trees and docks, they will burrow into levees, creating weak spots that may lead to a break. *(Collection of Christine Peterman)*

THORNTON
NORTHERNMOST TOWN IN THE COUNTY

Two nearly forgotten settlements are parent to this community, Benson's Ferry and Mokelumne City, both established during the gold rush. Floods in the 1860s plagued both towns, and higher ground was sought near the confluence of Dry Creek and the Mokelumne River. The new locale became known as New Hope Landing, but is not to be confused with the short-lived Mormon settlement of the same name at the opposite end of the county near the confluence of the Stanislaus and San Joaquin rivers.

The post office was opened in 1878, but by 1880 it was still a small place. Arthur Thornton built a two-story residence and operated a store, saloon and post office. There were also a hotel, blacksmith, livery stable and a brick works. Aside from water transportation, there was a daily stage (Sundays excepted) operated by Thornton to the railroad station in Lodi. This stage waited for the overland train in Lodi before departing.

With the coming of the Western Pacific Railroad in 1904, there was a new opportunity for Thornton to grow. Arthur Thornton, pioneer of 1855, donated a right of way through his land and worked to obtain the rest of the local right of way for the company. He was rewarded by having the station and large freight depot named after him. Soon the name was applied to the nearby town, and in 1909 the name New Hope became a thing of the past.

The agricultural economy of Thornton centered, at first, upon large ranching operations, one of which was on Thornton's 4,000 acres. Vegetables, barley and, most recently, asparagus were also grown and shipped to market in Stockton.

Encouraged by the growth potential offered by the railroad, a promoter named Patton subdivided considerable land around the town. He put in extensive concrete walks in 1908 and 1909. These saw little service in some sections until houses

were built in the late 1940s.

Development has been slow. Water service was provided by two private systems or various private wells until a public system was installed in 1978. There is no sewer district and street improvements have been limited. The biggest development in recent decades was a large housing unit for farm workers. This project consisted of 105 corrugated metal shacks measuring about ten by fourteen feet, built during President Franklin Roosevelt's administration. There were also thirty wooden "garden homes." This was one of the "Hoovervilles" offering shelter to 600 homeless during the Depression. The Louie Santini Manor now occupies the site, which was cleared of buildings in the early 1950s, after the eighty-one residences in present Mokelumne Manor were built by the San Joaquin County Housing Authority.

While there have been some improvements and expansion, recent decades have not been kind to Thornton. Enrollment in the school declined from 320 in 1965 to 140 in 1978 but increased to 200 by 1985. Many of the commercial buildings still standing in the business district are vacant. Others have been burned down by vandals. Commercial trade has stagnated from lack of demand. There is considerable activity from time to time at two social centers, Mater Ecclesiae Catholic Church and the two community halls owned by Our Lady of Fatima Society. The original hall, built in 1949, has a capacity of 400. About 1979 a facility accommodating 1,500 was completed adjacent to the earlier building. Many important cultural events for Portuguese residents have been held here. One particularly historic function was part of the dedication ceremony for the completion of Interstate 5.

Starting in March 1981 an occurrence considered by some to be a miracle began at Our Lady of Fatima Catholic Church. A sixty pound stone statue of Our Lady of Fatima would apparently

CONTRASTS AT BENSON'S FERRY, 1879 AND 1983

Travelers continuing north from Thornton would soon reach this major crossing of the Mokelumne River. The illustration above is from the 1879 *Illustrated History of San Joaquin County* by Thompson and West and shows, from left to right, the blacksmith shop, Gayetty House Saloon and the home originally built for John A. Benson. The latter was saved from destruction in the great flood of 1862 by being lashed to a tree.

In the photo to the right is the shell of the old Gayetty House Saloon, standing an uneasy vigil upon a crumbling foundation on the Mokelumne River levee. This is the same building appearing next to the blacksmith shop shown above. *(Photograph by Raymond W. Hillman with permission of Supervisor George Barber)*

THE THORNTON HOTEL

Above is the oldest known illustration of the town. It appeared in the 1879 *Illustrated History of San Joaquin County*, published by Thompson & West. Clearly seen to the left of Thornton and Borland's general store is the fifteen room hotel completed in 1876. Over the many decades the hostelry operated, it became known as a place where a penniless transient could obtain a meal and a bed for the night.

In the photo to the right, although the porch has been rebuilt, the old hotel buildinging is still readily identifiable from the above lithograph. When this photograph was taken by Celia Thompson in November 1955, the building had not served as a hotel since the late 1920s. It had long been the home of Arthur Thornton's daughter, Jessie, who did not marry and still lived in town during the early 1960s. She operated the Thornton Tavern in part of the old building; the extensive porch served from time to time as a dance floor. *(Courtesy Lodi Public Library, Celia M. Thompson Collection)*

GENERAL STORE AND POST OFFICE, 1920

Constructed in 1892 at the northwest corner of the intersection of Thornton and Walnut Grove roads with Oak and Sacramento streets, this was one of three general stores in Thornton. Built of brick made on the nearby George L. Barber property, this was the largest and most substantial commercial building in the community. It was the town gathering place for decades, as it not only housed the post office and general store but also a community hall which doubled as a gymnasium for the local basketball team at one time.

At the time this photograph was taken for a *Stockton Record* travel series, the store was operated by James M. Gibson and Ralph W. Driggs. Just below their sign, a billboard-type advertisement has been painted on the brick for a famous Stockton product, Sperry's Flour.

A market remained in business in the venerable structure until the lower floor was damaged by fire in 1978. The building was eventually demolished and the site is now an empty lot.

move closer to the altar by itself and was observed to have what appeared to be real tears. The movements, involving about thirty feet, occurred on the thirteenth of each month until the statue was given a place on the main altar in September 1981. Attendance at the church has tripled, reaching as many as 600 a week. There has been a formal investigation but no explanation for this incident that has brought considerable attention to Thornton.

A cannery has been the only major employer in recent years. Originally established in 1928 by Major W. P. Hammond because the area produced peaches, plums and other produce in abundance, the firm became the Thornton Canning Company under the ownership of Nowell, Clark and Hollenbeck. A tremendous variety of food was processed, including asparagus, onions, tomatoes, potatoes, apples and even Nehi and Hires beverages. This variety made year round operation possible, with 100 full time jobs and 400-500 seasonal positions. The firm was always very generous to the people of Thornton, donating fruit and candy to fill a Christmas stocking for every child in school, providing paint for the community hall and sponsoring Boy Scout Troop 231. From about 1957 to 1985, the cannery was operated by California Canners and Growers (Cal-Can) as one of seven fruit and vegetable processing plants it operates in California. At peak season 600 to 800 people are at work; 200 permanent jobs are provided. The bankrupt plant was purchased by Tri Valley Growers, Inc., the nation's largest canning cooperative.

Interstate 5 holds the key to some significant future industrial and residential growth. Undoubtedly, the proximity of tiny Thornton to this major artery is looked upon as a great new resource by local residents and investors.

ARCHITECT'S RENDERING OF NEW THORNTON PUBLIC LIBRARY, COMPLETED FALL 1985
Occupying a two acre site at the north end of the old business district, this building is a tremendous asset to the 700 Thornton residents plus those in the surrounding area of northern San Joaquin County. It replaced a room in a house rented by the county. The chimney-like structures on the roof are skylights. The column and lattice motif of the exterior is carried into interior design. There is shelving for 10,000 volumes in the adult and children's reading areas plus a community program room for both children's events and the public. Both federal revenue sharing and county funds have met the $365,000 cost of the facility, the most important building constructed on Thornton's main street since the completion of the huge, now demolished, brick general store across the street in 1892. *(Courtesy Stockton-San Joaquin County Library)*

VERNALIS
SOUTHERNMOST TOWN IN THE COUNTY

The name of this hamlet, population 400, is either a combination of the first names of Verna Carpenter and Alice Hamilton, daughters of a local rancher, or simply an application of a Latin word meaning springlike. Nevertheless, it was named by local ranchers who were offered the privilege, as they gave Southern Pacific a right of way through their land. This was part of a new line created to serve the West Side in the late 1880s.

The railroad drew commerce from the Old River Road, the San Joaquin River and the older towns all along its banks. With the creation of Vernalis, the life was drawn away from San Joaquin City, including its importance as a post office. Vernalis was never large. At its height, there were two stores, a lean-to blacksmith's shop, one house and a waiting shelter at the Southern Pacific stop.

Trains would stop at Vernalis through a special arrangement made by a local rancher, J. R. Russell, who also donated part of the right of way. The agreement was that any of the passenger trains linking Central and Southern California could be stopped at Vernalis if there were a need for the service. The train stopped at the tiny waiting station directly across the street from the store constructed by Russell; the site is the northwest corner of Highway 33 and Schaeffer Road. Congenial Tom Murphy operated the business for many years. The second story of the wooden building was a social hall that was the center of activity for the area.

At least once a month, a pot luck and dance were held—waltzes, the two-step, the Schottische and a local preference, the La Mode, were danced here. Square dances were not permitted as they tended to rock the structure. Music was provided by the accordion and piano and two local Hispanic musicians who played the guitar and fiddle. These dances were the only form of local recreation. If there wasn't a dance, nothing was going on. In the spring the togetherness of the tiny community was strengthened by an annual picnic at Gooseberry Flat in Hospital Canyon.

By local option, the town went "dry" long before national prohibition was in effect. In spite of this, a saloon of sorts was operated by Tom Murphy. The impromptu style operation was in a deteriorated house near the store, where Murphy stored ice. Sawdust and something more covered the ice. Mixed in the sawdust and hidden from view were bottles of beer and wine. Customers took the key from a nail in the store, found what they wanted and kept a tally of what they drank on the walls of the house, to calculate later payment to Murphy.

A quarter mile from Murphy's, a similar store with an upstairs dance floor was constructed by Jacob Ohm in 1912, to become a rival general mercantile. By 1915, Vernalis had become a station on the crude oil pipelines constructed from Bakersfield to refineries on the Carquinez Straits. The two separate lines were built by the Associated Oil Company and Standard Oil Company. Two pumping stations to promote flow of the crude by heating with steam were erected here close to the railroad track. There was friendly rivalry between the residents who were "pipeliners" and those who were farmers. This reached its peak during the baseball game on Gooseberry Flat.

The pump stations have long since closed, one of the stores is now long gone, and the little Southern Pacific waiting shelter was moved to the site of San Joaquin City to become a cattle shed.

The only activity of recent years that has brought unusual distinction to the locality took place on a 700 acre site in the southeast corner of the intersection of highways 132 and 33. During World War II, prisoners of war, mainly Italian, were interred here at a facility built for Hammond

Army Hospital of Modesto. Men were sent from the camp to work on local farms, including some with crops of guayule, an alternate source of rubber. After the war, the barracks were again a home for foreign farm workers. These Mexican Nationals, all participants in the United States government sanctioned Bracero Program, comprised the principal source of agricultural labor until 1964. After this time, the barracks and all other facilities were dismantled. Today, there is nothing standing but the wall of the handball court; the remainder of the site is an almond orchard.

Of greater importance was the Vernalis Naval Air Station, established in 1942 and a center of sporadic activity for decades. Activity here was extensive enough for the base to have its own post office, in service from February 1944 to January 1946.

Extensive training with navy fighters took place here, with countless flights from carriers moored at Alameda, California, headquarters for aircraft patrols over the Pacific. Starting in 1953, this obscure site became part of an extensive study of the stratosphere. This project, Operation Sky Hook, was done by the Cambridge Research Center of the United States Air Force. Balloons 300 feet long and 200 feet in diameter were equipped with electronic gear sending signals to ground stations from points in the stratosphere 50,000 to 100,000 feet above the earth's surface. More than twelve of these balloons were launched from Vernalis; some landed as far away as Spain. The base at Gaffery and Koster roads has been abandoned, and the remaining 5,000-foot section of the air strip is used to dry cannery waste for cattle feed.

The largest employer in Vernalis is Trinkle and Boys Agricultural Flying. There are ten employees, including six pilots and an equal number of planes. Founded by Carl Trinkle and George Boys, the firm has been part of Vernalis since 1950 and serves a region extending from Ripon to Tracy and from Mossdale across the county line to Westley. The firm has been particularly innovative to the agricultural flying industry in performing the first alfalfa seeding by air as well as pollination of trees by aerial application. During the mid 1960s, when air pollution controls dictated the change from dry to wet chemicals, Trinkle and Boys did significant work in developing new equipment for the planes.

Just south of the prisoner of war camp site is a firm important to Vernalis, Western Farm Service.

VERNALIS GENERAL STORE AND POST OFFICE, DECEMBER 1983

At present this is the last general store remaining in San Joaquin County with a post office operating in one corner, a once common combination. Inside, the old, varnished oak partition and wicket of the post office blend well with the atmosphere of the store constructed by Jacob Ohm in 1912.

This was once a two-story building; the now dismantled second floor was the regional social center. The Vernalis Social Club held its monthly pot luck dinners and dances there. The lively dancing made big beams tremble in the ceiling of the store.

For thirty-six years, starting in 1920, this business, including the post office, was operated by M. A. Schaeffer, his wife, Abbie, and son, Noel. *(Photograph by Raymond W. Hillman)*

This Walnut Creek based operation established one of its Central Valley Division agencies here about 1968. Agricultural chemicals are supplied to Trinkle and Boys in addition to that provided for ground preparation operations over a wide area of the San Joaquin Valley extending from Gustine and Madera to Lodi. The firm offers commercial service to the area, with six ground applicators and a "Big A" open ground spray truck. The latter covers 400 acres a day. In addition, a nitrogen phosphate liquid fertilizer is manufactured here known as 10-34-0; this clear chemical is marketed in California, Oregon and Washington and is also shipped to pineapple and sugar cane plantations in Hawaii via the Port of Richmond, California. There are eight year round employees plus a seasonal crew.

Today, Vernalis is strung over several square miles of the West Side of the San Joaquin Valley. Though widely separated, each of the above firms helps maintain an identity for this community.

NAVAL AIR STATION, VERNALIS,
MARCH 15, 1943

A United States Navy photographer flying at 7,000 feet recorded these facilities, which are shown from a point looking northeast. A confidential photograph until 1957, this view shows the paved air strip, which was 500 feet wide and 7,000 feet long; the structures included two hangars, ready rooms, headquarters and barracks. In October 1945, famous band leader Louie Armstrong and his orchestra played here.

None of the buildings remains at the base site today, Gaffery and Koster roads. *(Collection of the National Archives, Washington, D.C.)*

THE ORCHARD, 1983

A rest stop and attraction for travelers on Highway 132 near Vernalis features the c. 1890 Southern Pacific station from Newman in Stanislaus County. The venerable structure was purchased from the Southern Pacific Transportation Company for the remarkable figure of $156.00 and moved nearly twenty-five miles to its present location in 1980.

The Orchard, a development of long time area residents Albert and George Bogetti, occupies a site that the family has maintained for the sale of fresh produce since about 1964. While produce is still featured, growth in the late 1970s expanded operations into a restaurant, deli, weekly flea market, large water slide and an eighty-eight space recreational vehicle park. *(Photograph by Raymond W. Hillman)*

VICTOR
SETTLEMENT IN THE VINEYARDS

The planting of vineyards brought the first residents to what was to become Victor. This town was named in 1903 after the son of Albert Morden, a prominent vineyardist who was instrumental in securing a Southern Pacific stop here. Many of the early residents were of German ancestry and, at one time, there were two German churches, the Salem Evangelical and German Congregational.

With the establishment of vast acreage in vineyards, it was not long before the first industry, a winery, was founded by Frank A. West and Sons of Stockton. This soon became a co-op for local farmers and eventually was purchased by Jacob Knoll and named the Victor Winery. The operation, which employed five to nine men, eventually had a 5,000 ton crush and a half million barrel cooperage capacity. August Knoll, wine maker and plant manager, was particularly identified with this operation from 1933 until its closing in 1959. Tokay and Zinfandel as well as Carignone and Burger grapes were purchased to make sweet wines. The ports and sherry were sold under the labels Knoll, Sweet Adeline and Cable Car.

During the Second World War, considerable high proof alcohol was produced for medical use. Most of the old plant buildings still stand near the eastern edge of town, including the large, two-story structure erected about 1947.

Just a short distance west of town are two more wineries that are part of the local story. Particularly attractive are red brick buildings constructed in the early twentieth century for the Roma Winery; by 1935, it was the largest winery plant in the United States. This operation is now closed, but directly across Highway 12, operations still continue at what was originally a co-op founded in 1934 by local people, the East Side Winery.

Fruit packing and shipping have been part of local activity almost since the very beginning. At one time, there were five packing sheds shipping grapes, cherries, plums and pears under the labels Safety First (Peter Heil); King Victor Brand (Jacob Neis and Adolph Bechthold); Old Vine Fruit Company (David Wiegum, John Weiderrich); Northern Fruit Company; Valley Fruit Company (Albert Neis); JK (Jacob Knoll); and Pacific Fruit Exchange. The Knoll operation also shipped potatoes and watermelons.

The most prominent of the shippers and major employers for many years has been Victor Fruit Growers, now part of Tenneco West. Victor Fruit Growers was first established in 1920, with Jacob Neis as its long time president. Soon local Tokay grapes were being shipped to Eastern Canada. Peak of activity was at cherry harvest, when 200 would be employed; the average number of year round employees has been twelve in recent years. In 1978 the operation was purchased by Tenneco and has remained basically the same. As one of the northernmost of the eleven Tenneco plants in California, it is now part of the largest supplier of table grapes in the nation and a major marketer of tree fruit, strawberries and vegetables. Grapes and cherries are also sent to Los Angeles, Chicago and New York City, as well as eastern Canada. Some shipments of grapes are made to London, Hong Kong and Taiwan.

Considerable cherry brining takes place at Victor; this is a process utilizing a sulphur dioxide solution to preserve freshly picked cherries until they can be treated with sugar solutions and colored to become maraschino cherries. Such processing started in the early 1970s and has been expanded by Tenneco, which ships this product in plastic lined wooden bins and fifty-five gallon drums to wholesale customers. Twenty people are employed full time, with 250 at peak season. Many of the employees were born and raised around Victor.

DELIVERING GRAPES FOR PACKING, NORTHERN CALIFORNIA FRUIT COMPANY, c. 1922
The photographer is situated at Bruella Road and Highway 12 looking east across the site where the co-op plant still operates. The trucks are delivering field lugs, the contents of which are cleaned by women and crated again for shipment. During a season, as many as 500 refrigerator cars would be ordered for the eight day shipments east. At the time this photograph was taken, this growers' cooperative was just a year or two old and was shipping Zinfandel, Black Prince, Berger, Tokay, Emperor and Cornichon grapes.
The trucks and their owners are identified from right to left as follows: Emanuel Handel's Selden, H. G. Mettler's Republic, Gottlieb Mettler's Republic, Adam Mettler's Republic, William Pressler's Transport and D. D. Mettler's Federal. *(Courtesy Northern California Fruit Company, Victor)*

THE OLD VICTOR SCHOOL, 1983
Built in 1911 by contractor J. B. Fitzsimmons, this building had two classrooms. One of the classrooms was occupied by all eight grades while the remainder of the building was reaching completion. The building served into recent times until consolidation with the Lodi Unified School District.

It housed a second hand store for several years, then became a school again. Since 1981, the structure has been used by the Victor Learning Center. Directors Frank Wallace and Jon deLongpre have had forty-nine developmentally handicapped adults in attendance from care homes as far away as Manteca. Work is done with student/clients with special behavioral and communication problems. There is an opportunity to learn and play as well as to work in a vegetable garden.

One of the last growers' cooperatives left in the county is the Northern California Fruit Company. Arthur Mettler was a major figure in its operation with other growers in the Mettler and Pressler families. A cold storage plant was built in 1948 that could accommodate 1,900 tons of peaches or 123,000 boxes of grapes. Until 1981 this firm was a major shipper of peaches. It celebrated its sixtieth anniversary in 1982; up to this time the manager and plant superintendent were always one of the thirty-five member-stockholders of the firm.

Goehring Meat, Inc., now a prominent Lodi firm, was first established next to the United Market in the center of Victor. In 1955, five years after it was founded by P. J. Goehring, the operation moved to Lodi. "Victor Brand" is still used on product labels.

Twenty-five acres in the center of Victor were owned by Peter Heil, Jr., in 1906. Some of this land was sold to Lot Lachenmaier, who owned five acres of the townsite and built one of the first stores, in 1910, along with a few houses. This grocery business had an extensive delivery route that kept Lachenmaier's four sons and four wagons busy. In the 1920s, Jacob Knoll subdivided his acreage in the northeast section of town, resulting in the development of a significant portion of the present residential district. Victor was on a Lodi rural postal route until 1922, when it was able to establish its own post office.

Significant work took place at Victor in the development of a sulphur blowing machine for use in controlling mildew in vineyards and orchards. The machine was developed by John F. Schlotthauer and Peter Heil, Jr. Between about 1925 and 1929, Heil built 150 of these machines. One of the earliest was ordered by the deGeorgio farms near Bakersfield. The Heil Manufacturing Company had facilities in Victor and Fresno. During 1929, the business was taken up by Schlotthauer, and about two hundred "Victor Dusters" were made by Schlotthauer and his sons John, Jacob and George during the ensuing twenty years. Many are still in use dusting vineyards. They were made of second hand Model T Fords, Stars, Dodges, Model A's and others that were cut down, shortened and narrowed. This motorized device consisting of a powerful blower replaced machines carried on workers' backs.

In the 1930s, the Gallo Winery bought its first such machine from the Schlotthauers. Hundreds of truck tie-down winches were manufactured and there was also equipment for battery rebuilding and elaborate overhauling of engines.

In the late 1950s, Victor became the location of the Pacific Gas and Electric Service Center for part of Amador county and the northern part of San

A VICTOR-BUILT SULPHUR DUSTING MACHINE, c. 1928
This self propelled unit, known as a "Forduster," with an orchard attachment, was made from a Model T Ford. After the body was stripped down, the frame was narrowed. About 350 of these machines were built between the 1920s and the late 1940s. Some are still operating in vineyards and orchards, controlling mildew through application of sulphur dust. *(Collection of Ted Heil)*

Joaquin County. Three line trucks and three trouble trucks and other vehicles are stationed here. There are twenty staff members, including line crews and construction engineers.

The most prominent retail business building was constructed next to the Goehring plant in about 1949 by Adam Pressler. Grocery and hardware businesses located here; the best known was the United Market, operated by Walter Parkin and his family for many years. They were honest merchants and very popular in the area, taking particular interest in local softball. Tragedy struck in 1973, when Mr. Parkin, his wife, Joanne, and seven others were murdered in the family home as part of a robbery of the market. The act drew national and international attention to Victor. The two men responsible were apprehended and jailed. Local residents chose to remember the Parkinses by building a community memorial park bearing their name on Bruella Road just north of town. It includes a large softball diamond and since 1979 has added measurably to the facilities of the adjacent elementary school.

MAIN BUSINESS CENTER OF VICTOR, 1952
From left to right are the two-story building erected just a few years earlier for the Goerhing Meat Company, the United Market, hardware store and Victor Service Station.

THE VICTOR GARAGE, 1983

This building, above left, was originally constructed for blacksmith Johnathan Schmidt. A great deal of work on Model T Fords also was done here by Schmidt's employee, Frank Yankey. With the purchase of the business by J. F. Schlotthauer in the 1920s, the operation concentrated on automotive repairs and equipment manufacturing. The firm was also a Plymouth and Dodge truck and automobile dealership. Schlotthauer, a trained blacksmith, had three sons who helped him in the business, John, Jacob and George. Automotive work continues to this day, although the business was sold by the last of the Schlotthauers in 1971. The old "visible" pumps in front remained in use until about 1980.

In the photo to the right, John Schlotthauer is holding the hand crank Kellogg telephone that was used in the Victor Garage until about 1932. It was part of the Lodi Rural Telephone system. (*Photographs by Raymond W. Hillman*)

WOODBRIDGE
ORPHAN OF THE RAILROAD

A questionable Mexican land grant, a railroad right of way that moved and a neighboring upstart community have each had a part in molding the history of this tiny town. Half of what is now Elkhorn Township was claimed by Andrés Pico as an 1846 Mexican land grant. Its validity was challenged by the United States Land Commission, and the imperfect title affected development for nearly twenty years.

When the Pico grant was finally declared invalid, uncertainty was to continue with a Central Pacific Railroad claim to alternate sections considered to be part of an agreement with the government for building a rail line. This matter was not cleared until 1876, and settlers were finally able to buy their land from the government at $1.25 an acre.

Permanent settlement of what is now Woodbridge came when Jeremiah H. Woods and Alexander McQueen bought a barley field from the Sargeant brothers, forty acres of which was to become the townsite. They were very serious about developing their property and in 1852 drew attention to the area as Wood's Ford by laying rock on the river bottom to create a ford. Soon they established a ferry across the Mokelumne River at about where the irrigation dam is located. During 1858, the bridge for which the town was named was completed.

Within two years, a wooden hotel was erected to serve teamsters and travelers. The community had potential for further growth through its position on the Mokelumne River, which was navigable to steamboats, and its ready overland access to Sutter Creek, Jackson, Mokelumne Hill and other Mother Lode mining camps requiring great amounts of supplies. Shipment of goods was made through Woodbridge.

The town was particularly busy in 1853, when a flood rendered most roads impassable and the route to the mines via Woodbridge drew attention.

J. H. Woods, the pioneering attorney in San Joaquin County, had boundless enthusiasm and seemed determined to build a community of importance. In his estimation, being the head of navigation on the Mokelumne was not enough; he wished it to become a major settlement and, perhaps, overshadow Stockton. The county government was petitioned to establish a public highway to the state capital via Woodbridge along a route still known as Lower Sacramento Road. Stages were running on the Upper Sacramento Road via Staples Ferry, but this traffic was easily drawn away in 1854 when Woods offered the stage company free crossings of the Mokelumne on his ferry. In addition, he had a scheme to create a new county, Mokelumne County, extending from the Cosumnes River in Sacramento County to a point five miles below Woodbridge. His town was, of course, to be the county seat. The idea met with general disapproval in Sacramento and generated mass protest meetings in Stockton.

Despite Woods' imperfect land title, the settlement was to grow. Businessmen from Sonora, San Andreas and Stockton relocated to Woodbridge, known as Woods' Ferry until 1862. The town grew like a mushroom from 1859 into the 1870s. A flour mill was erected in 1862 by Ranking Brothers. D. L. Green was operating a custom grist mill with three run of stones, possibly Rankins', in 1878. Many wished to reestablish here because of plans by the Western Pacific Railroad (no relation to the present company serving in this region) to build through the town to connect Sacramento and San Jose by rail. The Western Pacific soon failed and was taken over by the Central Pacific. Late in 1867, much to the horror of the builders of Woodbridge, the "Big Four" selected a new right of way about three miles east of Woodbridge, working to the disadvantage of the established

CONTRASTS ON MAIN STREET, c. 1920 AND 1985

Horace Bentley's General Store of 1865, the first brick building constructed in town, stands behind the trees. Bentley first entered business during 1853 and soon was the most prominent merchant. In the late 1870s, his establishment was noted as the largest general store outside of Stockton. The Bentley residence was on the second floor.

In 1973 extensive restoration of this building took place after Wein's Tavern, located here for many years, was closed. It became Woodbridge Feed and Fuel, a popular restaurant.

On the corner, to the right, is the IOOF Hall. On the opposite end of the block, to the left, is a single story commercial building that was constructed by John Rutledge about 1868. Over the years, it has been a meat market, grocery, pool hall and church. It was extensively restored between 1970 and 1973 by Stockton architect and local resident Edward Merlo, and is now an office for a winery.

186

ODD FELLOWS HALL, c. 1920 and 1985

A major building in the historic business center, above left, this was the meeting place for Jefferson Lodge #98, IOOF, that once had a membership of 124. The building is now on the National Register. San Francisco investors financed restoration of the long vacant hall for John Sherman's Bar & Grill, featuring California cuisine (right). Tragedy struck the project in March 1983, when the entire two-story brick facade fell away, killing "Frenchy" Disdier, foreman. Once this project was completed, additional space for the establishment was created by the erection of the adjacent, architecturally compatible structure.

The lower floor of the original building is older than the upper floor, as this was a one-story commercial building in the 1860s. In 1874, the lodge added the second story. The store provided a steady source of revenue for the lodge; this was a common arrangement for most lodges owning their building. The express and post offices and a variety of stores were once located here. For many years, the ground floor housed Levinsky's General Merchandise, a firm starting with stock left by a steamer chartered by D. J. Locke that never completed its voyage to Lockeford.

Note the small enamel sign in front of the right doorway. This is a directional marker for the Lincoln Highway, completed in 1915 as the first coast to coast highway in the nation. About the turn of the century, the store was remodeled for use as a hall for dances and dinners. *(1985 photograph by Raymond W. Hillman)*

town and to the advantage of a new community soon to be known as Lodi. Jeremiah Woods did not live to witness this turn of events; he was killed in 1864 during an argument over the shooting of his hunting hound, and the region lost his leadership.

The new plan put a stop to much of the growth in Woodbridge. Its established importance as a stage stop, ferry crossing and river port long before any development at Lodi did not succeed in ensuring a position on the first transcontinental railroad. Some growth was to continue and rails were finally to reach the town through a line promoted by Woodbridge residents, the San Joaquin-Sierra Nevada Railroad. The line was completed from nearby Brack's Landing to Lockeford in 1882 and to its terminal, Valley Springs, in Calaveras County three years later.

After the disappointment of bypass by the railroad, efforts to develop a community of distinction took another direction with the establishment of Clark and Langdon's Sanitarium and the Woodbridge Academy. Dr. Asa Clark was a well-known physician at the Stockton State Asylum before he resigned to establish his own hospital at Woodbridge for the care of mentally ill sent by authorities in Nevada and Arizona. From 1871 to 1877, Clark operated the hospital in partnership with Dr. S. W. R. Langdon. The institution was successful, but it was decided to move to a newly built facility in Stockton. In 1878 there were three doctors practicing here, Drs. Tatton, Adlam and Dayton.

Just after the hospital closed in Woodbridge, plans were underway to establish a young people's school, the Woodbridge Academy. One hundred fifty investors, many of them local, thought their town had the advantageous environment of a small community at a time when most such institutions were located in large cities with influences that could adversely affect students. The school was built, but its operation did not start until the interest of the United Brethren Church was gained. This group held a statewide convention of their church at Woodbridge in 1879. Four years later, the school was chartered by the state and at this time became San Joaquin Valley College, the finest in a wide area surrounding Stockton.

MASONIC TEMPLE, 1983
Shown here in its 100th year, the Masonic building is particularly outstanding among the early brick structures of the community.
David Gebhard in his *Guide to Architecture in San Francisco and Northern California* (1973) praised it as " . . . one of the most unusual nineteenth century buildings still existing in Northern California . . ." The architectural style of this remarkably tall, narrow temple was described as late Gothic Revival.
Woodbridge Lodge 131 still maintains the building.

The social and cultural influence of the college upon the town was considerable. Over the years, there were many graduates who achieved positions of importance: Avery White, district attorney in Stockton; Edward Thompson, Stockton city attorney; Robert J. Beasley, state assemblyman; Alfred L. Cowell, editor of the *Stockton Mail* newspaper; and Marion de Vries, congressman and U.S. Court of Appeals judge. Enrollment, however, declined and the college closed in 1897.

In 1927 Woods Elementary School, named for the town's founder, was to bring educational distinction to Woodbridge once again. The State Department of Education selected Woodbridge as a state demonstration school. More than 1,500 teachers and supervisors visited Woods Elementary over a three year period to observe classroom procedures.

Local agriculture, as in other regions, was to change with the development of irrigation. In 1886, plans were made to irrigate 100,000 acres, a project organized by Byron Beckwith. A timber dam was built on the Mokelumne to supply forty miles of canals. The work was continued by the Woodbridge Canal and Irrigation Company, which completed a major phase of the project in 1891. A huge celebration attended by 3,000 people heralded the turning of water into the canal. This dam, as well as another, was replaced by a concrete structure in 1910, which is still a major landmark in Woodbridge. An irrigation district was created in 1924 and the system gradually expanded to 100 miles of canals. The reservoir behind the dam created a beautiful area between Lodi and Woodbridge known as Lodi Lake.

Vineyards and winery operations have long been part of agricultural activities here. Wine production over the years has taken place at Sebastiani Winery, Guild del Rio Winery and the plant of the Woodbridge Winery Association, which, for many years, shipped all its products to the California Wine Association in San Francisco.

One of the best known local residents of recent times is Elbert A. Covell, a Woodbridge and Modesto area vineyardist. Elbert's father first came to this area in 1887 while working as a civil engineer. He laid out the canal system for the Woodbridge Irrigation District. At age sixteen, in 1890, Elbert helped plant the first commercial vineyard of Tokays. The 160 acres were planted with cuttings from the Florin area in Sacramento County. Covell was very successful with his life's

FORMER SAN JOAQUIN VALLEY COLLEGE, 1922

Originally constructed for the Woodbridge Academy in 1878, this substantial building soon became known as the Woodbridge Seminary. A high school level program was offered by the United Brethren Church. With the addition of college degree studies in 1882, the name was again changed, to San Joaquin Valley College.

Within a few years after the college closed in 1897, the building became the Woods Grammar School, a purpose it served until it was demolished in 1922, the year this photograph was taken. The site, a registered California State Historical Landmark, is now occupied by the present Woods Elementary School.

SAN JOAQUIN VALLEY COLLEGE FOOTBALL TEAM, FEBRUARY 14, 1895
Celia May Crocker of Tuolumne County took this photograph while attending college in Woodbridge. The players are identified as follows: left to right, top row, Homer Burtner, Fenton Hain; center row, Walter Garrison, Frank Ralls, Walter Meyers, Solomon Blodgett, Arthur Thomas; bottom row, Ed VanVranken, Louis Powers, Will Thomas, Roy Powers, Humboldt McClelland, George Rutledge, Lannie Rhodes. *(Courtesy Lodi Public Library, Celia M. Thompson Collection)*

VIGNETTE AT SMITH'S LAKE (NOW LODI LAKE), c. 1915
The Model T Ford, the youngster tugging its crank, and the horse make an interesting trio, not to mention the ice cream wagon/real estate office at right operated by Charles Smith.

work as a vineyardist. He gave part of his fortune to the University of the Pacific; one of the famous "cluster colleges" there was named for him in the late 1960s.

In 1923 a real estate development started what led to the formation of the Woodbridge Country Club, an outstanding and beautifully landscaped golf course. In recent years, growth in the town had been curtailed by an under-developed water system. A 1967 installation serving part of the town made it possible to expand three mobile home parks and to start work on a major subdivision, construction of which reached its height in 1972. In the 1980s considerable residential development has taken place. River Meadows has completed 105 detached units. Construction started in 1984 by another developer for luxury single family homes under architectural control on the Woodbridge (Sebastiani) Winery site. Woodbridge Greens, as it is known, is a locally based twenty

acre project. The first of three phases involves forty-nine homes ranging in price from $140,000 to $240,000.

Of the new developments, the most spectacular thus far has been just north of the country club, where a series of spacious, well designed, mansion-size homes were built in the early 1980s. Further expansion is planned. Perhaps this will be aided by the Woodbridge Advisory Council, a form of local government authorized by the county board of supervisors in 1982.

The attraction of the community in modern times was well summarized by the *Stockton Record*: "Woodbridge is a town where everyone seems to be on a first name basis. There is still one grocery store that maintains charge accounts for local residents. Older residents may walk the streets without the concerns they might have in larger cities; it is still a small town."

PART III
ALMOST FORGOTTEN
THE LITTLE SETTLEMENTS OF TODAY AND THE GHOST TOWNS

Each of these places is included because it has had a post office. Please see the map and the Appendix for data on dates of post office operation. If there is no further data available other than that regarding the postal operations, the entry will read simply, "See Appendix."

ATLANTA ELEMENTARY SCHOOL, 1918

This building replaced the historic Zinc House School, shown below in a 1913 photograph, just three or four years before this photograph was taken. Many of the pupils shown in this picture were tending an unusually large "war garden" of flowers and vegetables as part of their patriotic activities during the First World War. The school also had a baseball team which played spirited games with its old rival, Lathrop.

(Courtesy Dale Baldridge)

ATLANTA

Before the communities of Ripon and Manteca were established, Atlanta was the trading center of this section of the county. There are two versions about how it was named. It is known that the first storekeeper, Lee Wilson, was a native of Atlanta, Georgia. The second, equally believable, version is that the first postmaster, William Dempsey, had fond recollections of Atlanta, Georgia, for he received kindness and hospitality there as a runaway boy.

The town was founded at a time just after the Civil War when the region was undergoing a change from cattle ranching to grain farming. It was located on French Camp Road, which was a major thoroughfare for grain farmers on their way to Stockton.

The first store, built in 1866 by Lee Wilson, was also a station for Fisher Stages bound for the Mother Lode in the late 1860s and 1870s. Near the store was a barn where fresh horses were kept.

Atlanta was never more than a very small town and between 1866 and the 1930s, when the last store closed, had a blacksmith shop, general merchandise, butcher shop, hotel, "Zinc" House School, Atlanta Methodist Church and Saint Patrick's Catholic Church. It is interesting to note that the Rev. William B. O'Connor was pastor at Saint Patrick's in 1891, just a few years before he founded Saint Joseph's Hospital in Stockton.

The hotel was first operated by a Mr. Powell and later by a Mrs. Davenport and was located just west of the general store. In 1874 it was purchased by store proprietors, J. D. Murphy and family. Seven houses, a blacksmith shop and a general store comprised the town at the end of the 1870s.

There was also a baseball team, with Lathrop its principal rival. Of all the businesses in Atlanta, the best known was the general store, which was the first and last commercial operation at this point. It was acquired the same year as the hotel by William John Murphy and his brothers and operated by two generations of the family.

This is remembered as a colorful place having the aura of an establishment that had seen long years of service. It was jammed with merchandise, not only on the floors, counters and shelves but also hanging from the rafters was an array of stock including pack saddles that had been there for a very long time. Several hand written Murphy ledgers from the 1890s to the early twentieth century

are preserved at the Haggin Museum in Stockton and offer an insight into the operation of a typical general store of the era. They obtained their fruit and vegetables from Hobbs-Parsons Company of Stockton. The Rainier beer came from John Tons Bottling Works, the paint from W. P. Fuller & Company, and the soap from Williams & Moore, soap manufacturers, all of Stockton. Commonly purchased goods in the 1890s were such staples as cheese, bacon, lard, potatoes, sugar, eggs, roasted coffee and, of course, tobacco. From the general merchandise department, customers selected gingham, brooms for the school house, axe handles, nails, rope, lamp chimneys, underwear, shirts, shoes, thread, buggy whips, bucksaws, blasting powder, axle grease and stationery. A colorful story recalled by an old timer was of the day a cat had her kittens in the cracker barrel.

In 1912, Atlanta became a stop for the Tidewater-Southern Railway, which carried passengers in electrically operated coaches. The town became the most important of the thirty-six passenger stops on the line between Stockton and Modesto. Briefly, it was thought there would be a boom, and eleven streets were surveyed. However, the growth of Manteca and Ripon drew settlers away. Auto competition plagued the railway passenger service, which ceased in 1932; the tracks are still there, serving Western Pacific freight trains.

In 1916, the store was rebuilt by John, Robert and James Murphy through acquisiton of the old Zinc House School, which had been replaced by new construction. Soon it housed the newly arranged store and post office. Many remember the business as being in a long, false-front wooden building.

The town gradually died in the teens and '20s. L. A. Sprague moved one of the stores a few miles to the west to Simms Station on the railway line. Today, all that remains of the town is the former Atlanta Methodist Church and nearby cemetery. The 1878 church closed in 1934 but was preserved through purchase by the Atlanta Women's Club. The structure, a well known meeting place, is located one mile northwest of the townsite at Five Corners. Expansion and remodeling have altered the building greatly so that it bears little resemblance to its original design of 1878. One of the club's activities has been to care for the old Atlanta cemetery near the church, which, more than anything else, helps preserve the memory of this little town.

BELLOTA

Yokuts Indians considered this point a fine gathering place for acorns and hence the town received for its name the Spanish word for acorn, *bellota*. Even into the early twentieth century, Indian women, locally known as "Wallies," came here for acorns.

The first distinction the area attained came with the establishment of the San Joaquin Female Seminary, a short distance west of town. The two story brick building was completed in 1854, and during the following four years about one hundred students were enrolled, coming from all parts of California and West Coast points. An early advertisement stated that "the seminary is designed to afford facilities for the attainment of a thorough English and Classical education in connection with the study of ancient and modern languages."

The school lasted only four years, but the building remained for over a century and served as a warehouse for Solari's store and restaurant. In 1940, the Native Daughters unveiled a plaque outlining the historical importane of the seminary, which, during the 1850s, was the only private school in this part of the state.

Growth of the town was to come later and centered upon the completion of a toll bridge across an unnamed arroyo that ran between Mormon Slough and the Calaveras River. William V. Fisher was closely identified with this bridge, which changed the wagon route on the Mokelumne Hill Road from the Davis & Atherton Ferry east of Bellota. Over the years, six bridges have been constructed at this place. The first was only thirty feet long, but the slough gradually widened and now a 200-foot concrete span is at the junction of the Linden and Escalon-Bellota roads.

Bellota was eighteen miles from Stockton, a day's travel for teamsters, who stopped here for wagon repair, horseshoeing and a bit of drinking and brawling before their overnight stay.

David F. Douglas was the first settler in this area and built a roadhouse of shake shingles, one of seventeen inns along the road. Douglas later became secretary of state, in the mid 1850s. Another inn was constructed by David Fisher in 1861.

Fisher's Hotel established a reputation as a good boarding house. Also part of the establishment were a corral, stable and Fisher's Dance Hall, a popular place on Saturday nights. Sarah Fanning's restaurant packed box lunches on order for teamsters bound for the mining country. The usual stopping place for lunch became known as "Lunch Box Hill," a few miles east of Bellota. Other businesses were founded at Bellota in the ensuing decades, including two more boarding houses. Before 1875, there was a blacksmith and wheelwright, Frank Fanning, as well as a general store operated for many years by Gilman Chase. By the early 1880s, the town had a population of seventy-five, two blacksmiths, two general merchandise stores (Gilman Chase's and Alfred Parker's) and Fisher's Hotel.

There was a school one-half mile southwest of town. Surviving records show that in 1882, for example, there were about fifty students, with an average daily attendance of thirty-one. From March through June, 322 tardy arrivals were recorded and 297 absentees. From September 1910 to June 1911, nineteen students were enrolled in grades one through eight, with no more than three in any one grade.

In the 1890s, aside from the other businesses mentioned above, a cheese factory was operating, and near the school was a slaughter house. With the twentieth century, commercial growth of the community was at an end. By 1919, the only business listed in the town was Sidney E. Walker's general merchandise store; about one hundred lived in the area at this time.

For years, peddlers served the needs of area residents. Particularly remembered are a butcher wagon from Linden, a vegetable man who always had a jug of wine to share with his customers and a tinsmith.

Even the arrival of the Stockton Terminal & Eastern Railroad on August 10, 1912, did not affect the town significantly; it became the eastern terminus. Large corrals were constructed near the tracks for shipment of cattle. There was no station building or even a platform; the line just ended in a field behind Walker's store. Considerable gravel was hauled from a pit near town for use by the line.

Bellota has always been associated with ranching and general farming. Due to the abundance of acorns in the area, hog raising was undertaken for decades. In the late 1870s, Latimer Farm was operated by Alfred Parker, who was a prominent importer, breeder and shipper of Berkshire swine. Occasionally, the pigs would break loose and start foraging in the gardens of residences. At least one was shot but the meat did not go to waste. Half was given the owner of the pig and the other half used by the family whose property had been invaded.

By 1915, the region was recognized for its grazing land, but as much of the soil was thin and gravelly, more intensive agriculture took place in the rich river bottom lands, where vegetables, pears and cherries grew well. The largest cherry orchard in the world is maintained near here by the Podesta family. Hundreds of acres of walnuts were planted near here by the Bellota Operating Company in the 1930s. This firm was composed of several prominent Stockton businessmen.

Of great benefit to the farming operations was the completion of a weir on the Calaveras River above the townsite. This project of the Stockton and East San Joaquin Water Conservation District provided flood control and some water storage upon its completion in 1948.

Today, Bellota is composed of widely scattered residences, with only the shell of a concrete block store of recent times, the rambling remains of Fisher's Hotel and, across from it, a picturesque old barn to remind the traveler there was once a larger settlement here.

A TIRED OLD GENERAL STORE IN ITS DECLINING YEARS. BELLOTA, APRIL 1937.

Sidney E. Walker, a plump, accommodating merchant, operated the last general store in Bellota, which closed in 1945. The building was originally the Fisher Dance Hall, a center of Saturday night activity with a local orchestra. It is remembered that there were two violinists, Jim Martin and Edgar Holman; the guitar and bass player was Nealie Holman, and "Jimmie" played the cornet.

After Parker and Chase's store on the north bank of Mormon Slough was threatened by flooding, the hall was converted into a store, later to become the Cody General Store. Before 1919, the building became the Walker General Merchandise.

About 1908 a man was killed in a shooting incident on the porch of this building. Just a few years later a buckeroo who lived in a nearby shack broke into the store. He set a charge of powder in the safe door, and in an attempt to muffle the blast, stacked bags of sugar against it. The effort resulted in a blast heard throughout the town, and after a brief chase from the schoolhouse through the river and back to the little shack, the culprit was apprehended and served time in San Quentin. *(Courtesy Lodi Public Library, Celia M. Thompson Collection)*

HORSE AND WAGON MEET THE "GAS BUGGIES" IN FRONT OF THE SCHLICTMAN STORE
AND POST OFFICE. BETHANY, JANUARY 20, 1916.

Claus Schlictman and his family operated this store for half a century, from 1893 to 1943. Schlictman was not only kept busy as storekeeper but was also postmaster and "banker" for the Chinese employed to harvest sugar beets. They would bring their wages to him to be sent via money order to China. This store was also "Central" for the local telephone service. (Courtesy Mrs. Clifford Koster)

BENSON'S FERRY

See Mokelumne City.

BETHANY

In the southwestern corner of the county, in part of the region known as the West Side, is the townsite of Bethany. Growth was first directed by water connections, and after a short move to the south, it attained importance as a shipping point on the Central Pacific Railroad main line.

First known through the 1850s as Burns' Landing (for Maurice Byrnes), it was renamed Mohr's Landing in honor of German emigrant and pioneer John Mohr. He established the settlement on the west bank of Old River. All went well until he lost everything in the floods of 1862 and 1864. Up until this time, it was the supply center of pioneer settlers of the area. Redwood lumber for many of the first buildings constructed in this region is believed to have been brought by boat to Mohr's Landing. The Pacific Coal Mining Company in Corral Hollow shipped coal to a barge loading facility here in the early 1860s.

After the destructive floods, Mohr decided to build on higher ground. In the late 1860s, encouraged by increasing travel through the area to the newly constructed railroad center of Ellis about seven miles to the south, he decided to build a hotel. Before long, railroad officials made plans for a "low level route" connecting the Bay Area via Martinez and San Pablo, and Mohr donated the right of way through his land, provided that a station would be built. This is how the town of Bethany grew from a single hostelry. The town was renamed Bethany, probably taking its name from the locality in Palestine.

The first train through the area was on September 8, 1878, and Bethany immediately started to grow. Employment in the region was not centered exclusively upon agriculture; there were some jobs with land reclamation projects to the east, particularly with the activity of the dredge *Golden Gate.* By 1880 there were a general merchandise, liquor store, blacksmith, wagon maker and a hotel known as Bethany House and owned by John Mohr, who was also the local blacksmith. The section crew of the Central Pacific was stationed here, and, during the early 1880s, a second black-

SOUTHERN PACIFIC STATION AT BETHANY, 1937.
Charles Guevara, the son of the local section foreman, took this unusual photograph from a vantage point atop the water tower looking south toward Tracy. Such a sizable station was erected here as railroad plans were for a trans-shipment point to the river landing half a mile away. It is believed high winds that plagued the area discouraged this development. At the far right can be seen the blacksmith shop and the Schlictman General Merchandise. *(Courtesy of Charles Guevara and Mrs. Clifford Koster)*

smith shop was established along with a butcher shop and shoemaker.

The principal business was James O. Hutchins, general merchandise, which also contained the post office. The town established its importance over several decades as a shipping point for hay, grain, sugar beets and, in later years, asparagus.

The well water available was too alkaline to use, and the railroad regularly brought a tank carful that was emptied into a cistern for the use of everyone in town. Crop diversification with the coming of irrigation was going to end dependence upon dry farming. This was made possible by the Byron-Bethany Irrigation District, organized in 1916 with Sam Schearer as a prime mover.

Lilly Schlictman Spiekerman, who grew up in Bethany, described the town at about this time: "There were four warehouses, two blacksmiths, our store and home and a large SP station and home for the station master. There was also a home for the railroad maintenance man. Across the track was a bar and dance hall and a residence. To us, that was the wrong side of the track!" Nearby there was also an oil pumping station, one of a series between southern San Joaquin Valley oil fields and refineries on the Carquinez Straits.

With improved roads, Tracy and Brentwood, both far larger towns, were much more readily accessible, and businesses gradually closed and families relocated. In 1929 the only business listed was Claus Schlictman, general merchandise. The post office closed forever on January 31, 1940. Today, there is not a trace of the large depot, church and other structures that once characterized the little village of Bethany.

BOULDIN ISLAND

Apparently, the height of development attained by this settlement was in the mid 1880s, when there were two butchers, two blacksmiths, Dr. Leander H. Lowe, and Henry Wrobioff's merchandise store. By 1893, only Joseph Zeller's merchandise store and a blacksmith remained in the town. The tiny settlement was located twelve miles west of Stockton. There were two townsites, apparently; in 1906 the post office was moved to the south one mile.

CONGREGATIONAL CHURCH AT PATTERSON PASS AND BYRON ROADS, BETHANY, 1920s
Circuit ministers conducted services here for families around Bethany who were predominately of German ancestry. The altar, hand decorated in oils, stood in front of a Gothic arch. A few years after this photograph was taken, the church was torn down and the lumber used to build an Associated gasoline station. *(Courtesy Patricia Davis)*

BURWOOD

Burwood was located in the extreme southeast corner of the county. Its beginnings can be traced to 1859. For years, its activities centered around Ishmael Monroe, who was postmaster and proud of the fact that he had received his commission from President Abraham Lincoln. The post office was at his ranch where mail was received two to three times a week from Stockton. The most substantial building in Burwood was the schoolhouse. The red bricks for the walls and other material were all donated when the building was erected in 1866. Sometime before 1891, the school was damaged by earthquake and had to be demolished. The new building, also a one-room school, was to serve until 1919 when replaced by a much larger structure with two classrooms, an assembly room and a library.

The earliest business on record was Twohy &

Brother, general merchandise, listed in the 1869 Directory. By the early 1880s, there were Elison N. Cahill's Hotel, two blacksmiths, two merchants, a butcher, a shoemaker, a clergyman (who was also a farmer) and two music teachers. By 1893, the county directory ceased listing any activity at Burwood.

CALAVERAS

Calaveras became Waterloo. See Appendix.

CARBONA

This is a railroad point located about three miles south of Tracy at the junction of the Western Pacific Railroad mainline to the Bay Area and the old Alameda and San Joaquin Railroad, long known as the Tesla Branch. This branch, now torn up, led to gravel pits at the mouth of Corral Hollow Canyon. Among railroaders this is also known as Carbona Wye and Carbona Pump Station.

At one time, there were stock yards and freight sheds here, along with a passenger depot. The town bears the name Carbona as this area originally had its start during the Treadwell Brothers coal mining development in Corral Hollow.

After collapse of these activities by 1910, Western Pacific purchased the trackage and rolling stock of the Alameda and San Joaquin Railroad including the site of Carbona. Little Carbona is still the residence for railroad section crewmen and their families who reside in company owned mobile homes. A tomato cannery is also operated here.

CARLTON

See Appendix.

A HOME OF DISTINCTIVE ARCHITECTURE. BETHANY, 1983.
The present home of Stan and Pat Davis with its distinctive hacienda style architecture is all that is to be found at the site of Bethany today.

The residence, built in 1931, is situated a short distance south of the site of the business section. While the extensive, thick-walled home is largely adobe, it also contains lumber from the old commercial buildings.

The home and adjacent office building, which also served as the Bethany post office until it closed in 1940, were constructed for William T. Kirkman, a nurseryman. He employed many Mexican laborers in his business who also made adobe brick for the house. Kirkman's fruit tree stock was purchased to establish orchards in the surrounding area. He is also remembered for developing a new peach, the "Kirkman Gem." *(Photo by Raymond W. Hillman)*

CARBONA, 1983

A rare sight today is a wooden water tower built during the era of steam. One of the few surviving is standing at Carbona. It is shown framed by a portion of the covered loading platform of the combination freight and passenger depot constructed in 1910. The deserted depot in the photo to the left had been demolished by the spring of 1985. *(Photographs by Raymond W. Hillman)*

CARNEGIE

In the Livermore Range foothills in the extreme southwestern reaches of the county is a canyon with a remarkable history known as Corral Hollow. Stories conflict regarding the origins of its name, some saying it could be a corruption of Carroll's Hollow; Edward B. (Ned) Carroll came here in 1850 and built the "Zink" House, a tavern. Other sources, Earle Williams and F. F. Latta, credit an extensive corral built for roundup of wild horses and used by the Americans and Mexican-Californians between 1848 and 1855. The latter is probably true.

The area was first viewed by Juan Bautista de Anza during his expedition in 1776 to found Mission Dolores in present San Francisco. A trail through the canyon was in use during Spanish and Mexican times for the transportation of cattle south to San Pedro. With the California Gold Rush, the same trail was to be used by gold seekers traveling over "Stockton Pass" between the Livermore and San Joaquin valleys on their way to the southern mines. To serve them, the famous "Zink" house was built at the mouth of the canyon. Because it was constructed of zinc coated sheets of iron, an unusual building material for the 1850s, it was so named.

Parts of the canyon were thick with undergrowth, and there was a natural fortification known as Castle Rock. It was here that desperados found excellent cover. Because of the remoteness of some of the country, mountain lions and grizzly bears were well established. This attracted a colorful frontier character and showman, "Grizzly" Adams. He established a camp in 1855 and trapped bears and lions for his animal collection.

Activity of a more lasting nature came with the development of the Eureka Coal Mine in 1857 and 1858, discovered a year earlier by Jack O'Brien, a sea captain. While some of the coal was shipped to San Francisco by barge, the activities of this San Francisco based operation and other mines nearby were sporadic and short-lived. Great changes came when the attention of John and James Treadwell was drawn to the unique resources of Corral Hol-

SAN JOAQUIN RIVER CROSSING OF THE ALAMEDA AND SAN JOAQUIN RAILWAY,
STOCKTON TO CARNEGIE, c. 1900
The ten-wheel freight locomotive was one of the two built especially for the line by the Richmond Locomotive Works in Richmond, Virginia. The drive wheels on this coal burner were fifty-seven inches in diameter. The locomotive was crossing a span built by the Pacific Bridge Company in 1895; it was a swing bridge with each arm extending 103 feet over the water. The tender has just been supplied with water from a spout fastened to the bridge. A pump can be seen on the bridge deck for taking water from the river.

THE HEART OF CARNEGIE, c. 1910 and 1983
Smoke stacks up to 175 feet high tower over the works. This is the second set of stacks over the plant; the first fell in the 1906 earthquake. Most of the stacks drew away fumes from the oil fired kilns that were housed in the long wooden buildings. The brick forming machines and other equipment were powered by a 400 horsepower Corliss steam engine built in San Francisco in 1882. It had a flywheel sixteen feet in diameter. *(Collection of Earle Williams)*

The same spot eighty years later offers little testimony to the tremendous investment of capital and effort upon this now obscure location. The plant was demolished in 1916.
In the photo on the facing page, a sidewalk in an old residential section of Stockton at Hunter and Vine streets helps keep the name Carnegie alive.

low. They had developed the famous Treadwell Mines near Juneau, Alaska, and with their fortune committed themselves to develop bituminous coal deposits. They were encouraged by reports of experts on the quality of the coal and they obtained the inactive Commercial Coal Mining Company's rights to the six mile wide strip of the coal field. A tremendous investment was made, and by 1897, there were 400 men working in two shifts at the Tesla Mine (named for Nikola Tesla, a great inventor of electrical power transmission equipment). The mine was located at the head of the canyon, which is in Alameda County.

The main shaft was 700 feet deep, and about 1,000 tons of "steam coal" a day was being produced. It is interesting to note that Chinese and Japanese were employed to pick out slate and other impurities from the coal as it slid down screens toward the tipple. Japanese were also employed underground as timber men. Coal was not the only product of the mine; high grade clay was interleafed with the coal like the pages of a book. This clay was the key to a major industry that was to develop just five miles down the canyon in San Joaquin County. The Carnegie Brick and Pottery Company employed sixty-five men at the brick works and another forty-five at a nearby pottery plant. The pottery produced sewer pipe and crockery products while the brick works manufactured architectural, fire and paving brick. The clay was creamy white and the product had a distinctive

light color. Fire clay, glass sand for the Pacific Window Glass Company, as well as gravel for street surfacing in Stockton and elsewhere, were also shipped from Corral Hollow.

Operations at the brick works started in September 1903 with a production of about 80,000 bricks a day. The product was used all over California and Arizona. Some of the brick was first class, intended for building facings and fire brick. Rough common red brick was also made. There was a tremendous demand for the sewer pipe in San Francisco and Oakland. By 1904, there were twelve kilns in operation. The brick was fired in eight kilns thirty feet in diameter; in addition, there were four muffle kilns especially designed for architectural terra cotta. Interestingly enough, the kilns were oil fired even though coal was readily available. Nearby, additional kilns were burning limestone brought from a quarry to make lime for mortar.

Around the brick works developed a town named Carnegie, more than likely named for Andrew Carnegie, prominent nineteenth century railroad and steel industry figure and the founder, in 1899, of the Carnegie Steel Company, which soon became the United States Steel Company. Carnegie earned a niche in United States industrial history as he introduced the Bessemer process to this country in 1868, which made it possible to produce steel in abundance for structural use, manufacture of machinery, ship hulls, etc.

By the early twentieth century, about 1,200 people lived in and around Carnegie. Aside from numerous single-family dwellings, there were two large bunk houses with over one hundred rooms each, occupied mainly by Italian workers. Across from these was Tom Graner's Carnegie Hotel. Nearby were a bakery, Carnegie Livery Stable and Tom Collins' Saloon. The hotel seemed to be the center of community activity. Postal service for this town was through the Tesla post office.

Even though the Alameda and San Joaquin Railway commenced operation on its thirty-six mile run to Stockton in February 1897, it never carried passengers. Stage coaches and other forms of transportation brought the workers and their families to and from the area. Three times a week this strictly industrial railroad carried products of the mine and pottery works and hundreds of thousands of brick out of Corral Hollow. The coal cars, as many as forty-five at a time, were loaded mechanically at the tipples of the mine and dumped their loads from an elevated position at

the huge coal bunkers on the Stockton Channel. Principal customers for the coal were the river steamers and the Southern Pacific Railroad.

The industrial might of Carnegie and the other Treadwell properties came to an end by 1910. Substantial beginnings here had but a short useful life due to several factors. Particularly crushing was the failure of John and James Treadwell's California Safe Deposit and Trust Bank. They had to make good to their depositors through their own fortune. Destruction of the business center of San Francisco by the earthquake and fire of 1906 might have been looked upon as a great opportunity to sell bricks for new construction, but this was not to materialize. Rebuilding was to be accomplished in reinforced concrete; the use of brick was relatively minimal. There was also a depression in

1907 that slowed construction state wide, and a boiler explosion at the brick works made matters worse. This was followed by major flooding in the Hollow in 1911 and 1913 that damaged facilities there, especially the vital railroad grade and trestles.

The brick works and the pottery plant were the first to close down and were bought by Gladding, McBean and Company of Lincoln, California, and dismantled completely in 1916 to eliminate a competitor. This was followed by the closure of the Tesla Coal Mine in 1910, as there was no demand for its product due to increased use of fuel oil, with the perfection of oil burners for locomotives, steamboats and other applications.

Today, the drive up Corral Hollow would reveal hardly a trace of the extensive developments

CARNEGIE STATE VEHICULAR RECREATION AREA, 1981
Hundreds of off road vehicle owners would find this a familiar landscape. In the distance at right, the park headquarters buildings can be seen along Corral Hollow Road. *(Photograph by Diana Vallario,* Tri-Valley Herald, *Livermore, California)*

that once existed there. Disturbed earth, a concrete slab and a few scattered, broken brick offer slight hint of the great brick works. Not a single wall of a house or other building remains intact. The only development surviving is the major part of the railroad between Tesla and Stockton. This was purchased by Western Pacific, and its line from Stockton to Carbona is still in use.

Although brick making and coal mining are all a thing of the past, the valley is not without activity. For decades, non-nuclear explosive tests have been conducted here by Lawrence-Livermore National Laboratory. Tests are made for various federal agencies at three underground sites.

During 1980, the Carnegie State Vehicular Recreational Area was established on 1,500 acres. Motorcycle and other off road vehicle owners seek challenges on various steep trails that bear names reminiscent of the hollow's past, such as Franciscan Loop, Pottery Loop and Kiln Canyon. It is not unusual to have 250 to 300 riders bringing life to this remote spot on Sundays in the spring and fall.

Starting in 1981, additional attention has been drawn to the area through the proposal to create a new community in the county to be known as Carnegie New Town. This is the plan of Tracy developers Dave Olmstead and Don Cose for about 7,000 acres along the east side of Corral Hollow Road, south of Interstate 580. The concept is to divert growth from prime agricultural land on the valley floor to this marginal land in the foothills. The town is planned to be not only residential but commercial-industrial as well, and the population could reach nearly 35,000.

During 1983, the plan was encouraged by county planning commission action, the preliminary environmental impact report was endorsed, the question of on-site water availability was resolved and the proposal was endorsed for the County General Plan. The board of supervisors approved a General Plan amendment designating 6,000 acres for development in December 1984. Actual construction is not expected to be underway for about ten years, due to Williamson Act agricultural land preserves. Who knows, a substantial community may, once again, take the name of Carnegie.

GRANER HOTEL AT CARNEGIE, c. 1905.
Hotel manager Mrs. Josephine (O'Leary) Leary is standing on the stoop at the main entrance. Coming at the start of operations in Corral Hollow, she was first a maid at the Hotel Tesla. When the Graner Hotel closed in 1911, she moved to Stockton to become head matron at the old county jail under Sheriff Carlos Sousa and Sheriff Mike Canlis.

Chinese were employed as cooks and kitchen helpers. Japanese composed the upstairs help as well as the pantry men and vegetable peelers. Japanese also ran the town bakery. They made an excellent French bread that was highly prized by the Italians, who would try to spirit loaves of bread out of the hotel dining room where the food was served family style. This became such a problem that those caught were fined an hour's pay, twenty-five cents.

Another story about the hotel was, unbeknown to the Treadwells, fairly high stake card games were held there. Two out-of-town men arrived in the early years of the twentieth century to join one of these games. After losing heavily, they left the game for a time to make some special preparations—they sabotaged all but one of the railroad hand cars kept nearby. Wheels and axles were removed and rolled down an embankment. Returning to the hotel, the players were held up at gun point and the robbers took off rapidly on the downhill run aboard the one operable hand car. Their pursuers were left trying frantically to put together one of the hand cars. Needless to say, precious time was lost and the robbers were never apprehended. *(Collection of Earle Williams)*

206

SCHOOLHOUSE AT COLLEGE-
VILLE, APRIL 1931
When constructed in 1875, this
building replaced an older structure on the banks of nearby Little
John Creek, as well as the old college building lost to fire. Originally known as the McKamy School,
it was renamed along with the district in 1889.
Shortly after completion, there
were about forty-five students in
attendance. Several of the graduates went on to lives of distinction,
including Avery C. White, district
attorney in Stockton; Charles
Merrill, gunsmith; and James
Barr, long-time superintendent
of the Stockton public schools.
*(Courtesy Lodi Public Library,
Celia M. Thompson Collection)*

COLLEGEVILLE

This crossroads community, eight miles east of Stockton, first gained distinction as a stopping place on the Mariposa Road, heavily used by freight wagons and stage coaches on their way to the Mother Lode.

Dr. L. R. Chalmers was a pioneer settler here in 1850 and within two years succeeded in attracting the business of passersby, and the stop became known as Chalmers' Ranch or the Eight Mile House. It was part of a series of such road houses that also included such places as the Lone Tree House and Heath & Emory's Ferry on the Stanislaus River.

Most of the businesses were run by local farmers and ranchers. The name changed from Chalmers' Ranch to Collegeville when Morris College was established on five acres by the Cumberland Presbyterian Church. It was built in 1867 and remained an active, co-educational college for six years. It was at this time that the village gained its height of prosperity. There were two boarding houses serving the college plus fourteen residences. The businesses included the general store, Wallace Kerrick's hotel and feed yard, Aust and

Gilgert's blacksmith and wagon shop and a medical doctor.

In December of 1874, the large wooden college building, by then the district school, burned in a blaze that started in a chimney while classes were in session. The fire not only destroyed the classrooms but also the Collegeville Grange Hall upstairs, where considerable records were lost. The blaze was so hot that the 350 pound bell was completely consumed. The tolling of the large bell was sorely missed by the residents. The school was soon rebuilt near the original site (see photo).

Despite the loss of the distinguishing feature of Morris College, Collegeville continued a role as a small commercial center, as it was at the intersection of two major public roads, Jack Tone and Mariposa. By the mid 1880s the town still had a physician, Andrew Lawson's General Merchandise, Gilgert's blacksmith and wagon shop, William H. Snow's butcher shop, employing four butchers, and a school house.

By 1937, the population had dwindled to thirteen, with three houses, a grade school, Presbyterian Church, a branch of the San Joaquin County Library and a combination store and filling station. This store was established at the intersection in 1914 by John D. Gilgert and his son,

Carlton, who moved their old blacksmith shop building to this spot and operated a meat route from it. Soon there were three daily routes for the delivery of fresh meat, at a time when home refrigeration was primitive. Later the Gilgerts dealt in groceries, general merchandise and auto supplies. The old, familiar building, which had survived for almost one hundred years, was torn down by the Gilgerts in 1957 and replaced by the present concrete block grocery store and filling station.

Across Mariposa Road from the store is a prominent reminder that Collegeville has been around a long time. This is the old Collegeville cemetery, bleak and overgrown until recent years when an ambitious renovation was undertaken as a Boy Scout project.

RESTORED COLLEGEVILLE METHODIST CEMETERY, SOUTHEAST CORNER OF JACK TONE AND MARIPOSA ROADS, 1982
A five dollar gold piece bought this one-acre site for a cemetery in 1871. It was cared for by the Collegeville Cemetery Association until the 1950s, when it was allowed to enter a long period of neglect. In 1979, restoration was undertaken with the leadership of Lyle Hughes of Troop 425, Boy Scouts of America, in Manteca.

COMETA

Southern Pacific maintained a siding here where there were once corrals and a grain warehouse. It was located about five miles northeast of Escalon.

DEXTER

Originally a Calaveras County location, this became part of San Joaquin County in 1876. It is believed to have been eleven miles northeast of Lodi. See Appendix.

EAGLE TREE

In the early twentieth century this was a California Transportation Company steamboat landing. A bald eagle nested in a nearby tree, hence the name. This site is five and a half miles southwest of Thornton.

EIGHT MILE CORNERS
See Appendix.

ELLIOTT

Situated six and one-half miles north of Lockeford, this town was first known as Hawk's Corners in the 1850s and 1860s and re-named Elliott in 1863 in honor of pioneer rancher J. Elliott. There was a Methodist Church by 1858, and an early commercial firm was Hutchins and Bovard, general merchandise. There were eight major buildings here including Hickey Brothers, a general merchandise store which was two stories high; the hall upstairs was for Grangers and Good Templars meetings. The former met on the first Saturday after a full moon. Other businesses were M. Bovard & Company (flour millers), a blacksmith and wagon maker, two saloons (one connected with a feed stable) and Mrs. J. J. Pinkerton's boarding house. Nearby was the Elliott School with two teachers.

During the mid-1880s, about one hundred people lived here. The town reached the zenith of its development in the early 1890s with tri-weekly stage connections with Galt and had two blacksmiths, two saloons, a machine shop, a veterinary surgeon, a butcher, a school with three teachers and two societies meeting weekly in the Odd Fellows Hall—Farmers Alliance and the Good Templars. In addition, there was an insurance and news agency operating with the post office in the general store. By 1902, there were only one store and the schoolhouse.

Today only a lonesome cemetery on a mound marks the site. Here a grave marker carved in Jackson, Amador County, in the 1860s, reads:

> Remember me as you pass by
> As you are now so once was I
> As I am now you soon shall be
> So prepare for death and follow me.

ELLIS

The town of Ellis is an example of how a railroad can make or break a community. This settlement quickly gained importance in 1869 as a point on the first transcontinental railroad built by the Central Pacific. It was located near the foot of steep, nearly 1,000-foot high Altamont Pass, a hurdle for trains bound for the Bay Area. It was here at Ellis that the trains stopped at a coaling station. A helper locomotive would be coupled to the passenger train and two freight trains heading west each day for the two-hour climb. Around the "railroad reservation" were many stores and homes for the railroad maintenance crews. Many of these section hands were Chinese; residences were provided for them on the edge of town.

By 1870, there were forty-five or fifty houses in Ellis, some of which had been moved from the community of Wickland, just north of Ellis. All looked good through the 1870s until the railroad completed the low level line that was to eliminate dependence upon the Altamont Pass route and create a new community.

The new town, Tracy, was in a more advantageous position where the new rail route crossed the still useful Altamont Pass line. In 1878, the rush was to Tracy, the populous taking most of Ellis' buildings with them. Finally, four years after the establishment of Tracy in 1878, the passenger station, too, was moved to the new town.

Ellis had a heyday of just nine years. At its height between 1875 and 1878 there were three hotels, the Ellis, San Joaquin and Commercial.

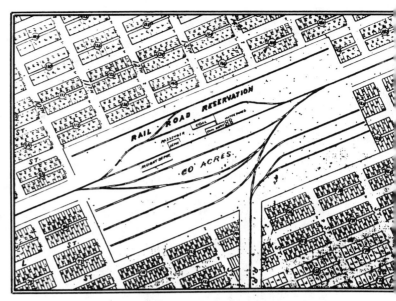

RAILROAD YARDS AT ELLIS, 1871
This is the official map filed at the San Joaquin County Recorder's Office. The Central Pacific Railroad mainline, part of the First Transcontinental Railroad, cuts diagonally through the map on its way between Lathrop, Stockton and points north (right) and Altamont, Livermore and points west (left).

The maze of main tracks, sidings and spurs served the passenger depot, freight depot, coaling station and livestock pens. The branch line to the southwest extended four miles to the mouth of Corral Hollow. The original intention was to bring coal from the Eureka Mine, but consultants' reports were negative and the branch line was used only to bring out ballast from a gravel pit. Also, very few of the finally divided blocks of lots surrounding the "railroad reservation" were ever developed. *(Collection of Robert Shellenberger)*

These were frequented by immigrants looking for opportunities to purchase farm land. In addition to the hotels, there were also a blacksmith shop, wagon builder, livery stable, two liquor stores, two variety stores, a saddle and harness maker, boot and shoemaker, two general merchandise stores (Philip Fabian's and Sebastian Questa's), lodge halls, community hall and a huge warehouse. For the extensive sheep raising area around Corral Hollow in the Diablo Range, this was an important supply and transportation center.

The 1883 directory for the county lists no stores in Ellis; all the residents were farmers. Today, the site of Ellis on Schulte Road bears no physical remains of the considerable, but short-lived, activity that took place there beyond a pepper tree, broken brick and a trackside sign with the number 35.

ELLISWORTH

Situated fifteen miles southeast of Stockton on the Santa Fe's transcontinental line, this tiny settlement was also known as Avena Station. *Avena* is the Spanish word for oats. Most of the residents were farmers; a few were railroad employees. Around the time of World War I, the principal business, a general merchandise store, was owned by Julius F. Holm, who was also the postmaster. A saloon was another enterprise in town. Mail was left here for the post office in Atlanta. There were warehouses for storing sacked grain, and this was also a grape shipping point.

FAIRCHILD

Located near an unusual bend in Roberts Road known as the "collar and elbow," there was once a large general store along with a barn used as a dance hall, and a school house. The post office had a small building of its own on the west side of the road. A cluster of nondescript old and newer buildings still occupy the site, which has been, in part, a heavy equipment repair and storage yard in more recent years.

FOREMAN'S RANCH

See Linden and Appendix. This was named for Samuel Foreman, pioneer rancher and first postmaster.

FOREST LAKE

The establishment of a Southern Pacific siding, a small station and platform created Forest Lake, also known as Collierville.

Activity centered upon the shipment of cattle and grain, starting about 1890. It was always a small place, having "flag stop" status, but there were a postmaster and butcher during the 1890s. After the turn of the century, the fledgling development was in retreat. However, the name Forest Lake is carried on nearby by a substantial, unincorporated residential area that has developed since the 1950s. The rural setting is studded with homes built on plots of a few acres each. Many are individual efforts, and no one builder has been in-

A FOREST LAKE RESIDENT
WITH HIS PONY CART, 1983

John Philip Sousa, his pony, Panch, and his dog, Paul, are a familiar sight on the county roads between his home and Elk Grove, Clements, Lodi and, occasionally, Stockton.

The yellow cart, trimmed with orange beads, is often seen enroute to Galt for Sousa's almost daily visits to his ninety-five year old mother. It is the only transportation used by this forty-five year resident of Forest Lake. His love of animals developed during many years of work with dairy herds in the area. *(Photograph by Raymond W. Hillman)*

volved with more than just a few houses. There is a volunteer fire department in a substantial, modern building, but the only commercial development is the inviting, park-like acreage of Forest Lake Golf Course, started in 1955 on the site of a nursery. This is a privately owned course with a 3,700 yard executive type short course open for public use. A spacious new clubhouse was completed in 1981. The large lake that gave this place a name so long ago still exists; it is at the confluence of Jahant Slough and the Mokelumne River.

14 MILE HOUSE

This was probably located where present Linden stands today. An 1862 map helps confirm this. See Appendix.

FUGITT

This was named for Chism C. Fugitt, first postmaster and later the founder of the town of Liberty in 1852. Fugitt was twenty-three miles north of Stockton, on the daily U.S. mail route of A. N. Fisher's stage line between Stockton and Sacramento. See Liberty.

HALF WAY HOUSE

This was a roadhouse on the Stockton-Sacramento route, twenty-five miles north of Stockton at the Mokelumne River crossing. See Appendix.

HAZELTON

Hazelton was one and a half miles east of Stockton. See Appendix.

HOLDEN

This place had a very short life. It was planned as one of five stops on the Stockton & Copperopolis Railroad between Stockton and Milton, but the town site, four miles west of Peters, was never developed. It was named after well-known Stockton pharmacist and president of the railroad, Erastus S. Holden. Next to Captain Charles M. Weber,

SANTA FE STATION AT HOLT, 1969
Shown here the year before it was torn down, this typical early twentieth century depot was the last reminder of the once busy shipping center of Holt. This building was moved in sections by rail to this site from another locality farther down the valley after the original Holt station was destroyed by fire in the early 1940s.
The company maintained a siding at Holt for decades with a capacity of seventy-five cars. Two agents were employed in the station. While freight traffic was busy, several daily passenger trains to and from the Bay Area also enlivened the community. In 1912 there were seven eastbound and seven westbound; this was reduced to four each way by 1942, including the Golden Gate, the Scout and the Grand Canyon Limited.
Passenger service came to an end about 1968. The train arrival and departure blackboard to the left of the telegraph bay was saved and donated to the Haggin Museum by Santa Fe. The waiting room section was moved in 1970 to become the clubhouse of the Holt Marching and Chowder Society on the Sonny Welser Ranch. (Photograph by Raymond W. Hillman)

Holden did more for the betterment of Stockton and adjacent areas than any other resident. Aside from establishing Stockton's first drug store and erecting the first two-story brick building in Stockton during 1853, he was vice-president of the State Agricultural Society in 1857. With his own resources, he beautified the grounds around the Courthouse in 1860 and, at about the same time, was the prime mover in establishing what is now the San Joaquin County Fair. It is unfortunate that the settlement did not develop to perpetuate his name.

HOLDEN'S FERRY

This place was named for William Holden, who established the ferry one mile northwest of present Oakdale. He soon launched a career in state politics, becoming a senator in 1858 and lieutenant governor from 1867 to 1871. See Loving's Ferry.

HOLT

A Sunset Home Seekers Bureau publication described Holt as the largest town in the San Joaquin Delta. It grew to importance because of its advantageous proximity to transportation resources. It was on the Borden Highway, the first through paved road in the Delta, it had water connectons to the entire Delta via Whiskey Slough, and was a busy car load shipping point and pas-

211

THE CHINESE SECTION OF HOLT, JANUARY 17, 1917

This unusual photograph was printed from the original, water damaged, glass plate negative preserved at the Haggin Museum in Stockton. It is the only early photograph of the town that has ever been located. It was taken by the San Joaquin County Sheriff's Department as part of an investigation. The first building, at left, is the Holt Exchange, a restaurant prominently offering Rainier beer. Additional businesses, including another restaurant and hotels, are in the distance. At the time this picture was taken, other businesses in town included two saloons, a butcher shop, blacksmith, two general merchandise stores, post office and a boat livery. *(Collection of the Haggin Museum, Stockton)*

COMMEMORATIVE CACHET ENVELOPE AND CANCELLATION, 1979

In 1904 the peatlands of Roberts Island, just north of Holt, were the site of the first successful test of the Caterpillar track-type tractor by Benjamin Holt. The seventy-fifth anniversary of the first test did not go unheralded. Hundreds of these envelopes were prepared as a joint effort of the local Caterpillar Tractor Co. dealership and the Haggin Museum.

Four hundred fifty-two of these souvenir items were cancelled in two separate post offices on the very day of the anniversary, first receiving the postmark of the Holt post office and then the special machine cancellation from the Stockton main post office. The latter cancellation was used in Stockton for several months on millions of envelopes.

senger stop on the Santa Fe main line to San Francisco Bay.

As the Holt Manufacturing Company owned considerable acreage in the vicinity, the community was named Holt in about 1902 when the post office was established. Contrary to popular opinion, it was not named for Benjamin Holt, who in 1904 conducted a landmark test on company property just north of town. This was the first successful test of the Caterpillar track-type tractor. It took place on November 24, 1904, with a steam powered unit and the assistance of his nephew, Pliny. From this experimental machine, Holt developed, perfected and mass produced such tractors in Stockton. Their production is continued to this day by the Caterpillar Tractor Company of Peoria, Illinois.

C. Parker Holt is much more closely related to this area. He bought the landholdings of the Holt Manufacturing Company prior to World War I and operated the 777-acre ranch along with responsibilities as vice-president and treasurer of the company. He was a scientific farmer and during World War I experimented with Red Milo Maize and developed hemp as a viable crop for the area. A large barn was converted into a hemp factory for

the duration and was staffed by employees brought in from the Deep South. Mr. Holt also raised successful crops of potatoes, beans, celery, corn, etc. over many years. Aside from the above activities he was also a prime mover of the Borden Highway project.

Dairying was also an important industry around Holt. One of the more innovative was the operation of John DeCarli, who introduced Ladino clover and the concept of piping milk from dairy farms into tankers. Sugar beets were brought to Holt and dumped next to the seventy-five car railroad siding for reloading into gondola cars. Beets and other produce were brought in by river craft, and Whiskey Slough was once alive with tugs, barges and small stern-wheel steamers.

Because of the large number of farm laborers employed in the surrounding area, Holt became a supply and entertainment center. By 1906, there were a saloon, the Farmers' Cash Store, a station agent who was also the Wells-Fargo agent and postmaster, a blacksmith and two produce buyers. The principal enterprise in the community, a general store, opened in 1908 and was financed by seven investors, each putting up a thousand dollars. It operated with David J. McAdams as propri-

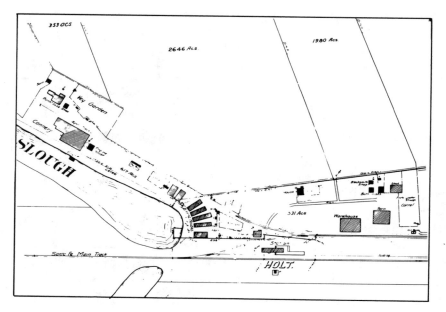

etor for twenty years before becoming the property of Ward L. Jones for almost as long a time. It was last operated by Terry Thomson, who ran it along with the post office into the 1960s, when it was closed.

It is interesting to note that in 1915, McAdams ran the only mercantile business in Holt operated by a Caucasian. A substantial part of the community was composed of a Chinese section and Japan Town. Chinatown started north of the tracks next to the general store. Japan Town, a smaller section, was on the opposite side of the tracks at the base of Whiskey Slough levee and consisted of one long block of buildings including a barber shop, restaurant and bar. Small vegetable gardens were cultivated throughout the town. The population reached about one hundred in 1918.

In 1917, an attractive stucco school house was donated to the community by C. Parker Holt. It was very well integrated, with Japanese, Mexican, Portuguese and Italian students. Its site today is only a tangle of blackberry bushes. A new Holt School, built in the 1960s, is at Holt and McDonald roads.

Holt was also a rough sporting town. Shootings were not uncommon. For the workingmen, there were gambling houses, and the five o'clock train would bring the girls from Stockton. During Prohibition a still was operated on a barge in a nearby waterway.

Holt's significance was gradually going to wane with ever improving highway connections to Stockton, just nine miles away. It simply became

much more convenient to travel to Stockton to do business, and the stores and other businesses gradually closed. During World War II, when lumber was hard to come by, some of the major buildings were town down for their materials.

Now all the buildings are gone. Whiskey Slough Resort/Marina occupies the site of the section of town along the levee. Pleasure boats and water skiers ply the waterway once busy with commercial river craft. Even the highway no longer goes through the townsite but has been re-located a short distance to the south where a tavern and a small, but very active, post office perpetuate the name of Holt.

HOMESTEAD

Very likely, this is the post office located in what is considered Stockton's first subdivision, an area south of present Charter Way roughly bounded by part of Wilson Way, French Camp Slough, the San Joaquin River and part of the Stockton Channel.

Changes in state finances regarding local schools no longer permitted children of families in this unincorporated area to attend Stockton schools. As a result, the residents of the Homestead area had to form their own school district, which was done in 1897. A six-room, two-story brick building was completed early in 1898 and named after General Ulysses S. Grant. As these dates closely correspond to the date of establishment of the post office, it is quite possible it was within this region of South

Stockton. In 1952 this name was reapplied to a postal station within this section of town.

KNIGHT'S FERRY

Knight's Ferry is now in Stanislaus County. See Appendix.

JAKESVILLE

Named for the first postmaster, Jacob "Jake" Small, this site is three and a half miles north of Acampo. See Appendix.

KERRICK'S RANCH

Collegeville occupies a portion of the J. Wallace Kerrick 400-acre ranch. Kerrick was treasurer and tax collector of San Joaquin County in 1888.

LIBERTY

Now a ghost town, Liberty was established in 1852 by C. C. Fugitt. Even at this time, there was a reminder that others had passed by and camped at this point.

This was a rose bush which marked the grave-site of Luís Andreas, a member of Jedediah Smith's fur party of 1826-1827. Andreas had a black slave with him, and there were several rose bush cuttings packed in his belongings that he intended to give to friends in the Northwest. When his master died, the slave marked the grave with a wooden cross and one of the rose cuttings. The bush flourished, not just in Fugitt's time but into the 1940s. It attained tree trunk-like proportions with branches covered with thousands of blooms. Unfortunately, construction of Highway 99 resulted in its destruction.

First known as Davis' Crossing, then Fugitt's, this settlement finally became Liberty in 1859. Located on Liberty Road, about one mile south of Galt, it existed from 1852 to 1870. During this time, it never had a population exceeding about seventy-five. The place owed its importance to the fact that one of the stage routes between Sacramento and Stockton crossed Dry Creek at this point.

The name Liberty was inspired by a town in Clay County, Missouri, the home place of Chism Cooper Fugitt. Meeting Fugitt once, one could not easily forget him, as he was six feet, seven inches tall. He arrived at the future townsite on the banks of Dry Creek with his wife, Elizabeth, and daughter in 1846. Six years later, the town started to materialize and it is believed that many of the first buildings had pre-fabricated frames made in Boston and New York. Among these buildings was a school erected in 1854; it had ten pupils on a subscription basis. When Fugitt was renamed Liberty, there were three stores, two saloons, two blacksmith and wagon shops, a hotel known as the Liberty House, two churches and the school.

Like most towns, Liberty experienced its set-backs, one of which was a fire that destroyed a blacksmith and wagon shop owned by Ireland Turnace. There was no insurance for the loss of $1,500.

Efforts to establish the Mokelumne as a river of commerce in the early 1860s helped facilitate de-

OLD LIBERTY SCHOOL ON THE NORTH END OF MAIN STREET, GALT, SACRAMENTO COUNTY, 1983
The heavy wooden frame of this historic structure is composed of studs that are joined together by mortise and tenon construction. Such technique is typical of prefabricated structures from the East Coast shipped around Cape Horn during the California gold rush. It is very likely this is the school house assembled in Liberty during 1854 and moved to this location about 1870.

For many years, this has been the home of Mrs. Baxter Sperry, who operates the Laurel Hill Press in the addition to the right. (Photograph by Raymond W. Hillman)

215

LIBERTY CEMETERY, 1984
Few travelers on busy State Highway 99 notice this reminder of old Liberty as they pass under the Liberty Road bridge. While badly vandalized, there are still many grave markers, some dating as far back as the late 1850s and 1860s.

livery of supplies to Liberty. The settlement was in direct line by road from Woodbridge, the major landing on the Mokelumne. In 1869, during the zenith of development, there were three merchandise stores, a shoemaker, a dentist, a livery stable, two blacksmiths, a wagon maker and C. C. Fugitt's Hotel.

The demise of the town came as a result of the Central Pacific Railroad establishing Galt as a stop. With this change in events, there was no need for another town just a mile or so away. New Liberty was established at trackside one and a half miles to the south during 1868 and soon became known as Acampo. Old Liberty remained a post office for six years before it, too, was abandoned.

Sawyer Brothers moved much of Liberty to Galt in Sacramento County. This was done by a horse driven windlass. The circular plodding of the horse was transferred to the drum of the windlass by cast iron gears. As the rope or cable was drawn in, the building would come trundling along the road on log rollers. One of these buildings was the hotel, relocated to Fourth Street in Galt, where it remained standing until demolition in 1970. It is also believed that a church and the school were

also moved into Galt in this manner.

Chism Fugitt eventually moved from the ghost town of Liberty to Galt to become constable and deputy assessor. He died as a result of an accident with his own gun in 1884.

Today, Liberty lives on only as the name of a township, a county road and a shattered cemetery overlooking Highway 99 at Liberty Road. Another physical reminder survives through the efforts of Mrs. Baxter Sperry, owner of a building in Galt believed to be the old Liberty School. The memory of the long-gone community has been perpetuated by her writings and successful efforts to have her property designated as a "Point of Historical Interest" by the State of California.

LIVE OAK

See Appendix.

LOCUST SHADE

This settlement was five and a half miles north of Waterloo. See Appendix.

LOVING'S FERRY

Now in Stanislaus County, this site is on the north bank of the Stanislaus River near the Highway 120 crossing. When the county boundary was changed from the middle of the river to the north bank, it became part of Stanislaus County. John Loving, for whom the place was named, was the ferry owner of this point that was once a major river crossing of the old Stockton-Mariposa Military Road. See Appendix.

LYOTH

This is the crossing point of Western Pacific with Southern Pacific trackage, two miles south of Tracy. By 1916, Southern Pacific had a switching tower here to control the crossing. Western Pacific, purchasers of the right of way established through here by the Alameda & San Joaquin Railroad, stationed a section crew in Lyoth plus a railroad agent for this "flag stop." The agent and two tower men were still stationed here in 1929. Standard Oil Company built a bunkhouse and had a crew here filling oil tank cars from its Martinez pipeline.

Near the small station was a tiny wooden post office. There were but three families in permanent residence here, and a big event of the day for the children was the morning flag raising and salute at the post office. Occasionally, they would be called on a "treasure hunt" when a fast moving train would fail to catch the mailbag and letters would be scattered all over the track.

In 1985 Lyoth is still identifiable by two very old but well-kept batten and board railroad dwellings. There is also a farm machinery storage facility and All Pure, a farm chemical supply firm.

MANDEVILLE

This place was probably named for James W. Mandeville, former assemblyman, state senator, U.S. surveyor general and state controller.

MARIETTA STATION

Three miles east of Farmington, this was a stage stop on the main freight route, the Sonora Road, between French Camp and the Stanislaus River. It was named for Marietta, Georgia, from which several of its pioneer settlers came. It is listed with other stops along the way such as 12 Mile, 26 Mile, Henrietta, Zinc House and Oak Grove Cottage.

McDERMOTT'S BRIDGE

A Mokelumne River crossing, this was also the halfway point between Sacramento and Stockton. William F. McDermott, first postmaster, built the bridge. See Appendix.

MEINECKE

From 1864 to 1882, this was a ferry crossing on the Stanislaus. At first, it was known as Burnham and Hillyer Ferry, then renamed Meinecke. Frederick Meinecke operated the ferry with his son for three years, starting in 1866. He was an immigrant from Germany, first arriving in California during 1849 after an overland trip from Wisconsin. He made a fortune as a freighter and in marketing dairy cattle. The settlement grew up along the north bank of the river close to the ferry landing and was a point on the road to Tuolumne City in Stanislaus County. After the post office was discontinued, this point became known as Taylor's Ferry.

MERRY OAKS

See Appendix.

MIDDLE RIVER

A Delta waterway known as Middle River is an important tributary to the main channel of the San Joaquin through the Delta; it also was an important asset to river transportation service. The community of Middle River was located on Upper Jones Tract along the Santa Fe Railroad line and gained considerable economic importance as one of the main shipping points of the Delta Islands. It was in the center of the potato growing region. By 1915, there was an asparagus cannery. Aside from the railroad depot and docks, there were a warehouse, school, a Pacific Gas and Electric station and meter readers' office and a

BOAT RENTAL ENTREPRENEURS, LIKELY AT MIDDLE RIVER, c. 1920
Middle River was a central point to the farmlands of the Delta islands. If one reached this point by train or by road and had more traveling to do, the trip would continue by boat. This firm rented boats to travelers and is very much indicative of Middle River and the times. Three of the men are identified as Arthur, Frank and Dave Planchon, but nothing more can be learned about the firm. *(Collection of the Haggin Museum, Stockton)*

BORDEN HIGHWAY (HIGHWAY 4) BRIDGE ACROSS MIDDLE RIVER, 1924
To early motorists, this was a familiar sight on the cross Delta trip to the Byron-Brentwood area. This crossing was about two and a half miles south of the community of Middle River.

fourth class post office which was operated by women for decades except for 1940 to 1944. PG&E did a substantial business in the area, as there were many electrically operated pumps and large labor camps. Except for a small resort and a few houses, Middle River is a ghost town. Collapsed homes on pilings sink into the water, and only one warehouse, relocated from a pier, attests to the once significant shipping activity.

MINGESDALE (MINGES STATION)

A native of Switzerland, John W. Minges, a farmer, is very likely the person for whom this place was named. Mingesdale may have been located near Lone Tree and Van Allen roads. Minges

arrived in California as a member of an overland party in 1849 and died in 1893. The Zinc House District School was located here for a few years.

MOKELUMNE

See Appendix.

MOKELUMNE CITY AND BENSON'S FERRY

These points are situated a very short distance from one another and are registered California State Historical Landmarks. Edward Stokes and A. M. Woods started this ferry on the Mokelumne River in 1849. It was an important crossing on one of the three routes between Sacramento and the southern mines. The ferry was sold in 1850 to

John A. Benson, who operated it for nine years until his work was abruptly ended by his murder at the hands of an employee. Ferry operations were continued by Benson's son-in-law, Ed Gayetty.

Just three-tenths of a mile east on the south bank is the site of Mokelumne City. It was located here as this is the confluence of the Mokelumne and Cosumnes rivers. The waterway was navigable for commercial traffic and Mokelumne City could boast deep water communication with San Francisco year round, in competition with Stockton and French Camp. The site was surveyed in August 1850 and, at this time, 100 lots were sold for commercial and residential use. Some of the lots brought as much as $1,000.

In a single week, five boats arrived with lumber and other merchandise. A famous Stockton ship builder, Stephen H. Davis, established a lumber yard here and operated the sloop *Mary Bowers*. He eventually built three of these river craft for the Mokelumne City-San Francisco service. Two of these sloops were the *Ceres* and the *R. W. Allen*. This fleet was joined by another vessel, Charles E. Wheeler, Jr.'s *Rhode Island*. Mokelumne City was serving as a trans-shipment center for the mining district around Camanche, Lancha Plana and Poverty Bar in Calaveras County. All were reached by good roads.

By 1861, Mokelumne City was the third largest community in San Joaquin County. It had three stores, two hotels, a blacksmith shop, saloon, a twenty-four by forty foot warehouse and other buildings, including some constructed of brick. In addition to commercial structures, there were twenty-three houses. The town, noted the *Stockton Republican*, was surrounded by a "stored agricultural treasure," the alluvial soil of the river bottom lands. Growth and promise for the area came to a rapid end with the flood of 1862, the result of a season with nearly three feet of rain. All of the buildings either floated away in eight feet of water or were demolished by wind and waves.

The town was ruined and it never recovered. A few stayed on, maintaining residences there, but the commercial importance was gone. The hotel was turned into a barn.

One commercial building floated about a mile to the south to a point near Thornton where it eventually became a residence. The original building still stands, and the passerby would scarcely recognize that part of this structure, now so long a residence, has such a colorful history.

THE OLD JUDGE HOUSKEN RESIDENCE ON BLOSSOM ROAD, SOUTH OF BARBER ROAD, 1983
There is quite a story to this house. It has been expanded considerably over the decades, but not all of it was built at this site and it was not always a house. Still standing among several additions is a structure originally built as a combination saloon, restaurant and general store, which was part of the business district of Mokelumne City.

During the flood of 1862, the establishment floated off its foundation and came to rest about a mile south of the townsite. It was remodeled for a residence, a purpose it has served ever since. Former river pilot and Justice of the Peace W. C. Housken is its best remembered occupant. *(Photograph by Raymond W. Hillman)*

MONTEVIDEO
See Appendix.

MOORLAND
See Appendix.

MORANO

Morano was a Southern Pacific stop eight miles southeast of Lathrop. See Appendix.

MORRISSEY
See Appendix.

FIVE BRIDGES ACROSS THE SAN JOAQUIN, LOOKING EAST
OVER MOSSDALE TOWARD MANTECA, 1977

Few places in the nation feature such a concentration of highway and railroad crossings. From left to right are the Southern Pacific lift span built in 1942, now welded shut; next is the Lincoln Highway span of 1926, part of the 3,332-mile automobile highway from New York to San Francisco; farther upstream is the old Highway 50 bridge dating from about 1950; the last two spans were completed in the 1970s as part of Interstate 5. A sixth span is just out of the photograph to the south, the Western Pacific Railroad crossing originally constructed in 1909.

At the point where the wakes of the motor boats can be seen in the river is the San Joaquin County boat launching facility, and directly across from it is the Mossdale Marina.

MOSSDALE

This river crossing has had a remarkably important role in San Joaquin County transportation history. The story extends from thousands of years before white settlement and continues to this day. It would be difficult to find a locality anywhere else in the county that has such a long, varied and significant history.

Mossdale has been a focal point because of a geological advantage. The San Joaquin River makes sharp bends in this region and its current is reduced, allowing sand and silt to collect and make the river bed shallow, an advantage creating good fishing and also providing a safe ford, virtues discovered long ago by the original inhabitants of San Joaquin County, the Yokuts Indians. They would pole their tule canoes into position in the river and spear fish through a hole in the thick bottom of the boat. For this reason, the earliest Spanish explorers called this point "El Pescadero" (fishing place). Later this name was applied to a

THE FIRST BRIDGE ACROSS THE SAN JOAQUIN RIVER. MOSSDALE, 1869.

One of the most historically significant events to take place in San Joaquin County was the completion of this Central Pacific Railroad bridge. Most people are informed that the first transcontinental railroad was completed at Promontory Summit, Utah, May 10, 1869. However, ocean to ocean rail travel was not possible as, at this time, the rails extended only as far west as Sacramento. Completion of this bridge made it possible for trains to reach San Francisco Bay and the terminal at Oakland. On November 10, 1869, the first transcontinental passenger train passed over this bridge.

The wooden tower rests upon a turntable that swung the adjacent sections of bridge deck parallel to the banks of the river so steamers could pass through on their regular runs to San Joaquin City, Hills Ferry and other river landings farther south. The remaining portion of the span was one of only two covered bridges to be erected in San Joaquin County. The other was on the Mokelumne near Clements. Covered bridges were desirable as the roof and siding kept the network of heavy timbers free from dry rot and extended the life of the span considerably.

An iron truss structure replaced this bridge in 1895 and served until the present span was completed in 1942.

J. P. Atwood, a Lathrop photographer, recorded this scene.

THE INTERSECTION OF OLD U.S. 50 WITH STATE HIGHWAY 120 AT MOSSDALE, c. 1925
These buildings are typical of roadside businesses that developed along the Lincoln Highway (U.S. 50). The garage could supply you with Coast tires or Red Crown gasoline. If your Ford broke down here, you were lucky, for this was a Ford authorized garage. The school across the road still stands, but not in Mossdale. It is now in Tracy at the Grace Baptist Church.

Mexican land grant encompassing 34,000 acres of this region; El Rancho del Pescadero was granted to Valentin Higuerra and Rafael Felix during 1843.

Mormon pioneers were familiar with this point on the river, for this was enroute to the New Hope settlement that was to be developed near the confluence of the San Joaquin and Stanislaus rivers. The *Comet*, the first sailing vessel to navigate the upper San Joaquin, could not navigate farther because of the shallows.

During the summer of 1848, an important river crossing for gold seekers bound for Stockton and the mines was established by John Doak with a boat made of tule elk hides stretched over a framework of willow poles. In November a more conventional ferry raft, built at Corte Madera Creek, many miles away in Marin County, was brought to the site after an arduous voyage. It was literally hauled up the last few miles of the San Joaquin by ropes run around trees on the river banks and pulling the ferry up against the current.

Doak and his partner, Jacob Bonsell, operated the ferry here until 1851, charging three dollars for a man and a horse, eight dollars a wagon and one dollar for foot passengers. As this was a very popular crossing, it was possible to make several thousand dollars a day. It continued operation under the name Shepherd's Ferry though still generally known as Bonsell's. In 1856, ownership passed to William S. Moss, who operated it for decades. The ferry finally ceased operation with the construction of an iron truss bridge in 1890. This was a very advantageous place to cross, as there were no more sloughs or rivers west of here.

Mossdale received its name from the last operator of the ferry and owner of over 10,000 acres of surrounding land. Moss was a native of Virginia and first traveled overland to California in 1856. Aside from his extensive holdings in the county, he also had a home in San Leandro and owned the *San Francisco Examiner*, which was eventually sold to George Hearst to become the first newspaper run by his son, William Randolph Hearst.

A town was gradually established over the years; there was a hotel in the late 1860s; even a post office was in operation, but only for a few months in 1911. During the 1930s, there were a school, Moore

222

Brothers Fountain-Lunch, a tavern, store and garage, all of which are gone today.

A major industrial enterprise was established during the 1920s by Stewart Moore. The dairy operation, near the west bank of the river, was unusually large, employing 100. The red masonry silos and barns, now in ruins, are plainly seen from Interstate 5. Today, Mossdale is known as the locale of Mossdale Marina, a resort and trailer park, and the Mossdale Boat Launching Ramp and Park, established by San Joaquin County in 1977.

By the side of the old Lincoln Highway, which borders this park, is a monument that testifies to the importance of the site. The monument was built in 1949 to accommodate the California State Historical Landmark plaque for the *Comet* landing and twenty years later, a second plaque honoring the importance of the crossing to the completion of the first transcontinental railroad. While small in size, Mossdale is a giant in historical perspective.

OAK POINT

Oak Point was ten miles southeast of Stockton. See Appendix.

ORR'S RANCH

This point eight miles southeast of Galt was named for pioneer rancher Fountain P. Orr. See Appendix.

PETERS

Reached by traveling five miles southeast of Linden, this former town was named for Italian immigrant Major J. D. Peters, who was a prominent Stockton grain buyer, riverboat operator and banker. The title "Major" was honorary and was bestowed upon him when he took an active part in the nation's centennial celebration of 1876. Peters was grand marshal of the huge Fourth of July parade that culminated the three-day event in Stockton. He owned the Peters townsite and had it surveyed before the arrival of the railroad. Peters became one of five stops on the Stockton & Copperopolis Railroad between Stockton and Milton.

They were, from west to east, Charleston, Walthall, Holden, Peters and #5. No sooner was the line completed in 1871 than Peters became the terminus of a twenty mile branch line to Oakdale. Within just a few years, the entire system was the Stockton & Copperopolis Division of the Central Pacific Railroad. The little town became a shipment and supply center for the surrounding region, including Linden. An underlying hard pan of the Peters area limited early agriculture to grain and stock raising. However, shipments of fruit were received from the Linden area, including the first peaches grown there.

The business district developed around a quadrangle adjacent to the tracks which still exists. In the early 1880s, there were a Wells-Fargo & Company Express office and Western Union Telegraph office in the depot, three blacksmiths, two saloons, grocery, liquor store, grain dealer and Martin McMahon's hotel. Several Central Pacific employees, including a section crew, resided here. In 1893, the telegraph office and depot were still active, as was the blacksmith shop, saloon and Isaac Webb's general store. There were also a Methodist Church and a one room school.

Just after the turn of the century, the population reached 100. In 1916, there were two major businesses, Thomas G. Dalton, general merchandise, and Miller & Lundblad, grocery and plumber. Dalton was also the postmaster. The only other business listed in the County Directory for the time was a harness maker. The section crew still resided at Peters.

Don R. Smith, in his book *Linden, From Stage Stop to Friendly Community*, describes Peters: "At one time, a nice park was located between the railroad station and the section house. The town also had a dance hall where they served soda pop cooled by putting the bottles on sacks in the tankhouse with water from the tank dripping on them. There were also three blacksmith shops, three bars, a skating rink, a hotel-restaurant and a baseball diamond. Some of the buildings originally in Peters were moved to Milton, but in later years, several were moved back to Peters from Milton."

A Citizens Promotional Association was organized in 1912, and the results of the cooperation it instilled were a church, school, town hall, better roads and a voting precinct.

Railroad passenger service continued in the 1920s with a Southern Pacific, diesel-operated passenger coach. It was called "The Peters'

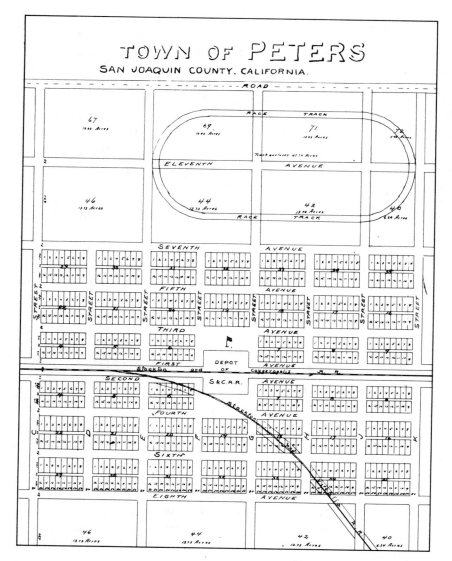

PLAT MAP OF PETERS AS FILED FEBRUARY 20, 1871

David S. Terry, a colorful but violent political figure, filed this map at the county recorder's office as part of his duties as trustee for the townsite owners. Present Fine Road is just west of the depot compound. Eighth Street, at the bottom of the map, is now Calaveras Road. Nothing is known of the race track; it probably had but a brief existence. *(Collection of Robert Shellenberger)*

Skunk'' because of the smell of diesel exhaust.

Loss of the post office and remaining businesses by 1951 ended the role of the town as a social and commercial center for the region. New houses have been built and the population has increased once again, but its days as a town are over. In 1976, local residents turned down a county planning commission's offer for re-zoning from ''general agricultural'' to ''rural residential.'' There was concern for growth overtaking the area, for the limited water supply and for restrictions on the number of animals owned.

In very recent years, considerable land in the area has been upgraded by ripping up the hard pan with heavy equipment and planting vineyards. The project is largely the work of a Fresno developer for Southern California investors. The vineyards are producing an exotic variety of wine grapes by drip irrigation. The result is a whole new dimension in agriculture which has always been so very much a part of the Peters area.

POLAND

Located about two miles east of Clements, this was a stage and teamsters stop on the Mokelumne Hill Road. George Poland established the station in 1852, and for decades the only hotel in the area of present Clements was located here. It was later purchased by Daniel Gillies, who developed the town of Clements. In 1865, a post office was established in the hotel building. Also of interest is that this community was the shipment point for the Lone Star Flour Mill owned by David S. Terry during the 1850s and early 1860s. All of the sacks shipped in the early days of its operation bore the name ''Poland, Cal.''

224

ROBERTS LANDING

This small river port in the Delta country was named for Martin Roberts, the postmaster. For additional information, see Appendix.

SAN JOAQUIN VALLEY

See Appendix.

SNUGVILLE

Probably little more than a crossroads roadhouse eight miles northwest of Lodi, the post office was established by Lemuel Josiah Dougherty, a settler of 1852. The hamlet, just a mile or so south of a now long abandoned Mokelumne River ferry crossing, appeared on the official county map as late as 1883.

STAPLES RANCH

See Staples Ferry references in Lockeford chapter and Appendix.

STATEN

This site is on Staten Island, three and a half miles west of New Hope. It was moved two miles south to Eagle Tree and its name changed. See Appendix.

TAISON

Lower Sacramento Road was once a stage route and one of the stops was just south of Thornton near Peltier Road. This was Taison. Captain G. P. Taison, for whom the town is named, was active here in the early 1860s, carrying lumber by schooner for Jacob Brack, farmer and major land owner. Captain Taison, a native of Denmark, had purchased one of Stephen Davis' sloops and operated it on the Mokelumne after Davis discontinued his service. The vessel, named the *Ceres*, hauled lumber and supplies for Woodbridge and other points. Before long, this vessel was joined with at least one more schooner sailed by George Hodgkins and several barges that not only operated on the Mokelumne but also on the San Joaquin and Sacramento rivers. About 1870 a ship canal was dug from near Taison to Hog Slough. It filled with tules in about a decade.

For pleasure, he had a racing yacht, the *Dorenda*, with which he won trophies in San Francisco Bay. He was a member of the Master Mariners Association and died in 1881 just before the town started to develop.

In the mid-1880s there was Arthur Thornton and Alexander Borland's general merchandise store and brick yard; a second general merchandise, grain buying and storage firm was operated by the Farmers & Business Association, which also was an insurance agency. In addition, there were a justice of the peace, a harness and saddle maker, a blacksmith and wagon builder's shop and a dance hall. Residents throughout this section traveled to Taison for dances.

The town gradually faded, more than likely being overshadowed by the growth of Thornton. Today the Lower Sacramento Road has been rerouted and no road passes the townsite.

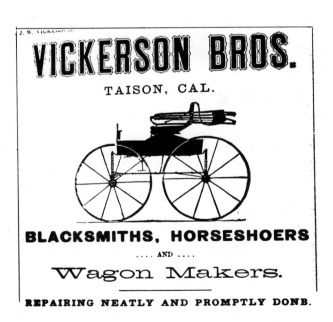

ONE OF THE FEW REMINDERS OF TAISON

L. M. McKinney & Company ran this prominent advertisement for Charles E. and Joseph W. Vickerson in their *Stockton City, San Joaquin County, Stanislaus, Tuolumne and Contra Costa Counties Directory* for 1884–1885. *(Courtesy Stockton Central Library)*

BUSINESS CENTER OF TAISON, c. 1890

A near-classic view of a now vanished part of small town America has been recorded here. Note how the cow has positioned herself for posterity better than the horse and the local residents. *(Collection of the San Joaquin County Historical Museum)*

TERMINOUS

Shortly before the turn of the century, a narrow gravel road extended west from Lodi to the Bouldin Island Ferry on Little Potato Slough. The road was largely the work of John Doughtery, who chose the name Terminus, as, at that time, it was the end of the road into the Delta. Doughtery established the first and only general store for years and also applied to the U.S. Postal Service for a post office, which was established in 1895. Unfortunately, the bureaucracy misspelled the name chosen for the town and it was forever Terminous.

The post office was to continue to 1918, when it was closed and transferred to Lodi. Doughtery sold the store, which eventually became the Terminous Tavern, a lively place remaining in business to about 1960. Proprietor Charlie Stone and his gun collection are particularly well remembered. The tavern was really a combined bar, pool room, restaurant, grocery store and barber shop. In the late 1930s, Valley Brew, absolutely the best seller, was

sold at ten cents a glass. Whiskey was fifteen cents a shot and a dinner of roast pork or roast beef with potatoes, soup, bread and coffee was thirty-six cents. A cook, dishwasher, two waitresses, a bartender and helper were employed. To the east of the tavern was a large wooden school, across from Johnnie Fiesel's grocery store, garage and motel. On the south side of the highway near the first warehouse was Ed Schopp's coffee shop. As this was the closest supply center for a large section of the Delta, it was a busy place. Some of the customers came from Frodsham, a nearby permanent commercial fisherman's camp.

Also just a mile north was a popular harbor known as Grindstone Joe's, named for a Portuguese fellow whose real name was Joe Atello. He was a classic "river rat," had two beautiful collie dogs as companions and a large circle of friends, particularly pleasure boat owners using his good anchorage. He originally developed the marina with a partner, using little more than wheel bar-row and shovel. The partnership quickly dissolved when Joe's prized grindstone was broken. Old Grindstone Joe died on the front porch of the Terminous Tavern in 1944.

A great boost to the activity at Terminous came with the construction of the Western Pacific freight line in 1927. It involved the building of eight miles of track from the main line at Kingdon, just south of the Highway 12 grade crossing, and the erection of a long string of wharf warehouses, a potato and onion loading wharf and other facilities. Similar to operations at Holt and Middle River, vegetables were barged in over a wide area for washing, trimming, crating or sacking. A lofty water tower, still standing, was built to supply vegetable washing operations with water from the adjacent slough. The washers were electrically operated. The produce was loaded into freight cars on spur tracks beside the warehouses. As many as seventy-five cars of celery would be loaded in one night. The most prominent label was Maurer & Sons "Red Lion Celery." During the 1929-30 season, 2,264 cars of celery, nearly 600 cars of potatoes, nearly 200 cars of onions and almost 200 cars of sugar beets left Terminous.

Competition from Southern Caifornia eventually eliminated the busy traffic in celery; it was replaced with asparagus. The produce would be sent via the Feather River Route through Portola, California, to Elko, Nevada, eventually reaching the auction tracks in Chicago. This was a particularly profitable shipping point for W.P. and the eight mile track was so busy that it had its own maintenance crew. It was said to be the best eight miles on the entire W.P. line. For years, W.P. #122 hauled vegetables from Terminous to Stockton. This steam locomotive was one of two originally bought in the nineties by the Alameda & San Joaquin Railway for service to the coal mines and brick works in Corral Hollow.

This shipping and processing point required a great deal of labor. While the population figures vary and are often exaggerated, they were, nevertheless, significant. At season's height, there would be about 350. About 150 of these drove in from the surrounding area. Approximately 200 lived in "Box Car City," which was situated at the base of the levee just across from the warehouses. It was composed of obsolete, wooden box cars taken from their wheels and set up somewhat haphazardly on old railroad ties, etc. Fresh water was brought in once weekly in two 100,000-gallon tank cars that were filled at the Stockton roundhouse.

"Box Car City" was a rough place. Brawls and cock fights were a regular order of business, as were the bleached blondes brought in Lincolns every pay day. All of this disappeared by the late 1930s. The freight business, by this time, was suffering badly from losses caused by the introduction of refrigerated trucks and competition

"BOX CAR CITY," TERMINOUS, c. 1941

Japanese and Filipino packing shed workers were housed in these ancient wooden box cars during the harvest season. Another group of box cars, still on wheels, was a familiar sight along the highway just east of Little Potato Slough and was reserved for Caucasian workers. The watch tower (photo above) was erected to control gambling. The view below was taken from the top of the conveyor hopper which still stands at the south edge of Tower Park Marina. *(Photographs by James A. Kirk)*

from smaller packing sheds throughout the Delta. State Highway 12 reached Terminous and became a through route to Rio Vista and points west in 1942 with completion of a bridge across the Mokelumne River a few miles to the west.

About 1959, a year after surrounding Terminous Tract flooded after a levee break, W. P. started phasing out the facilities, and Terminous became a ghost town when all activity ceased in 1964. The old corrugated iron warehouses along Little Potato Slough were again to be the center of activity as a result of an enterprise envisioned by avid boater Irwin Peterson. He realized there was need for a marina in the area and bought twenty-six acres from the railroad company. The existing improvements included the cavernous warehouses, a massive wooden hopper for storing trimmings for dairy farmers and a landmark water tower that inspired a name for the resort, Tower Park Marina.

Work began as soon as a use permit was obtained

in November 1968. The following June was opening day. Sid and Clark Wallace became owners for several years, starting in 1971. Development has been steady over the years, and the old warehouses now contain dry boat storage facilities, repair shops, launching ramps, a general store, restaurant and bar next to 178 covered berths. Nearby, on the site of old "Box Car City," are 250 camp sites well patronized by recreational vehicle and mobile home owners. A 200 unit mobile home park, Tower Park Village, was selling lots rapidly in 1985. Thirty-three people are now employed on a permanent basis, with another forty temporary employees during the summer.

According to Hal Schell, authority on the Delta, this is "easily the Delta's most complete marina." He also stated, "Tower Park has made Terminous as important to the pleasure boaters as the town once was to the Delta farmers."

ARRIVAL OF THE TERMINOUS-BOULDIN ISLAND FERRY, LATE 1890s
While the main road extended only as far as Terminous for many years, there was a ferry across Little Potato Slough to serve extensive farming operations on Bouldin Island. The ferry was still in operation during the mid 1920s, but it was to be replaced in 1936 by a steel bridge during construction of the State Highway 12 to Rio Vista. (Courtesy Lodi Public Library, Celia M. Thompson Collection)

OLD TERMINOUS LIVES ON
AS TOWER PARK MARINA

The graceful meanders of Little Potato Slough and the South Fork of the Mokelumne River dominate the landscape. On the levee top, in the photo at the top of the page, are the three long roofs of warehouses built by Western Pacific in 1927. These form the nucleus of extensive resort facilities. In the foreground is the series of covered docks providing berths for 178 boats.

In the photo above, the swing bridge beyond the resort is the Highway 12 link between Bouldin Island and Terminous Tract. The large white building in the upper right corner is the old Terminous School, built about 1919 and now a residence. Across from this building is the colorful false fronted Terminous Market (see photo to right). The Episcopal church that once stood in Terminous still exists but no longer in this locality; the trim, batten and board sanctuary was moved to West Lincoln Road in Stockton to become the Episcopal Church of Saint Anne.

229

TULEVILLE

See Appendix.

UNDINE

An interesting old sign and a ranch house on an Indian mound are all that mark the site today of this community, which was located six miles north of Tracy. William Hyde Irwin, in his book *Augusta Bixler Farms*, stated, "This spot was a natural stopping place for horsemen riding up and down the West Side of the San Joaquin Valley to and from Stockton via the Tracy Crossing Levee." This region on Union Island was of particular importance to agriculture. Immense grain "ranches" operated here, and of interest is the fact that what may be the first crop of pinto beans in the state was planted here in the 1880s.

The region had additional distinction by staging sporting events that attracted visitors to Undine from a wide area. Duck hunting was very popular. In addition, George Kidd operated a bear baiting pit during holidays. The bears fought to the death.

Horse breeder Thomas Williams, Jr., operated a race track on Undine Road just a short distance from town. It is said spectators were brought in by barge via the Grant Line Canal. The mile-long track was lighted by gas lamps at night; the methane or "marsh gas" came from a 350-foot well. The passerby and visitor alike could always be assured of a bed and a meal for fifty cents. Board for horses was a dollar.

The town bears the Norwegian name for water nymph—Undine. During the 1880s, I. R. Dickson's hotel and general merchandise was the principal establishment. There also were a dairy, a saloon, a harness maker, a blacksmith and a wagon maker. In the early 1890s, there were two blacksmiths, a machine shop, a butcher, J. W. Moore's merchandise store and the post office with a telephone. Telephone service came to the area by the early 1880s with a line to Stockton.

When the population reached about one hundred, just after the turn of the century, George Mowry was operating a stage line to Tracy. Aside from the merchandise store were the post office and telegraph, three blacksmiths, harness maker, machine shop and two liquor stores. The schoolhouse was located to the southeast toward the Mowry Bridge. Water for the town was pumped by a windmill until a gasoline driven pump was installed to fill the tank at the top of a fifty-foot tower, which was a landmark for many miles around.

With improved roads in the twentieth century, the town gradually died, and all of the stores were long out of business by the 1930s. All that remained in the late 1930s were an ice house made of planks, sawdust and an interior lining of brick, the gasholder tank over the well and the lofty, wooden tank tower, made of twelve-inch by twelve-inch timbers.

During World War II, this structure was used by aircraft spotters. It remained standing until January 1967, when it blew down during a windstorm.

WAKEFIELD

Eight miles west of Stockton was Wakefield Landing, on the San Joaquin River levee of Roberts Island opposite Rough and Ready Island. Into the twentieth century, this was a stop on the main steamer route between Stockton and San Francisco. See Appendix.

AN OLD SIGN—THE "LAST STAND" FOR AN OLD TOWN, 1983

Legend has it that a Chinese cook carved the letters in this two and three-quarter inch thick plank about a century ago. It hung in front of the general store/post office operated by John W. Moore. Relegated to a garage for years, it was re-erected at a point just about a hundred yards north of the townsite. Very faintly in the distance can be seen Livermore Range, of which Mount Oso is a high point.

WATERLOO

Eight miles northeast of Stockton, there was an important junction of two county roads. One (present Highway 88/12) continued on to Lockeford, and the other, Comstock Road, offered a direct route to the ranch lands and mining country of the foothills.

In the very early 1860s, it was known as Calaveras Post Office or the Waterloo House, a name typical of a wayside stop frequented by thirsty travelers. As the town was on a well-traveled route to the Sierra, it soon had a hotel, blacksmith shop and

from the original outside walls. The space between was filled with earth with three-inch square loop holes cut at strategic points. This was the beginning of the greatest excitement the town ever saw.

Balkwill had an arsenal of four shotguns, two rifles, a pistol and an axe. The local farmers were sure they could overcome this fire power by riding to Stockton and taking an old nine pounder cannon kept in front of the St. Charles Hotel and used to fire salutes during celebrations. This was loaded onto a wagon and spirited away to the "battle ground" under a load of hay. Their efforts, how-

This advertisement for a blacksmith, horseshoer and carriage and wagon maker appeared in the L. M. McKinney & Company directory for 1884–1885. *(Courtesy Stockton Public Library)*

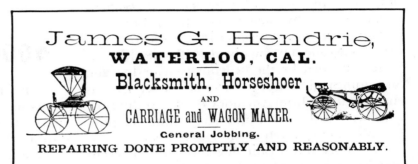

James G. Hendrie,
WATERLOO, CAL.
Blacksmith, Horseshoer
AND
CARRIAGE and WAGON MAKER,
General Jobbing.
REPAIRING DONE PROMPTLY AND REASONABLY.

four saloons. It was at this time that the locale was to gain distinction through two separate disputes with squatters.

These were the Battle of Waterloo and the Comstock Affair, which became the best known of a myriad of cases against squatters in San Joaquin County. The Battle of Waterloo in November 1861 came as a result of the filing of a petition in the land office by a thirty-year-old Canadian, John Balkwill. He was claiming 160 acres that were considered to be Almer Drullard's property. Drullard had title to an adjacent 160 acres, but other land owners in the vicinity informally claimed additional acreage for which the law would not allow them to file. He rented twenty-five acres of this extra land to Balkwill, who built a cabin, established a garden and opened a blacksmith and wagon shop. It was not long, however, before he discovered that his landlord did not have title to this land and filed for it. Local land owners were determined to make an example of Balkwill, whom they considered a squatter.

Balkwill, expecting trouble, fortified his cabin by building an additional wall of planks six inches

ever, were compromised by their fear of Balkwill's crack shot.

They situated themselves so far from the cabin that the shot they were using, composed of scrap iron from Balkwill's shop, scattered before it could hit the cabin. The cannon was fired four times and Balkwill returned fire five times. The most seriously injured among the farmers was Jack Tone, who lost a finger. The law soon arrived and about ten farmers were arrested for "riotous acts." The cannonneers, Jack Tone and J. C. Dodge, were fined $150 each and court costs of $500.

Balkwill obtained title to a portion of the land and was eventually bought out by Drullard. The battle was considered to be a colorful event, almost a comic opera. As there was a lot of good humored talk about the Battle of Waterloo, the place took on this name by which it has been known ever since.

The place gained more distinction in about 1870 with completion of the Waterloo Gravel Road, operated as a toll road. By this time, there were a post office, two hotels, three blacksmith shops, a Chinese laundry and two or three saloons. By the mid 1880s, the population had reached about fifty.

John Balkwill operated a hotel, the Waterloo House, and a saloon. There were three other saloons competing with him.

Other businesses were two wagon makers, a cabinet shop, pork packing house, butcher, print shop, farm implement agency, blacksmith shop, a brick maker, stone cutter and toll house. The town also had a physician, a teacher and a constable, as well as a justice of the peace.

Starting in the 1880s and increasing into the twentieth century, Italian truck gardeners and orchardists became established in the Waterloo area. However, the growth of Waterloo was to cease with ever improving roads, making Stockton and Lockeford more accessible. By 1908, there were only nine buildings in the town, but it became a stop on the Steiny Stage Service, providing transportation between Stockton and Lockeford. For nearly a decade starting about 1912, horseless carriages operated by the "Clements-Waterloo and Stockton Stage" stopped here, before service was ended by a line from Amador County. At this time there were still a blacksmith shop, store and public hall where church services were held.

The most important development in recent decades was the establishment of the Waterloo Gun and Bocci Club in 1955. Founded by marketing shares, the club now owns forty acres and a club house with a large dance hall and kitchen. The finest bocci ball courts in California are located behind the club house and occasional tournaments are held here. In 1985, the United States Bocci Championship Tournament was attended by more than 1,500 competitors and spectators. An extensive trap and skeet shoot facility also adjoins the building. All of these facilities can be rented by other clubs, thus attracting visitors to Waterloo from throughout the state.

Today there is a small business district, including the Waterloo Inn. In front of this bar is an historical monument honoring the Battle of Waterloo. It was unveiled by the Tuleburg Chapter of E Clampus Vitus in 1976.

WOODWARD

This point, seventeen miles west of Stockton, was named for Orville Y. Woodward, first postmaster and, after 1905, a partner in the San Joaquin Ditching Company, which undertook reclamation work in the Delta. Woodward was located on the Old River levee of Woodward Island a few miles west of Middle River. See Appendix.

APPENDIX
POST OFFICES IN SAN JOAQUIN COUNTY

The following information has been excerpted and modified from the now out-of-print book *A Century of California Post Offices 1848-1954* compiled by Walter N. Frickstad and published in 1955, and *History of California Post Offices 1849-1976* by Harold E. Salley, published in 1977.

Key to Code
Fr Name or site changed from
--- Still in operation
To Name changed to
M Mail sent to

Office	Established	Discontinued
Acampo	August 28, 1872	---
Atlanta	April 24, 1868	April 5, 1876
	May 10, 1876	May 16, 1887
	April 21, 1888	June 30, 1911
	March 12, 1914	**M** Ripon, May 31, 1915
Banta **Fr** San Joaquin Valley	April 11, 1870	---
Bellota	June 1, 1860	January 19, 1863
	July 21, 1870	February 27, 1871
	June 24, 1874	**M** Linden, April 15, 1918
Bethany	August 14, 1879	January 7, 1880
	May 25, 1880	**M** Tracy, January 31, 1940
Bouldin (Boulder) Island	January 29, 1878	**M** Frodsham, September 14, 1918
Burwood	November 17, 1859	**M** Oakdale, April 15, 1898
Calaveras	December 2, 1861	**M** Stockton, December 4, 1862
Carbona	October 28, 1926	**M** Tracy, March 31, 1927
Carlton **Fr** Clements	May 14, 1887	**To** Clements, June 22, 1887
Clements	October 9, 1882	**To** Carlton, May 14, 1887
Fr Carlton	June 22, 1887	---
Collegeville	April 22, 1868	**M** Ellisworth, August 31, 1903
Cometa	January 16, 1892	**M** Farmington, September 15, 1892
Dexter	March 8, 1876	**M** Stockton, August 16, 1876
Eagle Tree **Fr** Staten	February 2, 1903	**M** New Hope, May 14, 1904
Eight Mile Corners	January 8, 1861	September 29, 1863
Elliott **Fr** Orr's Ranch	November 25, 1863	October 9, 1871
	January 15, 1872	**M** Galt, June 29, 1901
Ellis	January 10, 1870	**To** Tracy, December 6, 1878
Ellisworth	April 10, 1901	**M** Escalon, September 15, 1927
Escalon	May 4, 1898	Rescinded June 24, 1898
	September 10, 1898	---
Fairchild	April 25, 1900	**M** Stockton, August 30, 1902

Farmington **Fr** Marietta	March 17, 1862	---
Foreman's Ranch	January 3, 1855	**To** Linden, February 19, 1863
Forest Lake (Forestlake)	October 1, 1890	**M** Galt, September 30, 1903
Fourteen Mile House	January 15, 1857	July 28, 1857
	March 19, 1858	**To** Marietta, November 15, 1858
French Camp	May 3, 1854	November 12, 1862
	March 22, 1865	April 13, 1870
	June 19, 1874	---
Fugitt	April 25, 1857	**To** Liberty, July 5, 1860
Half Way House **Fr** McDermott's Bridge	October 2, 1858	March 30, 1860
Hazelton	March 17, 1899	**M** Stockton, January 31, 1900
Holden	April 5, 1871	**M** Peters, July 14, 1871
Holden's Ferry	June 3, 1858	**M** Loving's Ferry, December 18, 1858
Holt	April 26, 1902	---
Homestead	March 3, 1898	**M** Stockton, January 31, 1900
Jakesville	January 6, 1917	**M** Galt, June 29, 1918
Kerrick's Ranch	April 16, 1858	**To** Oak Point, September 30, 1858
Knights Ferry	Prior to July 28, 1851	Became Stanislaus County town, March 30, 1860
Lathrop	February 27, 1871	June 21, 1875
	July 23, 1875	---
Liberty **Fr** Fuggitt	July 5, 1860	**M** Lodi, May 3, 1874
Linden **Fr** Foreman's Ranch	February 19, 1863	---
Live Oak	November 17, 1869	**M** Stockton, February 6, 1871
Lockeford	June 19, 1861	---
Locust Shade **Fr** Staples Ranch	December 28, 1863	**M** Stockton, January 23, 1868
Lodi **Fr** Mokelumne	February 25, 1873	---
Loving's Ferry	July 31, 1855	**To** Holden's Ferry, Stanislaus County, June 3, 1858
Fr Holden's Ferry	December 18, 1858	Became Stanislaus County town, March 30, 1860
Lyoth	March 15, 1912	**M** Tracy, April 15, 1938
Mandeville	May 23, 1876	**M** Stockton, September 6, 1876
Manteca	July 22, 1908	---
Marietta **Fr** Fourteen Mile House	November 15, 1858	**To** Farmington, March 17, 1862
McDermott's Bridge	June 17, 1854	**To** Half Way House, October 2, 1856
Meinecke	November 21, 1866	**To** Modesto, August 26, 1872
Merry Oaks	July 14, 1853	**To** Stockton, March 30, 1855
	November 17, 1859	**To** Stockton, November 6, 1860
Middle River **Fr** Moorland	July 1, 1915	**M** Holt, June 2, 1944
Mingesdale	March 11, 1914	**M** Manteca, June 15, 1915
Mokelumne	November 17, 1869	**To** Lodi, February 25, 1873
Mokelumne City	June 28, 1861	**To** Woodbridge, May 4, 1864
Montevideo	March 3, 1857	**To** Stockton, June 1, 1857
Moorland	July 21, 1902	**To** Middle River, July 1, 1915
Morano	March 29, 1872	June 4, 1875
Morrissey	February 28, 1881	September 8, 1881
Mossdale	March 29, 1911	**M** Lathrop, October 31, 1911
New Hope	November 12, 1878	**To** Thornton, November 26, 1909
Oak Point **Fr** Kerrick's Ranch	September 30, 1858	March 3, 1859
Orr's Ranch	December 17, 1858	**To** Elliott, November 25, 1863

Peters	June 22, 1871	December 1, 1873
	October 11, 1881	November 30, 1904
	April 10, 1908	**M** Linden, April 30, 1951
Poland	September 30, 1858	March 23, 1867
Ripon	December 21, 1874	---
Roberts Landing	December 12, 1877	February 24, 1881
San Joaquin City	Prior to July 28, 1851	January 21, 1852
	September 18, 1874	**To** Vernalis, December 11, 1888
San Joaquin Valley	April 2, 1868	**To** Banta, April 11, 1870
Snugville	May 5, 1864	January 22, 1869
Staples Ranch	Prior to October 21, 1851	**To** Locust Shade, December 28, 1863
Staten	April 16, 1894	**To** Eagle Tree, February 2, 1903
Stockton	November 8, 1849	---
Taison	May 3, 1883	**M** New Hope, April 10, 1889
Terminous	July 17, 1895	**M** Lodi, September 30, 1918
Thornton **Fr** New Hope	April 1, 1910	---
Tracy **Fr** Ellis	December 6, 1878	---
Tuleville	October 14, 1875	July 6, 1876
Undine	October 27, 1881	**M** Stockton, August 14, 1906
Vernalis **Fr** San Joaquin City	December 11, 1888	---
Victor	August 16, 1922	---
Wakefield	May 17, 1880	July 5, 1881
	November 4, 1889	**M** Stockton, November 25, 1891
Waterloo	September 14, 1865	February 12, 1875
Woodbridge **Fr** Wood's Ferry	October 7, 1862	---
Wood's Ferry	April 25, 1857	**To** Woodbridge, October 7, 1862
Woodward	May 27, 1901	**To** Orwood, Contra Costa County, March 15, 1913

BIBLIOGRAPHY OF MAJOR SOURCES

The sources of information for this book are more varied than the myriad of crops found growing in the fields of San Joaquin County. This book is a product of research extending from obscure clippings and documents at the Haggin Museum to newspaper index files at the California State Library in Sacramento plus dozens of old city and county directories, recollections of old-timers and scattered published accounts from the 1850s to the present, to mention a few.

Many references used are unique materials or items of such rarity they are difficult to obtain; however, the following are in the libraries of Stockton and elsewhere in the county and are particularly useful resources.

For books that are out of print we have not included all of the information that is usually offered in a bibliography.

Books, Booklets and Pamphlets

An Illustrated History of San Joaquin County. Chicago: Lewis Publishing Co., 1890.

Bahnsen, Robert H. "A Half Century of Lockeford, California." Thesis, College of the Pacific, Stockton, 1953.

Brotherton, I. N. "Jack." *Annals of Stanislaus County*. Vol. I. *River Towns and Ferries*. Santa Cruz, Calif.: Western Tanager Press, 1982.

City and County Directory of Stockton City and San Joaquin County. Smith and Co., 1883-84.

Davis, Olive. *The Slow, Tired and Easy: The Story of the Stockton Terminal and Eastern Railroad*. Fresno, Calif.: Valley Publishers, 1976.

Fisher, C. E. "San Joaquin County, California." *Sunset Magazine, Homeseekers Bureau*. 1913.

Frickstad, Walter N., comp. *A Century of California Post Offices 1848-1954*. Oakland, Calif.: Philatelic Research Society, 1955.

Herbert, Ruth Hewitt, and Arleen Groves. *The History of Old Farmington*. Stockton: Mills Press, 1977.

Hicks, Warren Braukman. *A History of Lodi, California from Early Times to 1906*. June 1954. Reprint, 1962.

"Historical Landmarks." Sacramento: State of California Department of Parks and Recreation, 1981.

Hillman, Raymond W., and Leonard A. Covello. *Stockton Through the Decades*. Stockton: Union Safe Deposit Bank, 1982.

Hoover, Mildred, et al. *Historic Spots in California*. Stanford: Stanford University Press, 1966.

Hope and Co. *Mercantile Reports from the Mercantile Agency*. San Francisco: W. G. Bawden, 1869.

Kennedy, Glenn A. *It Happened in Stockton 1900-1925*. Stockton, 1967.

Murphy, George, Jr. *Manteca Memories*. Stockton: Stockton Savings and Loan, 1972.

Nesbit, Freda Jahant. *Lodi: The Home of the Mokelkos*. 1960 (?).

Pacific Coast Directory. San Francisco: McKenney and Co., various years.

Salley, Harold. *History of California Post Offices 1849-1976*. 1977.

"San Joaquin County, California for the Farmer." *Sunset Magazine Homeseekers Bureau*, c. 1915.

Smith, Don. *From Stage Stop to Friendly Community: A History of Linden*. Linden, Calif.: Scio Odd Fellows Lodge No. 102, 1976.

Stockton City, San Joaquin, Stanislaus, Calaveras, Tuolumne and Contra Costa Counties Directory. San Francisco: McKenney and Co., 1884-85.

Thompson, Evelyn Prouty. "Manteca, Selected Chapters from Its History." Manteca, Calif.: *Manteca Bulletin,* 1980.

Thornton, Frank S. *History of the Escalon Community in California.* 1964.

Tinkham, George H. *History of San Joaquin County, California with Biographical Sketches.* Los Angeles: Historic Record Co., 1923.

———— *History of the State of California and Biographical Record of San Joaquin County.* Vols. I and II. Los Angeles: Historic Record Co., 1909.

Williams, Earle E. "Boom Days in Corral Hollow." Typescript. 1968.

———— *Carrell of Corral Hollow.* San Leandro, Calif.: Mines Road Books, 1981.

Woodbridge Middle School Seventh Grade Basic Class. "Lodi Area People, Places and Events 1869-1969." Typescript. (n.d.)

Newspapers

Byron Times. Annual Development Editions. 1908-1937.

Linden Herald. Centennial Edition, April 27, 1963.

Tracy Press. Centennial Edition, Sept. 6, 1978.

Other Sources

Morgenson, Laura. Series published in *Stockton Record* in 1935 on the history of various communities within the area.

Research papers by students of Delmar McComb, Jr., at San Joaquin Delta College, Stockton, 1972-1982.

San Joaquin County Historical Society Bulletins, 1965-1985.

Historical photo and clipping collection of Celia M. Thompson, 1889-1959. Lodi Public Library.

INDEX

Page numbers in italics indicate association with illustrations.

240

241

242